WOMEN IN THE TWENTIETH CENTURY WORLD

"Women hold up half the sky."

—Mao Tse-tung

WOMEN IN THE TWENTIETH CENTURY WORLD

Elise Boulding

SAGE Publications

Halsted Press Division
JOHN WILEY & SONS
New York–London–Sydney–Toronto

HQ
1154
.B7

Copyright © 1977 by Sage Publications, Inc.

All rights reserved. No part of this book may be reproduced or utilized in any form or by any means, electronic or mechanical, including photocopying, recording, or by any information storage and retrieval system, without permission in writing from the publisher.

Distributed by Halsted Press, a Division of
John Wiley & Sons, Inc., New York

Printed in the United States of America

Library of Congress Cataloging in Publication Data

Boulding, Elise.
   Women in the twentieth century world.

   Bibliography p. 245
   1. Women—Social conditions.   2. Women—Economic conditions.   3. Women.   I. Title.
HQ1154.B7   301.41'2   76-28162
ISBN 0-470-98947-5

FIRST PRINTING

CONTENTS

Preface	9
Part I. GENERAL OVERVIEW AND HISTORICAL BACKGROUND	
1. The World We of Women: Household Patterns and Women's Occupations Around the World	17
2. Nomadism, Mobility, and the Status of Women	33
3. Familial Constraints on Women's Work Roles: An Historical Overview	55
Part II. WOMEN AND PRODUCTIVE SYSTEMS	
Introduction	75
4. Economic Dualism: Women's Roles and Poverty Traps	77
5. Women, Bread, and Babies: Directing Aid to Fifth World Farmers	111
6. Women and Food Systems: An Alternative Approach to the World Food Crisis	139
Part III. WOMEN AND THE INTERNATIONAL SYSTEM	
7. Women and Peace Work	167
8. NGOs and World Problem-Solving: A Comparison of Religious and Secular Women's NGOs	185
9. Female Alternatives to Hierarchical Systems, Past and Present: A Critique of Women's NGOs in the Light of History	211
Part IV. THE FUTURE	
10. The Coming of the Gentle Society	221
Bibliography	245
Appendix	253
Author Index	257
Subject Index	259

To my husband, Kenneth Boulding, who has taught me to think in global terms about human history

and to Helvi Sipila, Assistant Secretary General of the United Nations, who is teaching us all the importance of the participation of women in global thinking about the future.

PREFACE

This book was born out of a resolve in 1974 to undertake only those conference and lecture assignments in 1975, International Women's Year, that would enable me to address important issues concerning the role of women in the twentieth century. The chapters that follow were a series of papers prepared, except for the opening and closing chapters, for a variety of programs focusing on world issues extending from the fall of 1974 to the spring of 1976. Each is intended to speak to policy issues in relation to the three International Women's Year themes: equality, development, and peace.[1] Because I was writing the macrohistorical *Underside of History* at the same time, historical background kept creeping into each paper. However, I was simultaneously working with my colleagues Shirley Nuss and Dorothy Carson on United Nations data on women for the *Handbook of International Data on Women*, and was therefore sharply aware of the picture emerging from that data on the situation of women in this decade. What ties together the historical perspective and the current statistical data is my own personal experience as a scholar and activist in the international community over the past decade and a half.

The book is a critique both of the scholarship and of the activism of my own time, in regard to women. It also points to possible future directions. Social scientists have obfuscated the dynamics of social change in industrial society by overvaluing urbanism and by failing to note the women's sector. This sector I have variously referred to as the fifth world, the underside of history, and the gender-based undergirding of structural dualism in the third world. Woman the breeder-feeder-producer somehow slipped by the scholar's eye when development models were being constructed. Since the scholar did not see her, the planner was not likely to either. Unfortunately women themselves have done little to redress the world system's perceptual imbalance perpetuated by scholars and planners. First world women, except for a small minority of internationalists, tend in both Europe and North America to be preoccupied with their status problems in the urban enclaves of their own countries—even often the status problems of their own class within those enclaves—although in theory they affirm the world rural-urban sisterhood of women. Third world women, rural and urban alike, have few opportunities to enter such a sisterhood, and even the internationalists in the world of women's nongovernmental organizations (NGOs) have done relatively little to foster the further participation of third world women in the world community. Partly this is due to lack of resources, but partly it is due to an incomplete development of world perspective on the part of even the best educated and most idealistic of first world women.

I count myself among those who have had this incomplete perspective. Every critical word I have to say about women's NGOs applies very personally to me as a participant in that world movement of women. I am a westerner, with all the limitations of insight, experience, and sensitivity that being a westerner in the late twentieth century involves. We all need a better understanding of complex, interlocking global systems and of the character of the local systems that make up the global entity. We need mental training in kinds of conceptualization and imaginings that present educational systems do not provide. We also need to know our own grass-roots as women around the world. Only with more knowledge and in a closer partnership with third world sisters can we develop an adequate ethic of responsibility, and a reasonable set of action priorities for world betterment. The World Conference of the International Women's Year held at Mexico City in June of 1975 was an important affirmation of that partnership, but it was the barest beginning. The partnership cannot be made a reality through United Nations action alone. It must be created through the activities of every NGO, of every kind of women's group everywhere.

Although the language is sometimes unavoidably technical, and the statistical tables sometimes formidable, I would like to feel that I am speaking to many kinds of publics in this book; not only to scholars,[2] planners, and policy makers, not only to women and men who are activists, but also to the large numbers of concerned women and men who do not consider themselves activists but who give a lot of thought to the kind of world they and their children and their children's children will be living in over the next century.

Throughout the book, I often sound critical. Criticism can either strengthen or frustrate. I have tried to make my criticism strengthening, by providing a great deal of material, both historical and contemporary, about the extraordinary adaptability and productivity of women under apparently the most adverse circumstances. These are the resources to build with, the energies which can be drawn on in creating the more just and humane society of the future. I do not accuse anyone—scholar, planner, activist, or concerned citizen—of willful blindness. I only say to each, and also to myself, let us open our eyes and *see*. Many of us did not even know that our eyes were shut.

Part I begins with a description of the world "we" of women, a world profile as reflected in United Nations data, and goes on to provide a comparative view of the human experience of women as nomads and settlers to set straight some of our misconceptions about the role of urbanism in social development. The third chapter gives a historical overview of women's work roles to contrast with the data given in the introductory chapter.

Part II focuses on the woman as producer, primarily in the third world, and is the section addressed most directly to planners and policy makers. On the one hand I am trying here to reconceptualize the meaning of economic productivity and to redefine work sites, on the other hand to point to women's roles in that productivity. Only in Chapter 6 does the analysis shift to the global level, in order to give a perspective on the relative importance of women as producers in each part of the world in the complex of activities associated with the production, distribution and consumption of food.

Part III focuses on women as actors on the world scene and points to the strengths and weaknesses of women's organizations and of women's perspectives on their own tasks. Because the issue is dealt with at the international level, there is no consideration of the activities of women in any individual country. Rather, considerable attention is given to the problem of learning to think in different kinds of transnational entities.

It was my privilege recently to be invited to a consultation at the United Nations on the establishment of an International Institute on Research and Training for the Advancement of Women, a follow-up on proposals stemming from the Mexico City International Women's Year Conference. As I read the background materials so ably prepared by Gloria Scott of the United Nations secretariat, surveying the existing world knowledge base regarding the situation and needs of women and existing resources with the United Nations family of agencies; as I listened to the future unfolding as Helvi Sipila, Assistant Secretary General of the United Nations, spelled out her uniquely practical yet far-seeing view of the tasks of the proposed institute, and watched the attentive faces of my colleagues from around the world who had all dropped what they were doing at very short notice in order to participate in this consultation, I knew that a significant threshold in modern history was being crossed. The cumulative attention focused on the role of women in the social process broadly conceived, and economic development narrowly conceived, which first began about a century ago in Europe and North America but has particularly crescendoed in the past decade, has now developed a momentum that cannot easily be stopped. In any one setting movement may appear to be very slow, whether we look at national policies, United Nations activity or action in the transnational world of nongovernmental organizations. Nevertheless, the movement is worldwide, and the slender infrastructure of the network of regional women's institutes linked to the projected United Nations institute for women will therefore have an impact out of all proportion to its size and resources. This infrastructure will provide a vehicle for concerted thought, research, and action on the part of the ablest women of our time on all continents, and a vehicle for linking these women with their own grass roots on every continent. I hope this book can contribute to the new momentum.

I have benefitted greatly from opportunities to discuss the issues in this book with my colleagues in the International Sociological Association Research Committee on Sex Roles in Society, with colleagues at the United Nations, particularly Gloria Scott in the United Nations Statistical Division, and with colleagues at the Institute for World Order, in the Consortium for Peace Research, Education and Development (COPRED), and in the International Peace Research Association (IPRA). I am particularly grateful to the women of the twenty-one national sections of the Women's International League for Peace and Freedom for the decade-long apprenticeship to world community they provided. The women I have been privileged to know in women's NGOs—the YWCA, the WCTU, the Girl Guides and Girl Scouts, the Associated Country Women of the World, Zonta, Business and Professional Women, International University Women, the Women's International Democratic Federation, the International Federation of Women's Clubs, the International Council of Women, and others of the forty-seven women's NGOs mentioned in this book, have also been my teachers. So have the women associated with the World Council of Churches, with national and transnational denominational organizations, and women of transnational religious orders. I regret that the statistics on women's NGOs captures nothing of the dynamics of caring of any of these women's groups. The picture of these women at work must be saved for another book. I hope my colleagues in the women's NGO world will agree with me, however, that the exercise of submitting those NGOs to the type of analysis I have undertaken is useful in developing a perspective on the nature of the tasks at hand.

Since the work of preparing the data for the *Handbook of International Data on Women* with Dorothy Carson, Shirley Nuss, and Michael Greenstein has been intimately associated with the preparation of these papers, I want to thank each of them for their part in making this book possible. Dorothy Carson is the one who has been the most closely involved with the details of this book, and the compilation of the women's NGO data by country has been done entirely by her. Robert Passmore has assembled some of the data not directly associated with the data handbook. Anita Cochran, librarian at the Institute of Behavioral Science, helped me find the books on women in development used in Part II. Suzy Tessler helped prepare some of the tables. Alanna Preussner's work with manuscript detail has been invaluable, and Kathy Hamilton of Boulder Graphics went to a great deal of trouble to create just the kind of maps we wanted for the book. Judy Fukuhara's beautiful typing climaxed the arduous efforts with manuscript.

Preface

Kenneth Boulding and I dialogued continuously about the subject matter of this book. His continuous critical questioning of my commensalist philosophy has helped me strive for greater analytic clarity in identifying what I perceive to be the critical elements in the dynamic of growth toward a more just and stable world order.

To the many people, named and unnamed, who have helped make this book possible, I say thank you.

—Elise Boulding
University of Colorado

NOTES

1. Chapters 2, 3, 5, 7, 8, and 9 appeared in a mimeographed International Women's Year series issued from the Program of Research on General Social and Economic Dynamics of the Institute of Behavioral Science at the University of Colorado. Each of the papers in that series has been reworked to varying degrees for this book. Where necessary, the data on which the tables are based have also been reworked. Chapters 1, 4, 6, and 10 were not issued in mimeographed form and therefore appear here for the first time.

2. Because of the policy orientation of the book, the reader will find no review of relevant literature on women's roles here. A number of such reviews are now available elsewhere, and my own review of this literature will be found in Chapter 1 of *The Underside of History* (Boulder, Colorado: Westview Press, 1977).

PART I

GENERAL OVERVIEW

AND HISTORICAL BACKGROUND

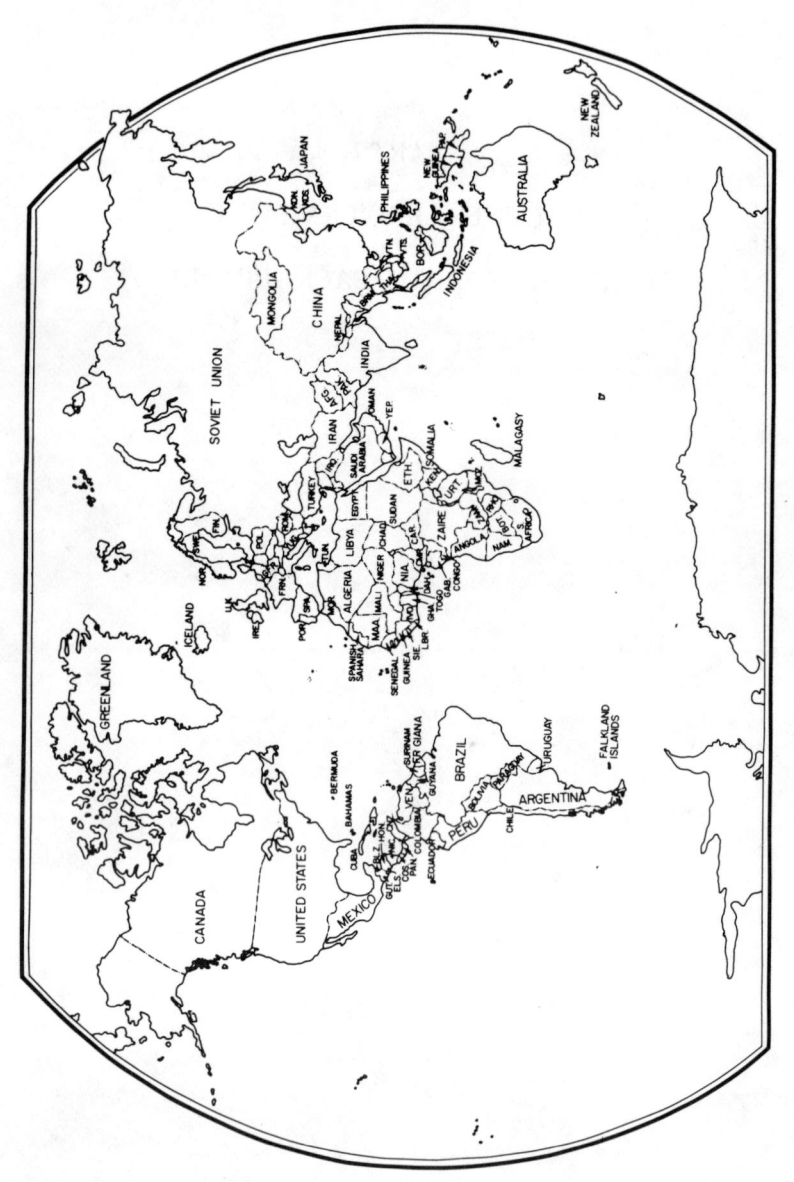

Chapter 1

THE WORLD WE OF WOMEN: Household Patterns and Women's Occupations Around the World

Throughout this book we will be moving back and forth between statements about the life situations of women based on contemporary observations and the historical record, and the coding of these life situations into "lifeless" numbers. Statistical tables are like topographical maps. They tell us in a general way where the hills and valleys are, and record the heights and depths, but they give few clues as to the character or quality of the landscape. Yet they are useful to hikers who need to allocate energy and resources according to the heights they will be tackling. Even when the heights are not accurately recorded, the maps give a general idea of the terrain.

In studying the situation of women in the twentieth century, we urgently need a general idea of the terrain. Most of us see the world from where we sit and have little idea of the general human condition of women. This introductory chapter will therefore be devoted to an examination of the larger picture. The contour lines I will be drawing are based on the numbers provided by the UN statistical offices about women in families, in school, and in the labor force. We face a dilemma immediately in interpreting these numbers because one of the major problems for women is their invisibility. They are invisible to the enumerators of employed persons because much of their productive labor takes place in what in this book we call the fifth world: the world of the kitchen, the kitchen garden, and the nursery. Economists do not assign a monetary value to this labor, but use a category called "not economically active homemaker" to cover women in this type of occupation. A second, more elusive category is that of "other not economically active women": students, pensioners, and "others." A third category of women's labor, hard to pin down, is that of the "unpaid family worker." A fourth vague category is that of "own-account" (self-employed) workers. What determines whether an enumerator will count a woman who is not in the regular paid labor force in one or another of those four categories? There are rules for enumerators, but they are variously interpreted in various countries.

Our problems continue when we move into regularly recognized occupational sectors. A majority of the world's population still lives in rural areas. What determines whether a woman who farms, alone or with a partner, will be listed as a "farmer," "unpaid family worker," "not economically active homemaker," or "not economically active other"? Again, there are rules, but they are not applied in the same way from country to country.

Even when we move into the industrial sector there are enumeration problems. In the third world there are still a number of home industries that employ wage labor. How accurately are the women who are nonfamily wage laborers counted in these home industries? How accurately are the women counted at any work site where they are employed? Since they are often considered auxiliary labor, the same care may not be taken to count them as their male counterparts. This means that in all but the most modern employment settings, there may be substantial undercounting of women. Women professional and technical workers (a large proportion of whom are teachers) are probably the best-counted women workers, and agricultural and own-account workers are probably the most poorly tabulated.

Apart from the problems of the social invisibility of women and the variety of ways in which enumeration rules are applied from country to country, there is also the problem of the basic capacity of the census offices in third world countries to do systematic counting of any kind, including the counting of births and deaths. Statistical offices are a luxury for poor countries with little governmental infrastructure. Sampling techniques can be substituted for complete counts, and frequently are, but these techniques, applied with inadequate knowledge of the total population being sampled, produce numbers that must be used with great caution.

The final problem stemming from the use of numbers has to do with whether the categories for which numbers are collected represent significant indicators of any aspect of social and economic conditions. What numerical categories would give us significant information about the situation of women with regard to the three arenas of social process covered by the International Women's Year themes of equality, development, and peace? The development of new measures that will come closer than the old measures of GNP, urbanization, etc., to telling us about the quality of life of a population and particularly of its women is a top agenda item for scholars, and for every UN agency. In this book, however, we will use the categories for which numbers are already collected, and try to take from these numbers what clues we can about the situation of women.

We see from the above discussion that national statistics have many weaknesses, and that national statistics about women are doubly uncertain. Nevertheless, in an uncharted terrain it is better to have some clues than none at all. In the spirit of setting out into uncharted terrain, therefore, I offer the following world profile of women. Readers who care to may consider this the "world we" of women. In the chapters that follow, many of the numbers given here will be disaggregated to create regional profiles. The world figures literally represent the world average for women for each characteristic enumerated. Since the figures are world means, it must not be forgotten that some countries will have higher figures for their women, while other countries will have far lower ones, even approaching 0.

For each category of activity where both men and women are involved, the world figure will be given in two ways: (1) as a femaleness index—i.e., how many women there are engaged in that activity as a percentage of all women and men engaged in that activity; (2) as a distribution index—i.e., how many women there are engaged in that activity as a percentage of all women in the relevant group (women in the labor force for occupations, women of school age for school enrollment, etc.).

GENERAL ECONOMIC ACTIVITY PROFILE FOR WOMEN

How "female" is the world labor force? That is, of the world's enumerated workers, how many are women? We see from Table 1.1A that 29 percent of the officially enumerated world labor force are women. Of that group in the labor force who are counted as employers or as working on their own account (self-employed), 18.6 percent are women. Of all workers who are employees, 23.6 percent are women. Of all unpaid family workers, 45 percent are women. Given all the forces operating to ensure the undercounting of women, the fact that roughly one-third of the world's enumerated labor force is reported to be female suggests that more figures on working women are available for planning and policy-making purposes than are paid attention to.

If we ask a different question, "What is the employment status of the world's female population?" we find in Table 1.1B that of all women to be counted as part of the potential work force of that society (females over ten years of age in some societies, over fifteen in others, not indicated in still others), 24 percent are in the officially enumerated world labor force. These 24 percent are in the *exchange* economy. Women in the subsistence economy are not counted in the labor force. Of the other 76 percent of women, 48.5 percent are homemakers. (These data, it should be noted, refer primarily to

Table 1.1A: World Economic Activity of Women by Status: Femaleness Index (Women as a Percentage of Total Labor Force)

Economic Status	Percentage Women
Women in the Labor Force	29.1
Women Employers and Own-Account Workers	18.6
Women Employees	23.6
Women Unpaid Family Workers	45.2

SOURCE: Boulding, Nuss, Carson, and Greenstein (1976).

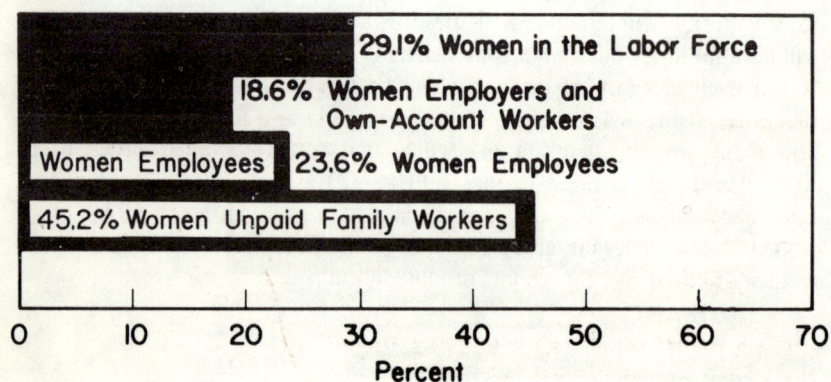

the industrialized world of Western Europe. Similar figures are not reported for much of the third world.) The rest are unlabelled, unpaid family workers, children, students, the elderly, and "other." An unknown number of these women live by their wits on the margins of society, in the subsistence economy, some as prostitutes, some as scavengers, some in other ways. (It would be interesting to do a study of the women who live by their wits around the world, outside the recognized categories of employed women, homemakers, unpaid family labor, and dependents.) Within the category of employed women—i.e., women employed in the exchange economy (second, third, and fourth categories in Table 1.1B)—we find that nearly 20 percent are self-employed. Another 20 percent are unpaid family workers, and 60 percent are wage workers.

In other words, 80 percent of the women who are listed as being in the labor force have an ascertainable cash income. We know nothing about the economic situation of the 76 percent who are not enumerated in the labor force. Many of them are active in the subsistence economy, particularly agriculture. The 50 percent who are homemakers presumably engage in uncounted home production, and possibly in extensive barter or uncounted cash transactions. They may receive intrafamily "grants" from male partners.

Table 1.1B: World Economic Activity of Women by Status: Distribution Index (Women as a Percentage of All Employed Women)

Economic Status	Percentage Women
Women in the Labor Force:	24.1
Women Employers and Own-Account Workers	18.9
Women Employees	60.2
Women Unpaid Family Workers	21.3
Total Employed Women	100.4*
Women Not in the Labor Force Who Are Homemakers	48.5

SOURCE: Boulding, Nuss, Carson, and Greenstein (1976).
*Error due to rounding.

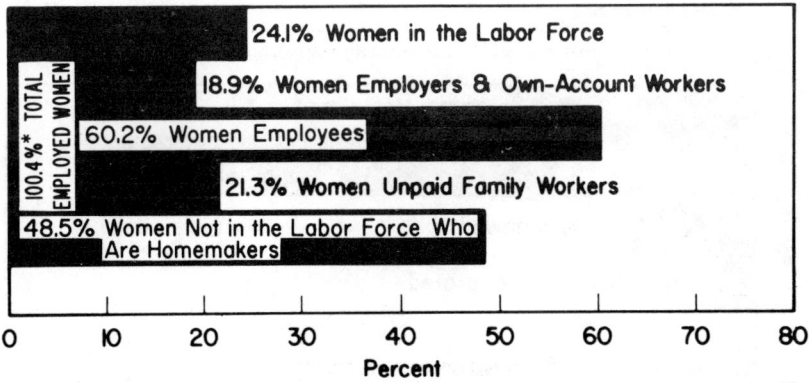

The other 50 percent may also engage in barter or uncounted cash transactions. Chapter 4 throws some light on how these transactions outside the official trade networks can operate. While figures for income by sex are not available on an international comparative basis, from an examination of the status categories just discussed, it is not hard to see that a large number of the world's women have no easily ascertainable regular sources of income.

FAMILY AND HOUSEHOLD SITUATION OF WOMEN

Table 1.2 provides an alternative perspective for viewing the world economic situation of women. At any one time, about 62 percent of the world's women over the age of fifteen are "legally" married. (Consensual unions are excluded from the data.) This is a padded figure, since many women report themselves as married who are not, or who no longer have partners living with them. On the other hand, it is also true that many women are living in consensual or other socially approved unions that are not defined as legal by

Table 1.2: World Family and Household Situation of Women

Marital Status	
Percentage Never Married	23.0
Percentage Married	62.3
Percentage Widowed	11.5
Percentage Divorced, Separated	3.5
Household	
Average Size of Household	4.6
Child Woman Ratio	635.7
Child Woman Ratio, Urban	571.6
Child Woman Ratio, Rural	702.4
Migration	
Percentage Female of Long-Term Immigrants	42.3
Percentage Female of Long-Term Emigrants	45.3

SOURCE: Boulding, Nuss, Carson, and Greenstein (1976).

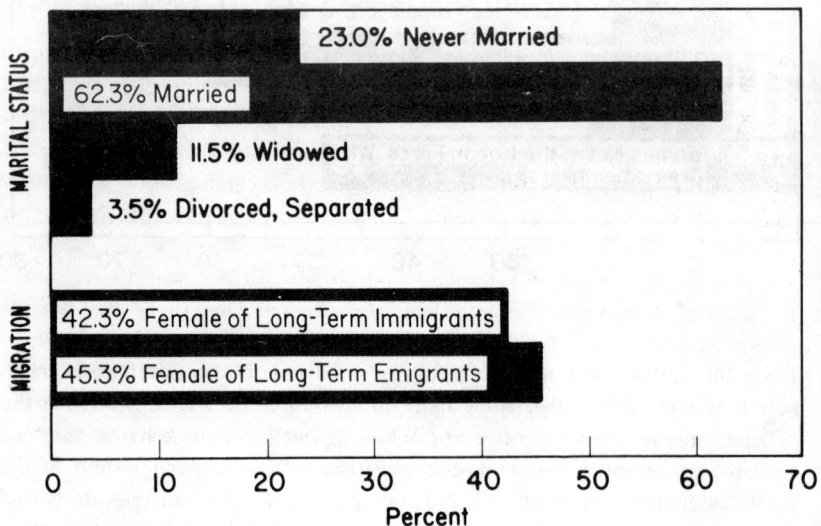

census rules and are therefore not counted, although the women are in fact "partnered." "Partnered" would be a better term than "married," since there is no necessary presumption of ritualized union in these "marriages." An unknown number of the 23 percent who have never married (many of whom will be married later—or may already be in consensual unions), of the 11.5 percent widowed, and of the 3.5 percent divorced or separated, have responsibility for children. These phenomena will be explored regionally in later chapters. For now it is enough to remember that at any particular time, roughly 40 percent of the world's adult women are legally unpartnered—perhaps more, perhaps less. An unknown proportion of these women, particularly those with children, suffer severe economic deprivation. The world child-woman ratio tells us that for every 1,000 women in the world, there are 635 children *under five* to be cared for. In rural areas, the figure is 702, in urban areas, 571. The breeder-feeder responsibilities carried by the world's women is a heavy one.

However heavy it is, women do not simply dig in where they are and try to make the best of it. We see from Table 1.2 that 42 to 45 percent of the world's migrants, whether counted as coming into a country or leaving a country, in major long-term moves of over one year, are women. No one knows how many of these women are partnered, but since it is generally recognized that many migrants are unpartnered men, then it must follow that there are also many migrants who are unpartnered women. These figures undercut the conventional images of women as sedentary nest builders.

EDUCATION AND TEACHING ROLES FOR WOMEN

While illiteracy is no bar to employment for women in the traditional sector, it is a barrier to modernized employment. We note in Table 1.3A that women carry a larger share of the burden of illiteracy in the world than men, and have relatively fewer opportunities as adults to take literacy training. Their opportunities for third level education (high school level or its equivalent[1]) are even more severely limited, except in the field of teacher training, in which approximately one-half of the world's third level graduates are women. The next best training opportunity for the world's women is in the field of social science, which produces one-fourth of the women graduates from third level institutions. However, women are one-seventh of the graduates in law, one-tenth in agriculture, and one-twentieth in engineering. It would appear that the participation of women in the world's labor force is not welcomed at higher professional levels. Yet as teachers they are widely employed in the world's primary schools, somewhat less so in the world's secondary schools. Nearly half of the world's elementary school teachers are women, as are just over one-third of the world's secondary school teachers. The incongruity of the low status of women as expert professionals when it comes to policy-making about social systems, and the intensive use of women as teachers and shapers of society's youth, will bear serious reflection.

If we look at the educational picture from the point of view of how many girls of school age actually get to school, we see that for elementary school the world picture is not as bad as we might have expected. Seventy-seven percent of all girls who could be enrolled in elementary schools evidently are so enrolled, although I suspect overcounting here (Table 1.3B). If we consider day-in, day-out regularity of education, and the frequency of dropouts,

Table 1.3A: World Educational Attainment of Women: Femaleness Index (Women as Percentage of All Those Educated, and All Those Who Are Teachers)

Educational Status	Percentage Women
Women Illiterates	59.3
Women in Literacy Courses	38.8
Women Graduates of Third Level Training in:	
Education	48.8
Social Science	25.0
Law	15.9
Agriculture	10.7
Engineering	5.1
Women Teachers at First Level	48.3
Women Teachers at Second Level	35.2

SOURCE: Boulding, Nuss, Carson, and Greenstein (1976).

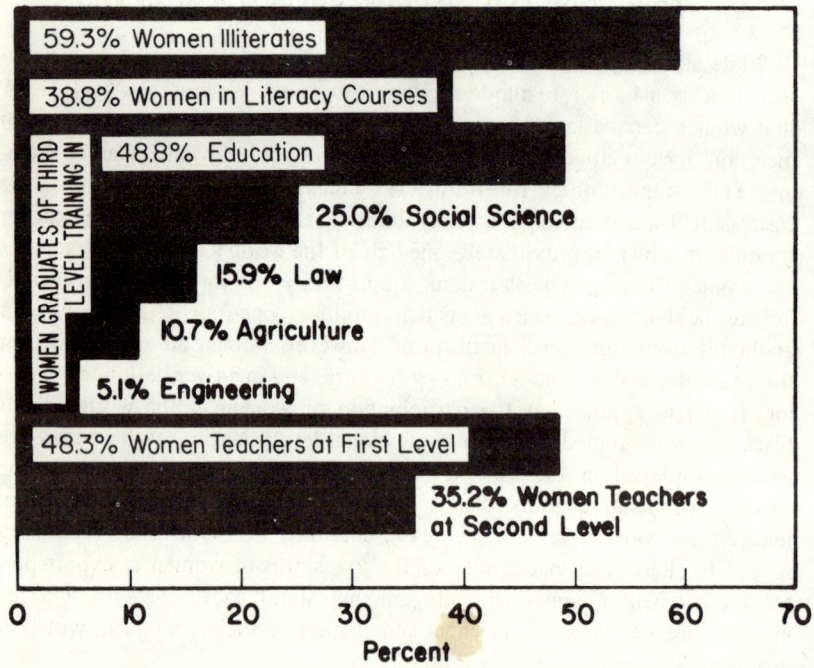

now a statistically noticeable phenomenon in upper elementary grades in the United States, the picture would not be so bright. However, as an order-of-magnitude figure, this 77 percent should be noted as expressing the intentions of the world's policy makers to give a rudimentary amount of education to the "future mothers" of the world society.

Table 1.3B: World Educational Attainment of Women: Distribution Index (Women as Percentage of All Women)

Educational Status	Percentage Women
Female Enrollment, First Level Education	77.4
Female Enrollment, Second Level Education	26.5

SOURCE: Boulding, Nuss, Carson, and Greenstein (1976).

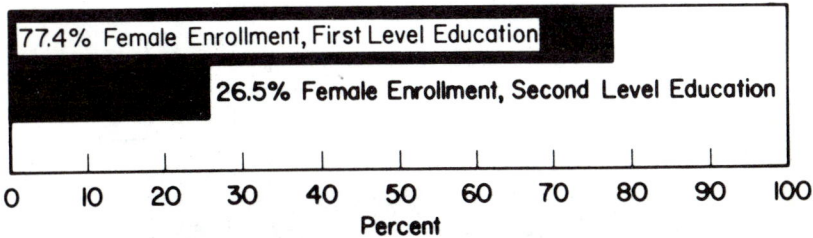

It has been stated more than once by development planners that when you educate a male you invest in only one person. When you educate a female you invest not only in that one person, but in all the children she will bear. This procreation-linked view of education that keeps women in the world's kindergartens will only disappear as economists and the societies to which they belong learn to give male parenting its proper weight along with female parenting in estimating investments in child-rearing, and female productivity its proper weight along with male productivity in estimating labor force investments. When we look at the percentage of girls who are able to go on to the second level of education, we quickly see that policy makers have very limited aspirations for the daughters of the world community. Only one-fourth of school-age girls receive this additional training. With only elementary education available to three-quarters of the world's women, opportunities in the more skilled sectors of the labor force remain very limited for them.

WOMEN IN THE LABOR FORCE BY OCCUPATION AND INDUSTRY

It comes as no surprise to discover that one-half of the world's service workers are women, as Table 1.4A indicates. This category includes domestic service and a variety of other types of service including "sports and recreation," services that are generally (not always) rendered at low or intermediate skill levels. That 38 percent of the world's professional and technical workers are women comes as more of a surprise. However, it is the vast world army of women elementary school teachers which swells this category. There are

Table 1.4A: Rank Ordering of Women by Occupation in the Labor Force: World Femaleness Index (Women as Percentage of All Persons in the Occupational Category)

Rank Order	Percentage Women	Occupation
1	50.1	Service
2	38.3	Professional, Technical
3	33.9	Sales
4	33.7	Clerical
5	21.7	Agriculture
6	15.3	Production
7	10.2	Administrative, Managerial
8	2.3	Armed Forces

SOURCE: Boulding, Nuss, Carson, and Greenstein (1976).

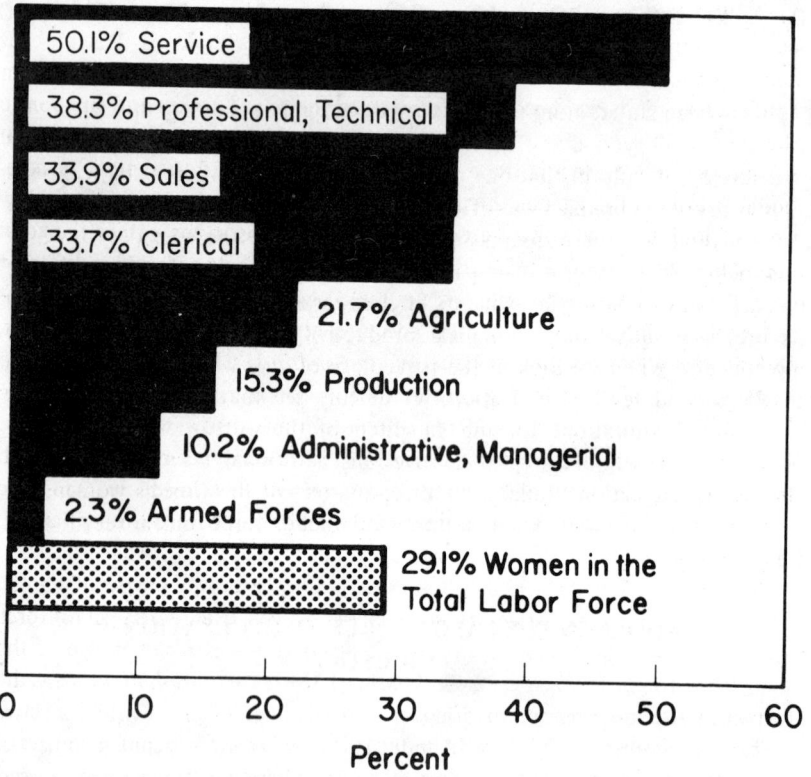

relatively few nonteaching professionals in this category, as we can infer from the paucity of women graduates from third-level training institutions (Table 1.3A).

That one-half of the world's clerical and sales labor force are women is not surprising. I shall dispute later the figure of one-fifth women, in agricultural labor as being more than ordinarily undercounted. The 15 percent of women in production certainly does not include an adequate count of women wage laborers in home industries. The 10 percent figure for women in administrative and managerial positions contrasts sharply with the 38 percent figure for women in professional and technical occupations. The figure on women administrators reflects better than any other figure in this series the low status of women in the world's labor force. Women participate least in the world's military, as we see from the 2 percent figure at the bottom of Table 1.4A. While this may not be a sector in which we want to increase anyone's participation, women or men, it must be at least noted as a significant arena of human activity where few women are present. Since only fourteen countries in the world both admit women to the armed forces and enumerate them separately in their national statistics, this mean of 2 percent women soldiers is only based on these fourteen countries.[2] The foregoing occupational profile is for women as members of the total world labor force. Now we will look at how women are distributed by occupations within the total population of employed women (Table 1.4B). The rank ordering is different here. We see that more women are employed in agriculture than in any other occupation. If they were counted better the figure would be even higher. Service ranks second, and production ranks third among occupations for women, as contrasted with a rank of six for women in production in Table 1.4A when women were considered as a percentage of the total world labor force. Professional and technical, clerical and sales occupations all loom much smaller when compared with women's involvement in other sectors, ranking fourth, fifth, and sixth. Administrative and managerial work, not surprisingly, ranks at the bottom, just above participation in the armed forces.

It is clear that we get a very different picture of the employment of women when we compare occupational involvement within the female labor force than we do when we compare women's occupations as a percentage of the total labor force. From the point of view of the life situation of women, the former figures are more illuminating.

Tables 1.5A and 1.5B look at women in the labor force not in terms of occupations, but in terms of industries. Tables 1.4A and 1.4B showed what women actually *do*. Tables 1.5A and 1.5B show what industries women are employed in, regardless of their actual occupation in that industry. (For example, a woman could be a *secretary* in a factory or a mine, rather than a production worker or miner, and still be counted in the manufacturing or

(Text continued on page 31)

Table 1.4B: Rank Ordering of Women by Occupation in the Labor Force: World Distribution Index (Women as Percentage of All Employed Women)

Rank Order	Percentage Women	Occupation
1	29.8	Agriculture
2	24.2	Service
3	18.7	Production
4	12.8	Professional, Technical
5	12.1	Clerical
6	10.4	Sales
7	7.1	Administrative, Managerial
8	0.1	Armed Forces

Percentage Women in the Total Labor Force: 29.1

SOURCE: Boulding, Nuss, Carson, and Greenstein (1976).

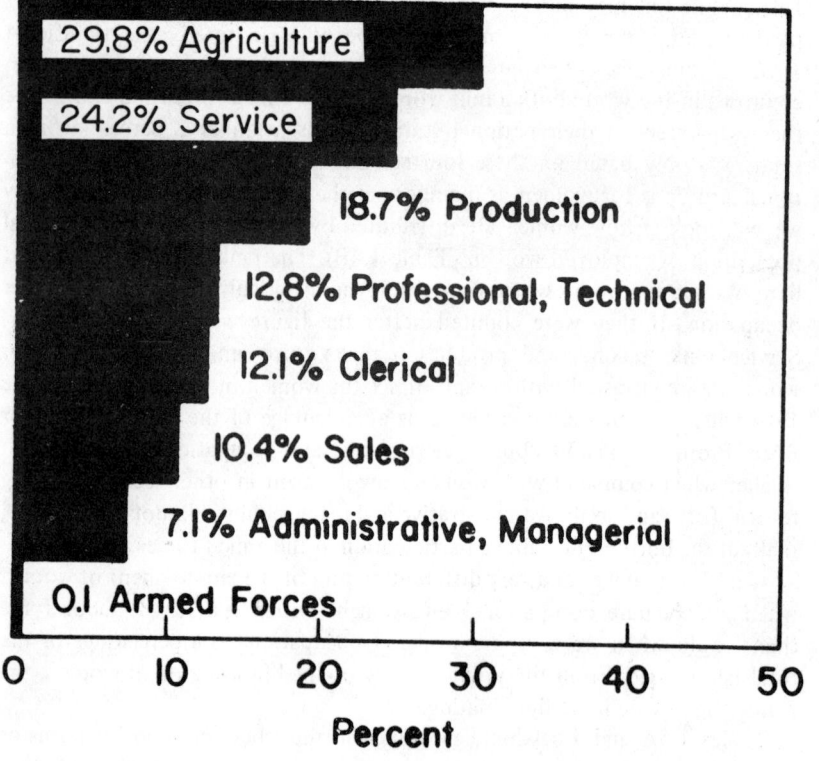

Table 1.5A: A Rank Ordering of Economic Activity of Women by Industry: World Femaleness Index (Women as Percentage of Total Labor Force, Women and Men)

Rank Order	Percentage Women	Industry
1	41.2	Finance, Insurance, etc.
2	30.6	Wholesale and Retail
3	25.5	Manufacturing
4	22.8	Agriculture
5	7.9	Electricity, etc.
6	7.7	Transport
7	7.6	Mining
8	3.5	Construction

SOURCE: Boulding, Nuss, Carson, and Greenstein (1976).

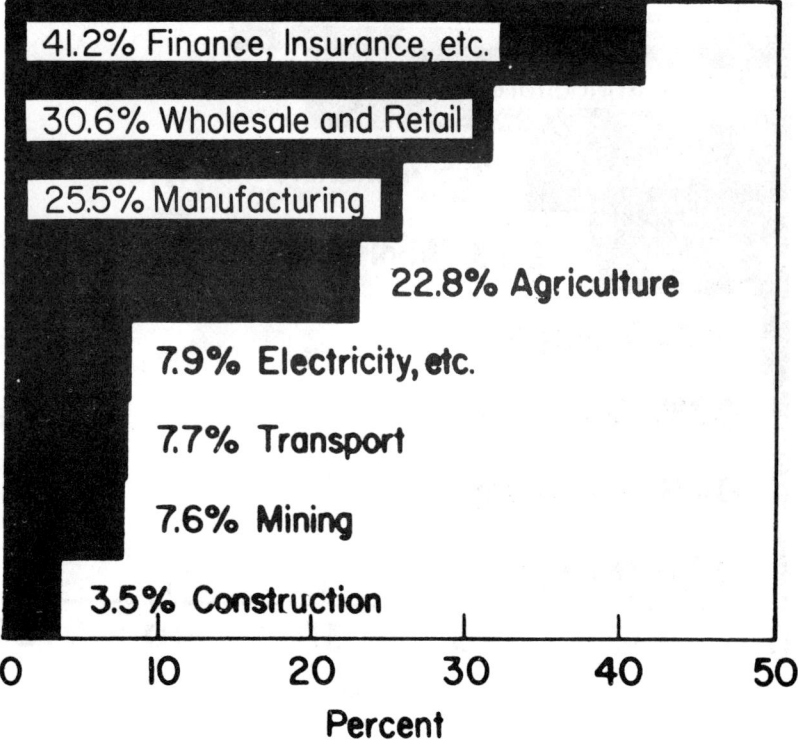

Table 1.5B: A Rank Ordering of Economic Activity by Women by Industry: World Distribution Index (Women as Percentage of All Employed Women)

Rank Order	Percentage Women	Industry
1	36.2	Finance, Insurance, etc.
2	31.2	Agriculture
3	16.9	Manufacturing
4	12.6	Wholesale and Retail
5	1.5	Transport
6	0.7	Construction
7	0.4	Electricity
8	0.3	Mining

SOURCE: Boulding, Nuss, Carson, and Greenstein (1976).

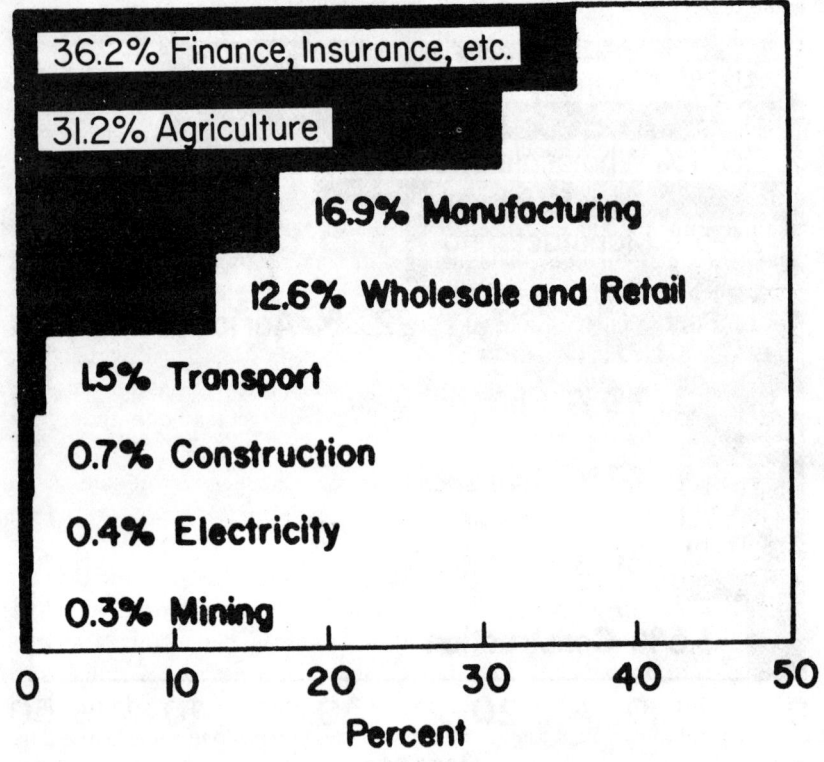

mining sector.) Table 1.5A thus provides another way of looking at the femaleness of the world labor force. From the industry perspective, women are most frequently found in the somewhat unwieldy combination labeled "finance, insurance, real estate, and community and personal services." Women are next most frequently found in wholesale and retail business, with manufacturing and agriculture ranking third and fourth. They represent under 10 percent in the remaining industry categories. The picture does not change very much in Table 1.5B when we look at the distribution of women by industry within the female labor force. Finance is still first, but agriculture has moved to second place, showing the importance of women in agriculture-related employment as well as in direct agricultural employment. Participation in the other industries is roughly equivalent to the rank ordering in Table 1.5A.

We know something more about the status of the world "we" of women than we knew before we started, although the reader must again be reminded how very rough and approximate any of the figures given here are likely to be. The participation of women in a number of occupations is higher than we might have expected. Even though women are certainly undercounted, there appear to be more data for planners to work with than are generally taken account of. The evidence is clear that in relation to the extent of their labor force participation, their higher skill training opportunities and their employment status at the administrative level (even for those who have higher education) are very disparate indeed. The data on number of unpartnered women, and the large question about the situation of that half of the "not economically active" female population who are not classified as homemakers, suggest severe hardships for substantial numbers of women not in the regular labor force. An unknown number of these women also have children to care for. Substantial numbers of the world's women lack *equality* of status with the men of their society, do not participate in *development* processes, and are excluded from public peace-making roles.

What in fact do women do, then? Since we know they are more than 50 percent of the human race, and we see from the numbers presented in this chapter that many of them are absent from the enumerated sectors of society, it becomes necessary to turn to other kinds of information and to informal speculation to uncover where they are and what they are doing. In the chapters that follow in Part I we will explore their productive roles historically and in the present. In Part II we will pay particular attention to their food-related roles since provision of food is always associated with women's roles. Since, as John Muir says, when you take hold of anything you find that it is related to everything else, we will find that it is impossible to isolate women's roles in the domestic arena even when the focus is on food. Everywhere the lines lead out from food and babies to every arena of human activity. In

Part III we will shift the focus directly to the international arena and see how women do in fact function as creators of the public order. In every chapter we will point out untapped resources and unnoticed potentials. New problem-solving approaches related to the women's development decade themes of equality, development, and peace will be pointed out wherever possible, and the entire book is pointed toward the creation of a different and better future as further delineated in Part IV, called The Coming of the Gentle Society.

For the remainder of Part I, we will explore the historical background for a consideration of twentieth and twenty-first century problems.

NOTES

1. The meaning of third-level education varies from country to country. In Europe it is usually equivalent to junior college training in the United States, and is sometimes actually equivalent to a four-year American college course. In the third world, third level education may approximate the European model, or it may approximate the American model.

2. A number of countries report women in the military, but lump those figures together with other occupational categories such as construction or mining, making it impossible to ascertain what percentage of the women are actually in the military.

Chapter 2

NOMADISM, MOBILITY, AND THE STATUS OF WOMEN

The data we generally use as indicators of women's status are based on the industrialization-as-emancipation model of women's participation in society. In this chapter some questions will be raised as to the adequacy of these measures in measuring the participatory quality of women's roles. An examination of the situation of the nomad woman becomes the point of departure for raising these larger questions. Specifically, we will look at the contribution of nomadism (and secondarily migration) to the rigidity—or fluidity—of power differentials between the sexes. It will not be argued that there is less gender-based role differentiation among the nomads than among settled peoples. In a continually moving society everyone needs to know his or her part in breaking and setting up camp, and there are clearly identifiable male and female role clusters, though the content of these clusters varies considerably from one nomadic tribe to another. The exercise of authority, however, may be somewhat different. Nomadic women have always felt freer than their settled counterparts (this is apparently still true today), and though they would not use such a term, they may think they live in a more participatory society.

The scale of nomad society has something to do with this participation level, since nomadic groups that travel together as a body may be as small as twenty people. At the other end of the size scale are the "ten thousand

Author's Note: Paper presented to the session of Working Group 13, Research Committee on Sex Roles in Society, International Sociological Association, Toronto, Canada, August 20, 1974; an abbreviated version of this chapter will appear in French in a volume entitled *Roles des Femmes et Stratification Sexulle,* Andree Michel, editor (Paris: Presses Universitaires de France, 1977).

tent" camps. Most bands have about 200 people in them. Only among nomads do we find a small population living together intimately and yet at the same time meeting a wide range of adaptation problems. A comparable village settlement would meet a much narrower set of problem-solving situations.

Materials on the role of women in nomadic society from a longer macrohistorical study of women's roles (Boulding, 1977) will be reviewed and contrasted with the situation of women living an urban life of enclosure in the gynaeceum[1] and harem of the first millennium A.D.

By deliberately choosing the extremes of mobility and settledness we will see some of the characteristics of urban life that often escape us. The situation at the end of the first millennium will be contrasted with the situation at the end of the second millennium—i.e., the twentieth century, both with regard to a general mobility of population, extent of nomadism, and the status of women by conventional measures.

Mobility is an interesting condition under which to view the social structure of any society, because the dynamics of mobility lead to a stripping down, though by no means an abolition, of stratification structures. People on the move have to travel light and cannot carry cumbersome stratification systems with them. Furthermore, mobility leads to a reshuffling of roles both for those who move and, in the case of migrants, for those who remain behind. The degree of mobility and accompanying reshuffling of a society may have more to do with an egalitarian relationship between women and men than with the level of technological sophistication of the society.

Nomadism, migration, and the permanently settled condition can be thought of as points on a mobility continuum. Most studies of nomadism by international agencies today deal with herding societies, but our definition will be broader.[2] I will treat as nomads all those who do not live regularly in settled abodes, but move their complete households from place to place in pursuit of a livelihood. The movement may be a perfectly regular one as between summer and winter pastures, a herding practice known as *transhumance.* It may be the irregular movement of hunting and gathering peoples through a relatively limited terrain where there are familiar campsites revisited periodically. It may be the destinationless movement of the gypsy, who travels from continent to continent following roads without end. It may also be the wandering of the seafarer, though movements of sea peoples tend to be migrations in search of new farmland. The migrant is looking for a place to settle, and is not a nomad in our definition. The term "nomad" for us here represents households more or less continually on the move. Since the woman in settled societies is often bound to her household, a comparison of her situation with that of women in societies where the very household is in motion will be of particular interest.

As a background to the analysis of women's roles in nomadism, it is necessary to say something about the function of nomadism in human history. We tend to think of nomads as marginal—people pushed off to undesirable fringe areas. If this were true we would expect women to be even more marginal. Research on nomadism since the 1930s, however, has made it clear that the transition to a herding way of life, whether it is directly from hunting or after a period of engaging in settled agriculture, is a choice made by preference. Nomads in every age of history have felt contempt for farmers and city dwellers. At the same time the farm and the city produce goods useful to the nomads, and nomads find various ways to procure these goods. Perhaps as much as 90 percent of all nomad-settler contacts have been peaceful. The nomad trades with the settler, or offers an exchange of services.

Herding societies naturally develop very different characteristics from settled societies. There is an egalitarianism of steppe and desert that is different from the egalitarianism of the village. At the same time, the taming of horses (after 2500 B.C.) modified nomad egalitarianism. There is a tendency to develop an aristocracy on horseback and a warrior class, at least in areas like the Asian steppes, where people can ride great distances at high speeds without any barriers of nature or human habitation to slow them down.[3] (Did horses teach men to become warriors?) This produces a three-layered society: the chiefly family or families, the people of the tribe, and slaves captured in raids. In less open terrains, or with few horses, nomads remain more peaceable and more egalitarian.[4]

The very fact of the distances that nomads cover in their daily lives year by year gives them different perceptions of society than people can have living inside walls and boxes. Seeing any one city or state in the context of other cities, other states, makes it possible for the nomad not only to act as social organizer and communications network, but also to perceive possibilities of alternative modes of exploiting environmental resources over the wide geographical areas.

The nomad has provided a society with a unique set of adaptations to problems of increasing scale of social interaction from the time of the first major human settlements. On the one hand, the nomad can remain outside the "social order problem" entirely by finding micro niches that will seal her off from contact with other populations, and using resources not desired by those populations. Within her niche she can have autonomy. This is the hunting and gathering adaptation which has survived all the way into the twentieth century. The more common adaptations involve some sort of relationship with settled society, while retaining a degree of autonomy and freedom of movement which settled societies do not have. Nomadic tribes may develop a series of beachheads in cities, establishing formal or informal contractual relationships which permit them not only to transport what they need out of the city, but also to play leadership roles among the settlers. They may even assist in the federation of formerly separate cities. Arabs, Turko-Mongolians, and Indo-Europeans have all played such roles, probably from the beginnings of the first pristine civilizations in Egypt and Sumeria.

One could argue from the historical record that the social organization and patterns of movement of the nomads, for all their fluidity, have provided the true infrastructure of history. Maybe cities and states represent the "debris," and nomadism, the actual social development of the human race!

There appear to be three main types of nomadism: (1) hunting and gathering nomadism; (2) herding nomadism of steppe and desert; and (3) craft and trade nomadism.

Hunting and gathering nomadism is the oldest, with two million years of human experience behind it. Today it represents one of the most highly evolved approaches to resource utilization in submarginal land that we know of, and it is now receiving a fair amount of research attention.[5]

Herding nomadism of steppe and desert evolved contemporaneously with agriculture. Early farmers with growing herds came to specialize in moving with their herds to less fertile regions, as the need for food led to the more intensive use of local land. This was the beginning of the competition between "the desert and the sown." Three major groups are known to us: the Bedouins of the Afro-Arabian steppes, the Turko-Mongolian groups of the Eurasian steppes, and the Indo-Europeans clustered more toward the European side of the Eurasian steppes. Bedouin and Asiatic herding nomadism continues to the present day, but European herding nomadism has disappeared except in enclaves such as the Lapps in northern Scandinavia.

The craft and trader nomads—the gypsies who originated in India and developed a complementary role to that of the Turko-Mongolian hordes, traveling with them and "servicing" their almost craftless societies; the Bedouin peoples who shifted from herding and became the intrepid Muslim traders, penetrating everywhere in the Mediterranean world; and the "beaker folk" of Europe—all live on in the twentieth century, most easily recognized in the gypsy caravans of Europe, Turkey, Africa, and the Americas.

THE ROLE OF WOMEN AMONG THE NOMADS

While nomadic societies differ considerably from one another in structure and role patterning, there are some characteristics that are found among nearly all nomads. We will examine some of these general characteristics here; readers interested in descriptions of individual societies are referred to the book-length study (Boulding, 1977).

The Family

One of the most widely recognized features of herding societies is their patriarchal structure. The herding mentality and culture have sometimes been blamed for the overthrow of the "Golden Age of Women" and for their subsequent subjection. Yet one of the most consistent features of each of the herding societies we will look at—the Arab Bedouin, the Turko-Mongolian, and the Celtic—is persistent traces of matrilineage and of some significant public roles for women. There are tribal stories of a time when women remained in their own tents after marriage and received visiting husbands (Smith, 1966: 126). Tribal genealogies mention the name of the king's mother as well as father in far more instances than we would expect if the mother were of no importance. When the head of a tribal group dies, be it chief, khan, or king, his mother and his widow play an important role in nomadic tribal societies in Asia today. While a king or khan usually has more than one wife, there is never any question as to who is the "ruling wife" and who thus plays the chief political role in the tribe (Grousset, 1970).

The man "heads" the family, but when there are plural wives, each wife has her own tent and her own herds. A women's relationship with her husband has many of the characteristics of a herding partnership, although usually men do the physical tending of the cattle. Women care for goats and sheep, and frequently milk the cattle. Among pastoral nomads, only the well-to-do warrior-aristocracy tribes practice polygamy. The average pastoral female nomad and her husband would find partner-wives an economic drain (Dupire, 1963: 47-92).

The rate of population growth in a nomadic tribe depends on the resources available to the tribe. Tribes with few pack animals and no wagons may keep close to zero population growth, using infanticide as the ultimate means of population control. Tribes with substantial wagons and draught animals have no problem in transporting children and are less inclined to practice exposure of unwanted infants at birth, though there may be some attempt to keep down the number of girl babies raised. Girls cannot be used for herding, which is as physically rigorous an occupation as hunting and which often requires long absences from camp.

Nomads tend to be sexual puritans, whether gypsies, Mongols, or Arabs, and they punish both women and men for adultery. Marriages are usually arranged, and if there is divorce, there are usually rights to divorce on both sides. Property rights of both sides are protected in divorce.

In general, then, within the family there is an egalitarian husband-wife relationship and an economic partnership based partly on individual ownership, partly on shared holdings.

Political Structures

The tribal chief, khan, or king usually has a khatun or queen as co-ruler; they are usually advised by a council of elders. The council of elders is not a mixed group, but there is usually at least one woman who serves as senior adviser to the council; she is partly political adviser, and partly forecaster (Chadwick, 1970: 135-136). Sometimes these roles are separated. The khatun rules until the next khan is designated and when necessary acts as regent during the minority of the next designated ruler (Prawdin, 1940: 287). In rare cases, as during the height of the Mongol empire, the institution of the harem has appeared, having the characteristics of a woman's court, with diplomatic retinues in attendance. Women are also important as conductors of ceremonial activities, and in some nomadic societies only the women chant and sing, never the men (Drinker, 1948).

Women of the elite also play important political roles in settled societies. It is difficult to compare the two, since records on the participation of women in nomadic societies are even scarcer than those for settled societies, but political participation of women often appears more formalized in nomadic than in settled societies. Among the Mongols, a woman *always* rules between khans as a matter of tribal custom. There are traditional spheres of authority allotted to women as co-rulers, advisers, regents, and participants in the choice of succeeding rulers. In general, women of the urban Middle Eastern elites who have gotten into political action have had only one formally recognized position to work from—that of priestess. Other activities have depended on their own wits, rather than on a tradition of participation. There is some evidence that outstanding women who appear in the Mesopotamian chronicles are second generation nomads.[6] When nomadic elites have entered cities, the women have both activated the traditional priestess roles and generally expanded the sphere of their political participation in the city.

Economic Roles

There is a gender-based division of labor in nomadic societies, but it is not as rigid as it often appears to be. While herding is usually done by men, milking is done sometimes by men, sometimes by women. Men are more engaged in fighting than women, but since war is often fought while the entire tribe is on the move, the campground can become the battlefield and women must also be trained to fight (Grousset, 1970; Chadwick, 1970). Among the gypsies, women and men are both craftworkers and traders, but they specialize in different products. In general, women have more camp-based activities than men, since they rarely do herding or raiding. Camp-based tasks, however, have a different social setting from the home-based tasks of the sedentary woman. Breaking or setting up camp, the woman's task, occurs frequently and is always done in close proximity to other women. Preparation of food, garments, containers from wool and skins goes on in the spaces between tents as well as inside them. There tends to be women's space versus men's space, rather than private domestic space versus public space. On ceremonial occasions, women's spaces and men's spaces intersect, although there are also all-female and all-male ceremonies. The community of women, girls, and boys under twelve can be a strongly knit group that provides inputs to the men's community via the woman elder.

Religion

All types of nomad societies seem to have a deep religious strain, but it is a generalized religious responsiveness that can fit a wide variety of institutional forms. The Mongols were extraordinarily tolerant of all religions, having Nestorian Christians and Catholics, Buddhists, Zoroastrians, and Moslems in their courts. The gypsies adopt the religion of the country or region they are in at the moment. Their religious fervor is matched only by their acceptance of many ways to express it. It seems to be particularly the woman's job to identify and support the appropriate variety of cults in a given setting, and to "take in" new religions (Grousset, 1970: 280). The underlying faith is shamanistic, and the tribal shaman may or may not outrank the prophetess. To the extent that ceremonies reflect the basic belief structures of the society, however, the leading role of women in ceremonies belies the formal prominence of the shaman. The rites of childbirth, baptism, marriage, death, and coronation are often women's rites.

In general, the skills that keep a nomadic society functioning smoothly on the road and in the making and breaking of camp, and those that enable nomads to scan and utilize their environments in ways that settled peoples often occupying the same general space do not, seem to be skills that also create a unique social bond among these people. This bond delineates nomad society as clearly in social space as settled societies are bounded in physical space.

Within this space there is indeed a man's world and a woman's world, accentuated by the need to provide protected space for bearing and rearing children in a camp environment that does not easily allow for protected spaces. Women's participation in the total life of the society, however, is not less, and may be greater, than it is for women in settled societies. The common orientation of both sexes toward the "world as one's backyard" and the common experience of living out of the nomadic equivalent of suitcases are a more powerful bond between women and men that the separateness of their tasks would indicate.

THE MIGRANT: TEMPORARY NOMAD

The migrant, at least during the period between leaving home and final resettlement, must have the scanning skills of the nomad. Women and men must both learn to "read" alien environments and to create adapted role patterns that will utilize new resources in new settings. In family sociology vocabulary, migration is a "family crisis," old patterns won't do (Hansen and Hill, 1964: 782-819). Authority becomes much more fluid under such circumstances, and everything depends on competence, not on social status. The pioneer era of the United States is perhaps the one time for which the favorite sociological model of modernization as a movement from ascribed to achieved statuses was historically descriptive. That American pioneer women had "achieved" statuses is perhaps best documented in *Democracy in America* (1945). De Tocqueville never tired of describing the free, autonomous ways of American women, who presumably had lived in subjection to their husbands back in Europe. (Why else would De Tocqueville have been so surprised?)

There are two sides to the migration phenomenon, however. One is the effect on women who migrate; the other is the effect on women who stay behind. Prior to 1000 A.D., as far as we can tell, migrations tended to be family migrations. During the prolonged period of social disorganization that included the Crusades, however, many individuals were detached from households, and many men went to the holy land to seek their fortune. These were settlers, not crusaders, though some set off in a dual role. Women went, too, but there were far fewer women than men. From 1000 A.D. on, then, we have women left behind in areas from which male migrants have poured out, women who faced opportunities to reorganize and administer the remaining resources. What happened to these women?

The evacuation of the men seems to have given women a much freer hand than they had before. Here we turn for evidence to a study by Herlihy of women's status as revealed in documents relating to European land transfers, 701-1200 (1962: 89-120). His data point to an increasingly high status for women, by two indicators: (1) extensive use of the metronymic in legal documents (identification of persons through mother rather than through father); and (2) substantial increase in the amount of land registered directly in a woman's name, as well as in land she administered on behalf of heirs—presumably her children. By 1100, 25 percent of all land covered in the survey was controlled by women. While many of the women who show up in these documents belonged to the upper classes, we can assume that the general loosening of men's control over resources during this period gave women of every sector of society new economic opportunities and increased personal freedom. This is the period of the great flourishing of women's guilds

(Renard, 1968), as women entered into a whole range of craft and professional occupations which they were not eased out of until the 1400s, when the prolonged "fluid period" of European society ended.

THE ENCLOSURE MOVEMENT FOR WOMEN

It is difficult to know when the enclosure of women first began. It has always been associated with urbanism and also with high status. In Egypt the harem was actually the women's court, from which national and international affairs were administered; originally, it may have been an indicator of women's power, rather than the reverse. The gynaeceum in Athens, the woman's quarters of the house, represents the opposite extreme, and had its counterpart among the Jewish merchant families of Syria. While a woman was indeed "mistress" of her own quarters, she was so powerless to move outside them that to dwell on her power *in* the home is almost meaningless. The gynaeceum apparently became the civilizing model for the way women of status should live for both the Persian and the Hellenic empires. It was very widespread in the Byzantine Empire, and Moslem writers blame Byzantium for introducing the idea of purdah to the much freer Arab (nomad) women (Ali, 1899: 755-774). The institution probably was brought to India and China via Greek and Persian traders. For the top aristocracy, purdah was indeed the women's court. The mother or wife of the emperor or caliph had her own prime minister and a retinue numbering in the thousands. But for the wife of the ambitious middle class merchant, there was no busy court life, only enclosed space, and the company of the women of her own home.[7]

If only the top layer of elite women had been affected by this practice, it might not have had such a deleterious social effect. But when seclusion of women became the model that every upwardly mobile family aspired to, large numbers of women were removed from effective participation in society. This is a phenomenon that grew with urbanism. We will see shortly how this effect continued into the twentieth century.

What is there about urbanism that contributes to enclosure for women? There are many answers to this, but the one that might concern us most is women's removal from significant productive activity by being placed in a setting where the raw materials for craft production are no longer available. The bakery around the corner is found as far back as the cities of Sumer, 2000 B.C., so urban woman's release from home production activities is not a new thing. It is one of the primary features of urban existence everywhere. By the same token she was (and is) removed from the public spaces of villages and rural settings in which the work of production went on communally. This removal from communal work spaces is as significant as the release from production tasks, since in these spaces her political skills were developed and her communications networks activated.

Where is the communication network for the woman in the city? Being ingenious, Moslem women developed them in the public baths. Since these spaces had no productive function, however, the quality of the interaction between women deteriorated. The secluded home puts on the individual mother full responsibility for child-rearing with none of the communal child care available in normal village life, and this only reinforces the isolation of the woman and sets up additional barriers to her exploration of the public spaces in the urban setting and her search for new productive activities. This is true chiefly for the middle class woman, of course—and all cities have middle classes. Women among the urban poor must find their way into productive activity, and they do. *They* run the corner bakeries! Their children grow up under their feet, wherever they work. The fact that there are parallels between women in cities one and two thousand years ago and in the era of new industrial urbanization suggests that the structures of urbanization did not change very much with the advent of mass production.

Given the seclusion of middle class women and the economic slavery of poor women, the contempt that nomad women have felt for their city sisters is understandable.

THE TWENTIETH CENTURY AND THE GREAT SETTLING DOWN

One of the most startling aspects of twentieth century life is that it is becoming increasingly sedentary, at the same time that we have the illusion of great mobility. The nomadic societies described earlier are fast disappearing. For the most part this is because modern nations feel that nomads represent a backward element in their respective populations and that they must be settled in order to participate in the good life of the modern world. Not all students of nomadism agree, and some effort is also being made to learn quickly (before it is too late), the special resource-utilization skills that arid-land nomads have developed over centuries on land that cannot be turned to other uses.[8]

Herders as well as gypsies are the target of settlement schemes in almost every country where they are found. More studies are urgently needed of women's roles in these societies before they disappear entirely, for there are strong traces of an egalitarianism in them which is rare in industrial society. The material on women's roles in the recent hunting and gathering studies as cited earlier in Note 5 is suggestive, but not nearly detailed enough.

The experience of mobility, so prominent through recorded history, is diminishing. With its diminishment, we may be losing a certain set of social skills.

We don't feel less mobile—if anything, the self-image of the "developed" countries in the twentieth century is one of great geographic and social mobility. Social mobility is not in question here, but geographic mobility is slowing down. The era of great "development migrations" from Europe to North and South America and Australia is essentially over.[9] The era of internal frontier migrations—such as the push west in North America, the pushes from European to Asiatic Russia and from China to Manchuria—is also over.

Finally, the great rural-urban migration is over as well. By 1950 from 60 to 80 percent of the rural populations of many European countries had emptied into the cities (United Nations, 1953: 109). One reason for the rapid growth of the "enclosure movement"[10] for American women in the early to middle part of this century was because of the rapid urbanization that took place in the United States between 1880 and 1920. The United States went from 28.6 percent urban in 1880 to 63 percent urban in 1960, but most of the change occurred between 1880 and 1920. The percentage of increase in the first twenty years was 38.9, the second twenty years it was 28.9, and then the percentage of increase slowed down to around 11 percent for the last two twenty-year periods (Taeuber and Taeuber, 1971). The speed of the early stages of the change was enough to render large numbers of women "helpless" in strange urban environments.

Migrations have certainly not come to an end. There are still substantial intracontinental migrations in Europe and also in Africa. They could be considered as residual to the major population shifts that took place in the preceding century, however. It has been suggested that there has been a general decline in adventurousness (United Nations, 1953: 162), and an increase in population shifts determined by government policy rather than private initiative (United Nations, 1953: 122).

The United States is apparently typical in the general disinclination of populations to move further away than the next town or country. In 1960 only about a third of all Americans were born outside the state they were living in, a proportion that had not changed since 1920. In fact the 1960 U.S. census tells us that four-fifths of the American population was still living in the same county as five years previously. Most migrations, in whatever part of the world, are to the nearest town, involving a minimum of upheaval.

This gives the general mobility picture. What about women? The U.S. census report states:

> Men were more mobile than women, particularly so as the distance of the move increased. In 1960, the numbers of men per 1,000 women was 933 for stable, 940 for movers within counties, 1,031 for movers between counties and 1,089 for interstate migrants ... sex ratios were lower in urban than in rural populations [Taeuber and Taeuber, 1971: 814].

This lesser mobility of women holds in general for all twentieth century migratory movements.[11]

If settled life is becoming the norm, what does this mean for women? On the one hand, the slowing down of intercontinental migration means that women have the opportunity neither to share in the egalitarianism of building up life in a new locale, nor to gather up the resources left behind by others who emigrate.

On the other hand, migration to the city, whether from rural life or from nomadism, often means a loss or atrophying of a set of valuable skills and competencies for women (Boulding, 1969b: 549-554). The trap of urban poverty is very real for women. It is assumed that they gain new skills to replace those no longer relevant, but do we know this? Studies indicate that child-rearing in the city does not produce the autonomy in children that rural child-rearing does, so women pass on their skill-loss to their children, both female and male (Graves, 1971).

The third generation urban woman develops a new set of skills; thus, it is no accident that the women's liberation movement in the United States is the product of the sixties. The young women of this movement grew up in urbia and suburbia. Not their mothers, but their grandmothers came from farms. (Some women have been smart enough to do the whole thing in one generation!)

This new urban-based development model for women, however, comes at some cost; costs in community (not knowing the neighbors), in simplicity of life style (everything tends to be bought prepackaged) and in simple intergenerational enjoyment (day care centers are one further step in providing a totally age-graded life so that each individual from infant to aged spends most of her waking hours with her age peers). Those same male achievements that women have decried become the performance model for the urban woman.

PROBLEMS OF MEASURING PARTICIPATION OF WOMEN

One of the basic social values pursued in every modern society is *participation*. The ideology of participation means that all mechanisms which assist individuals in making the decisions that shape the pattern of their existence get serious attention. It is hard, however, to get meaningful measures of cross-national participation. We use what is easily available to us, which is information on women in the labor force, and education of the women. We do not even have access to good cross-national information on the political participation of women, although this is of great concern to us (Boulding, 1966, 1972). When we have drawn the best picture we can, based on this kind of information, what do we really know about the status of women in the countries so described?

Nomadism, Mobility, and the Status of Women

To clarify the nature of the problem I am pointing to, I have constructed a table showing the rank order values for women in the labor force, and for women's literacy, for twelve countries which in the year 1968 had a substantial nomadic population and active nomadic traditions, in Africa and Asia.[1,2] There are in fact twenty-two countries with substantial numbers of nomads in Africa and Asia today, but eight of them had no information on women in the labor force or women's literacy in the International Labor Organization and United Nations Yearbooks used for this purpose, so they had to be excluded. Table 2.1 gives a list of the excluded countries in a footnote.

The Case of Somalia

Before discussing the implications of Table 2.1, I will discuss briefly one country which is excluded for lack of UN data, Somalia. Somalia has been the object of UN attention, in urging the enfranchisement of women, on behalf of "the resolute pursuit of a policy of nomadic betterment, a nomadic welfare society" (Silberman, 1959: 569).

The Somalis live in an environment

> where rainfall is low and there is so far no likelihood of irrigation . . . nomadic animal husbandry—in default of mineral wealth or advantageous trading opportunities—is the natural and efficient form of human adaptation to the environment. The Somalis have reached a high level of competence as herdsmen. . . . By natural selection [he] has proved himself a skilled ecologist [Silberman, 1959: 559].

The Somalis live spread out over several countries which now abut the "nation" of Somalia, and wherever they live, from 65 to 85 percent of them follow the nomadic way of life (Silberman, 1959: 560). Somalia has substantial trade in leather and forest products (90 percent of the world's incense comes from there). There is agriculture in Somalia, of course, but the true nomadic tradition looks down on agriculture. The Somali does not require vegetables; his main food is milk, and, on festive occasions, camel meat. Monteil comments that he has seen sturdy old men—and presumably women! —who have never known any other food than milk (Monteil, 1959: 575). Keeping mobile is important for these people, both to prevent overgrazing and to prevent the human diseases that come with too much interhuman contact in that environment.

> Respiratory complaints are rampant and tuberculosis rates would be higher still if people lived in great proximity for longer periods. It may be merely an instinct that makes Somali women such keen partisans of nomadism—so tragically at times goading their menfolk to fight, as in

the massacre of Italians, in Mogadishu in 1947, as symbols of town and sedentary life, but . . . they know that the first consequence of the transplantation of a nomad group into an agricultural region (in Africa) is an enormous increase in the habitual unrequited work of the women. In Arabia it means, of course, veiling and seclusion [Silberman, 1959: 568].

Why would a woman trade relative health and freedom for agricultural or urban "slavery"? Everything she owns can easily be piled on a couple of camels, and she is the one who decides where the tents will be erected when camp is moved. She is interested in a politics which will maintain her freedom of movement and her children. A Somali child of five is

> alert, and is not afraid to go thirty miles alone; it knows the geneology of its clan over 17 generations; and it can milk. All through [her] life the Somali invests in brain rather than brawn. The satisfactions of nomadism are such that senior members of the education department at Hargeisa, as a good Somali should, return periodically to their herds in the interior [Silberman, 1959: 568].

What are the alternatives? Settlement brings disease, unemployment when "settlement schemes" run out of steam, and anomie, a loss of social energy and enjoyment of life. The favorite way to deal with unemployed and demoralized ex-nomads is to create warrior groups to augment standing armies. As a general contribution to peace and welfare in this part of the world, this is certainly a questionable policy (Monteil, 1959: 583). Some of the Somalis themselves have a vision of a continuing nomad society using communications technology to improve their information system about conditions of the land and the herds; using schools to create a nomad-centered education where girls and boys will learn "on the move" about how to live better in their arid land. Somali women and men are an education-oriented people. But they want education on *their* terms. Who among development sociologists are listening to and learning from Somali women? Remember that the Somali are considered so "backward" that they have no data on women at all; therefore, according to the conventional view, they could only be considered as objects needing help. A similar picture might be presented for Saudi Arabia, where 50 to 60 percent of the population is nomadic, and up to 80 percent come from a nomadic tradition.

UN Data on Countries with Nomads

Now let us turn to an examination of the countries with substantial nomad populations who do report on the occupations and education of women. In Table 2.1 they are grouped by continent, and also by the degree of emphasis on rapid assimilation indicated in writings on national policy. It happens that

Table 2.1: Percentile Rank Ordering* of Twelve Countries** of Africa and Asia with Significant Nomad Populations on Occupation, Literacy and Modernization Variables, with Associated Role Status Ratings, Based on Their Position in a Total Rank Ordering of 165 Countries

Country	GNP	% Urban	Females Economically Active	% Female Non-Agri.	Female/Male Ratio White-Collar	Female/Male Ratio Literacy	I Scale	R-S Scale
AFRICA								
(Slow Assimilation)								
Algeria	59.6	53.2	99.4	95.3	88.3	85.3	Low	Med.
Libya	19.9	43.1	96.3	89.8	97.1	94.9	Low	Low
Morocco	65.8	46.8	90.5	84.3	79.6	83.8	Low	Low
Sudan	80.1	95.4	37.4	81.1	—	83.4	Low	Med.
Tunisia	59.6	56.9	95.7	87.4	85.4	77.2	Low	Low
(Rapid Assimilation)								
U.A.R.	69.9	30.3	92.3	82.7	89.3	84.6	Low	Med.
ASIA								
(Slow Assimilation)								
Jordan	52.0	62.4	96.9	94.5	81.6	82.4	Low	Med.
Pakistan	80.1	78.9	85.9	92.9	—	86.8	Low	Med.
Syria	52.3	28.4	48.5	96.1	96.1	86.0	Low	Low
(Rapid Assimilation)								
Iran	45.9	51.4	86.5	74.0	86.4	79.4	Low	High
Iraq	52.0	43.1	97.5	93.7	—	88.2	Low	High
Turkey	45.9	64.2	22.1	91.3	83.5	74.3	Low	High

SOURCE: Boulding Global Data Bank. Fuller information on the I Scale and the R-S Scale can be found in E. Boulding (1972). See note 13, p. 53 for other sources.

*According to the usage in this paper, a percentile rank of 90 for a country means that 90 percent of the countries in the total group of 165 rank higher on the variable in question.

**The following countries also have important nomad populations, but are not included for lack of data on the status of women: Ethiopia, Kenya, Somalia, Afghanistan, Lebanon, Mongolia, Saudi Arabia, and Peoples Republic of China. The USSR and Israel, which also have nomadic populations, are excluded because they are so much more modernized than the other countries that it is difficult to make meaningful comparisons.

only the UAR among the African countries has a strong policy of rapid assimilation. In Asia there are more rapid assimilators than not. For each country, percentile rank order information is given, locating the country in its position in a total list ranging between 100 and 165 countries (coverage varies) and territories in regard to the following economic and literacy variables: economically active females as proportion of total female population; percentage of all females who are employed in nonagricultural work; female to male ratio of number of professional, managerial, and clerical workers; ratio of percentage female literates to percentage male literates. The information is taken from 1971 and 1972 yearbooks, but for the most part, the data are from 1968.

In addition, the rank order percentile is given for GNP per capita for each country, and the percentage of the population living in urban areas. To the far right are columns giving the country ratings on the individuation scale and the role-status scale derived from an earlier study (Boulding, 1972)[13] which utilized Human Relations Area File data and status of women reports to make judgments about the traditional freedom and autonomy of the women of the majority tribes in a given country, at a baseline date of 1900, and of their current participation in public life. The following items are included in these scales.[14]

Women's Individuation Scale
Age at marriage
Divorce rights
Freedom to be traders
Range of movement from hearth
Money handler or food provider
Marriage choice
Property rights
Inheritance rights

Women's Role-Status Scale
Right to vote and to run for office
Women having been elected to the national parliament
Women having held high governmental posts
Women having held high diplomatic posts
Women having held high judicial posts
States parties to convention on discrimination in education

The value of using rankings instead of the raw data, percentages, and ratios on which the rankings are based is that it is possible to tell at a glance whether a country is uniformly high or low among the total population of countries, with regard to all the variables listed. The use of percentile standardizes the rankings on a base of 100.

It will be noticed that ten out of the twelve countries have substantial discrepancies in rank percentile between modernization level and the participation of women in the labor force and education, and that the discrepancies are equally great for rapid and slow assimilator countries. Sudan and Pakistan are the only countries with comparable ranks for modernization and nonagricultural labor force. Sudan is discrepant in the other direction for women economically active, ranking higher than we would expect. Within the women's employment figures, the countries divide into those with a relatively high number of women in the work force—Sudan, Syria, and Turkey—and the remaining countries, with fewer women in the work force. Even in the three countries mentioned, however, the rank differences disappear when we look at nonagricultural or white-collar employment. None of the twelve countries rises above the eightieth percentile in nonagricultural employment for women, except Iran, which is just slightly above at 74. The picture is about the same for literacy, with three countries falling just above the eightieth percentile.

Table 2.2 makes the lack of relationship between modernization and participation in the nonagricultural labor force and in literacy skills clearer. Countries are grouped according to whether they fall (1) above the fiftieth percentile in GNP and urbanization, (2) below it, or (3) are low in GNP, but high on urbanization. Sudan, one of the least modernized countries (Group II), joins Turkey (Group I) in ranking high on economically active women. In general, the picture is one of low participation of women except in agriculture, and of low traditional autonomy for women (these countries all rated low on the individuation scale). The role-status scale, measuring current participation in civic roles, gives a better showing, with medium to high ratings for some countries in each of the three modernization groupings.

Group III, low on GNP and high on modernization, has the poorest role-status showing, suggesting that areas anciently urbanized with no substantial recent growth in the modern sector offer the least opportunity for women to participate in the public sphere. Only Egypt of these three anciently urbanized countries achieves even a "medium" rating on role-status.

Table 2.3 gives medians for the modernization, employment, and literacy variables for the world and for each region. This gives an idea of the data values behind the rankings and makes possible the comparison of the nomad-harboring countries of Africa and Asia with the rest of the world. All of the Asian nomad countries are from the Near East, except Pakistan, and it will be noted that the Near East medians fall well above the African ones in GNP, yet well below in labor force participation. Only literacy ratios are similar. It is oil wealth that raises the GNP, and this increased wealth has not yet affected other sectors.

The "nomad-harboring" countries are in general among the less modernized of the world's countries, but in most cases they are more modernized by

Table 2.2: Countries Grouped by Levels of GNP and Urbanization

Country	Females Economically Active	% Female Non-Agri.	Female/Male Ratio Literacy	I Scale	R-S Scale
GROUP I **At or Above 50th Percentile** *(Relatively High GNP and Urbanization)*					
Libya	96.3	89.8	94.9	Low	Low
Iran	86.5	74.0	79.4	Low	High
Iraq	97.5	93.7	88.2	Low	High
Turkey	22.1	91.3	74.3	Low	High
GROUP II **Below 50th Percentile** *(Relatively Low GNP and Urbanization)*					
Algeria	99.4	95.3	85.3	Low	Med.
Sudan	37.4	81.1	93.4	Low	Med.
Tunisia	95.7	87.4	77.2	Low	Low
Jordan	96.9	94.5	82.4	Low	Med.
Pakistan	85.9	92.9	86.8	Low	Med.
GROUP III **Below 50th Percentile in GNP** **Above 50th Percentile in Urbanization**					
Morocco	90.5	84.3	83.8	Low	Low
UAR	92.3	82.7	84.6	Low	Med.
Syria	48.5	96.1	86.0	Low	Low

SOURCE: Boulding Global Data Bank. Fuller information on the I Scale and the R-S Scale can be found in E. Boulding (1972).

Table 2.3: Median of Occupation, Literacy and Modernization Variables by Region*

	In US $'s GNP/Capita	Females Economically Active	% Female Non-Agri.	Female/Male Ratio White-Collar	Female/Male Ratio Literacy
World	280	.250	12.01	.535	.730
Africa	100	.324	3.32	.244	.302
North America	460	.205	15.17	.725	.988
South America	340	.144	11.06	.548	.891
Asia	130	.234	8.47	.218	.494
West Asia (Near East)	360	.048	2.18	.199	.372
Europe	1320	.280	18.95	.737	.926
Oceania	330	.183	11.49	.723	.946

SOURCE: Boulding Global Data Bank.
*Percentage Urban not included in this table because of ambiguities of data.

GNP and urbanization measures than by women's participation measures. It is unlikely that the nomad women were taken account of in the estimate of employment or literacy, since these women are hard to count and keep track of. They stand outside all measurement, one might say. Even the I scale rating doesn't take account of nomadic women, since it is based on ratings of the majority settled tribes in each country, and the nomads are too small a minority to take account of in these twelve countries.

The one place where the nomad-harboring countries show up well in women's participation is in the ratings on the role-status scale. Only four of the twelve countries have a low rating on this scale. In general, it takes an active urban elite to produce a high rating on this scale, though not necessarily; the types of participation it measures are for the most part urban-generated activities. There are more of medium to high R-S scale ratings in this group of twelve countries than in the nonnomadic countries in the total N of the 58 countries of Africa and Asia so rated.[15] The countries given a high R-S rating include the four with a rapid assimilation policy. There is really no basis in our data for saying that women from nomadic traditions take active roles in urban-based civic affairs, but it is interesting to speculate whether the ancient tradition of the nomad on horseback contributing to civic infrastructure still applies to some extent.

More important, the kind of civic participation which nomad women do engage in is not being picked up in the labor force and literacy figures. In the absence of additional measures of women's participation, I cannot say that a false picture of the nonparticipation of women is being presented. But the question can be raised as to the possibility that this is true. If nomad women develop special skills and bring these special skills to the city with them, we should discover what they are.

THE OLD MOBILITY AND THE NEW

The "case" for the civic skills of the nomad women developed in the historical section and in the discussion on the Somali is based to a considerable extent on her experience of mobility, and an associated skill in making comparative assessments about different kinds of environments, and developing participation skills that deal with changing environments.

It could be argued that I have presented a very misleading and unrepresentative picture of Euro-American twentieth-century style mobility as contrasted with nomadic mobility and that the Somali woman knows very little about the larger world she lives in. Certainly typical "modernized mobility" includes a great deal of international travel, increasingly by plane, of persons involved in nongovernmental activities, such as the international professional associations[16] and other of the over 2,500 NGO associations.[17] There is travel by students, business people, and tourists. This is in addition to a great amount of IGO (intergovernmental) travel (including military movements). The study of transnational encounters is of major importance in understanding twentieth-century-style mobility. It is time for some careful analysis of the significance of this kind of movement, however. It is possible that the kinds of contacts represented by the networks mentioned above are so specialized and restricted that those who move about are understanding less and less of the complexity of the world they live in while they travel more and more. The new cosmopolites move from airport to airport, hotel to hotel, tourist site to tourist site (and, in the case of the sociologist, from university to university). The travelers are encased in an elaborate set of cultural formulae, guaranteed to prevent any drastically new perceptions of reality.

When nomads move, they go by camel, by horse, and by foot. (Now also sometimes by truck and car.) There are tribes in Syria that make 1,500 mile migrations routinely, carrying their households with them. Tribes in Algeria and the Sudan find 2,000-mile migrations routine.[18] (Some tribes, it should be added, move no farther than to the equivalent of the next county.) When they are on the move, they are in intimate relationship with their environment, scanning it closely, knowing intimately features of it which our untrained eyes could never see. They are also passing all kinds of different societies on the way. They see "how people live." They make comparative judgments of many kinds. Since the women and the men are moving through the same spaces, exposed to similar stimuli, both must be adaptable and responsive to new situations in terms of their separate responsibilities. Some of these environments may appear monotonously similar to the untrained western eye, and some may in fact be homogeneous over wide areas, but many nomadic tribes do experience a series of highly differentiated environments. It would be interesting to compare the total skill and knowledge stock of the American housewife still living in the county of her birth, complete with all her education and access to mass media, with the total skill and knowledge stock of the average Somali nomad woman.

This is not a pitch for a return to housekeeping with camels. Modern women have certain nomadic skills, too. Some, at least, know how to travel light, how to "scan" new social environments, and how to adapt to new role patterns as required. The wife of the business executive is a past mistress of this art. But there is a certain standardization about urban environments, and our social scanning skills encompass a narrow range of phenomena. Moderns are not nearly as "cosmopolitan" as they think, and, after all, it is mainly about cities that they are knowledgeable.

If women are to participate in the shaping of the future, at the level of both national and international society, there must be a careful examination of the adequacy of the social spaces they have "won" in the economic and educational systems of each country, and in the political systems. There must be an evaluation of these spaces in terms of the perspectives and skills women are gaining for the development of alternative social environments and institutional infrastructures.

A careful comparative study of women's roles in societies on the move might give clues about new kinds of indicators to look for, to reveal participation levels in society. The view from camelback is not enough either. However, when we can *measure* the extent of participation of Somali women in the society in which they feel so free, and yet which does not even provide the basic information about women in terms that our computers can digest, then we may come to understand more about the dynamics of the urban enclosure process that even today continues to capture women in modernized societies—and we may learn how to counteract it.

NOTES

1. Women's quarters of the Greek household.
2. For two widely used definitions of nomads, see Turnbull (1968b) and Toynbee (1935).
3. The camel has a similar effect on the desert.
4. It has been suggested that "most higher societies with a nobility as leading elite, and therefore, most classical and modern urbanized and industrialized societies, are the result of military conquest or peaceful penetration by nomadic groups" (Eberhard, 1967: 279). In other words, peaceable or warlike, people who come into the city from the steppes or desert come in feeling superior and manage to achieve the ruling positions in the societies they penetrate. If it is the view from horseback that has caused all the concentrations of power in successive civilizations, horses have a lot to answer for! Reality, of course, is much more complex than that. It is interesting, however, that stratification may have a basis in the matter-of-fact experiences of physical elevation!
5. Notably Lee and DeVore (1968), Turnbull (1968a, 1968b), and the special issue on nomads of the *International Social Science Journal* (1959).
6. King Sargon's priestess sister, for example.
7. For discussions of the harem, see Wenig (1970), Penzer (1935), and Lacey (1968).
8. Monteil writes that "the nomads of the Sahara usually keep a list, either in writing or by oral tradition, of the places where they have found pasture for many years past. In 1958, J. Petit found the list kept by the Mekhadma of Ouargla since 1884." Monteil goes on to list seven different tribal chronologies, each at least 100 years old, about pasture, wet and dry years, etc., which if attended to would let westerners in on the knowledge of long-run support capacities of marginal land, now known only by nomads and in danger of being lost by them under pressure from urban-based technologists (1959: 572-585). Articles dealing with both the skills and the problems of the nomad are given in the references (United Nations, 1966; Awad, 1959; "Nomads and Nomadism in the Arid Zone, 1959).

9. Immigration to the United States went from a peak of 8,795,000 in 1900-1910 to 426,000 in 1946-1948. In Latin America, Argentina's population went from 1,764,000 in 1901-1910 to 175,000 in 1941-1948 (United Nations, 1953: 102).

10. This is another way of labelling what Betty Friedan called *The Feminine Mystique* (1963).

11. The differences are not large for the world as a whole, however. In the previous chapter we noted that 42 to 45 percent of migrants between countries were female.

12. The judgment on extent of nomadism comes from the International Labor Organization and the *International Social Science Journal* articles cited earlier. Exact figures on nomadic population are not available for any country, but the twelve countries in our list have up to 10 percent nomadic populations.

13. Fuller information on the scales can be found in Boulding (1972). Data for GNP are from *UN Statistical Yearbook, 1971;* data for employment are from *Yearbooks of Labor Statistics;* data on education are from *UNESCO Statistical Yearbooks;* data for literacy are from *UN Demographic Yearbooks.*

14. Fuller information on the scales can be found in Boulding (1972). See note 13, above, for other sources.

15.

R-S Scale Ratings (in percentages)

	58 Countries of Africa and Asia	12 Countries of this Study
Low	42	33
Medium-High	58	67
Total	100	100

16. The International Sociological Association, for example. Professionals, of course, belong to an elite that travels far more than the average citizen.

17. NGOs are nongovernmental organizations, private international associations with members in at least three countries, and an autonomous international headquarters.

18. The migrations, of course, cross national boundaries ("Nomads and Nomadism in the Arid Zone," 1959).

Chapter 3

FAMILIAL CONSTRAINTS ON WOMEN'S WORK ROLES: An Historical Overview

The nature of the familial constraints on woman's role as worker in every type of human society is perhaps best captured by the triple role concept of "breeder-feeder-producer." From the earliest and simplest hunting and gathering folk to the most industrialized society of the twentieth century, the breeding of babies[1] and the feeding of humans of all ages is almost exclusively the work of the woman,[2] above and beyond other productive processes in which she is engaged. In addition, the woman participates in certain producer roles, usually but not always differentiated from male producer roles.

It should be clear that all three categories in the breeder-feeder-producer triad are in fact producer roles, but I am distinguishing between the first two categories, which are assigned to women only, and the third, which is divided between women and men. In a subsistence society, the producer role exists primarily to create material for domestic consumption. It is only when trading begins that sticky questions about the agents and measurements of production arise. Woman's production is normally noticed by statisticians only when it leaves the home. Man's production is more apt to be noticed whether it leaves the home or not.

At the simplest level the producer roles for women outside the breeder-feeder complex have to do with the gathering or growing of food, carrying water and fuel to the hearth, erection of shelters, making domestic utensils

Author's Note: Paper presented to the Workshop Conference on Occupational Segregation: Past, Present, and Future, Wellesley College, Wellesley, Massachusetts, May 21-23, 1975. Reprinted with permission in revised form from *Signs: Journal of Women in Culture and Society,* Spring 1976, Volume 1, Number 3, Part II, pp. 95-117. ©1976 by the University of Chicago.

and clothing, and the creation of ceremonial objects. The triple role tends to give women more hours of work in a day than men, although this is not universally true. We will begin by examining the working day of women in different kinds of societies.

DIFFERENT WORK SETTINGS FOR WOMEN THROUGH HISTORY

Hunting and Gathering Societies

In hunting and gathering societies the producer role of the male encompasses hunting and the making of tools associated with hunting. These activities consume all of his working hours and generally provide about 20 percent of the food of the band (Lee and DeVore, 1968). Hunting has been described as a high-risk, low-yield activity, in contrast to food gathering as a low-risk, high-yield activity (Lee and DeVore, 1968). Women seem able to provide the other 80 percent of the band's food through gathering activities and still carry out the breeder-feeder roles, the procuring of water and fuel, building of shelters, making of utensils, etc. They also catch small game close to the campsite with their bare hands, but do not run great distances after game—an impractical proposition when small children are being cared for. That the hunting and gathering way of life is sometimes described as the leisure society by contemporary ethnographers because of its easy rhythms of work, rest, and play. Reports from many of the 250 hunting and gathering bands extant today indicate that women and men work shorter hours than in any other type of society and have more time for ceremonies and celebrations (Lee and DeVore, 1968).

Due to the constraints of the nomadic life, there is a strict limitation on family size. Hunting and gathering bands manage zero population growth through a combination of abortion, infanticide, and infant mortality. In the hunting and gathering way of life, there are few sex-differentiated reward systems. Women and men have different ceremonial roles but participate equally in ceremonials and band decision-making, including decisions about marriages. There is no accumulation of resources to serve as a power base for individuals of either sex, and monogamy is the rule. Although it is said that twenty hours of work per person per week may meet all maintenance needs, it is not clear whether the anthropologist observers have actually clocked the full working time of women around the campfire after the food has been brought there. There is probably a component of "invisible" work which needs to be more accurately recorded before this way of life disappears. It is also difficult to clock time spent in care of small children. When are they being "cared for" and when is interaction with them pure recreation and enjoyment? When all these considerations are taken into account, the chances are that even in this most egalitarian of all types of human societies the women are "working" longer hours than the men.

The Early Agrovillages

Agriculture probably emerged out of discoveries of stands of wild grain at revisited campsites—stands that represented accidental harvests of the previous year's gathering activities. This was clearly women's work and still is wherever simple digging-stick types of planting in the slash-and-burn cultivation pattern are found, notably in Africa. In the agrovillage existence that developed when people began settling down near good supplies of wild grain —and planting their own crops besides—the workload began to shift more heavily toward women. Men in these agrovillages were still contributing their share of the food through hunting. Because of game scarcity by 12,000 B.C., the contributions of the now sedentary hunters, even with improved tools, were probably kept to 20 percent of the total food supply. Men would be gone for days at a time in pursuit of game, and women's producer roles in the agrovillage multiplied. The herding pattern for men, which was an offshoot of hunting, involved similar movement, although it may have increased the economic contribution of men toward family sustenance. With settlement came buildings, courtyards, the making and accumulation of domestic objects and ceremonial materials. The following outline summarizes women's daily activities in the agrovillage based on my interpretation of archaeological evidence in the Near East from 10,000 to 6000 B.C., along with more contemporary anthropological evidence (Boulding, 1977).

The Daily Life of the Woman Villager in Peasant Societies

(1) The Hearth
    (a) Cooking, feeding, and care of small infants
(2) The courtyard
    (a) Production processes
        (1) Food. Processing of foods to be cooked (sometimes cooking, baking also done in courtyard, combining 1a and 2a)
        (2) Crafts. Sewing, weaving, basket and pottery making, stoneware and implement making, jewelry, production of cosmetics
        (3) Building. Houses, cult centers, etc.
    (b) Social organization
        Council meetings, ritual and ceremony preparations, teaching, general administration of the village
(3) The Fields
    (a) Gathering and collecting of fruit and nuts

(b) Clearing, planting, cultivating, and harvesting food
(c) Caring for sheep and goats
(d) Collecting fuel for hearth fires
(e) Collecting material for building
(f) Carrying water

These first agrovillages had populations of one hundred to two hundred people. If the workload assigned to women seems improbably heavy, compare it with the summary of workloads for women (Table 5.1) based on surveys of women engaged in subsistence agriculture in Africa today.

I suggest that the point of transition from these early agrovillages (such as Eynan, Jarmo, Hacilar) to the larger trading towns (like Jericho, Beidha, Catal Huyuk) was the point at which the woman's economic contribution started to "weigh" less than the man's, even though the sheer quantity of productive labor was greater. Initially, the egalitarianism of the hunting and gathering society must have carried over into the earliest agrovillages. The sheer fact of the continuing presence of women and long absences of men may have given rise to occasional examples of a "rule of women" during this first village life. Aberle suggests that matriliny arises in situations where there are all-women work groups, where women control the residence bases, and where there is "a certain range of productivity and a certain range of centralization—ranges narrower than those of either patrilineal or bilateral systems" (Aberle, 1962: 655-730).[3]

The Trading Towns

Historically, women's range of productivity narrowed increasingly as men, during their hunting journeys, began locating sources of flint and other materials valued for tools and ceremonials. This immediately gave them a competitive advantage over stay-at-home women. The first specialization between villages, according to the archaeological evidence, appeared when hunters (some from agrovillages, some probably still nomadic) began supplying other villages with flint and receiving craft and food products in return. Women were too busy with production for family consumption to work the trading networks to the extent men could. Some of women's craft products entered the trading networks, but by and large the diversity of women's tasks prevented specialization. Thus, products which did enter the market were marginal and probably did not command "prices" comparable to those of the male specialists in the new stone and bone shops of the later trading towns.

The Rise of Urban Civilization

By the time major urban centers arose in Sumer and Egypt, a system of social stratification had developed that complicated the picture. In Sumerian

Erech, 4000 B.C., there were few distinctions between rich and poor. There were "street scribes" available to any woman or man for business purposes, and there were no great differences in housing style or size. By 2500 B.C., however, nomadic incursions, wars, and gifts of land and booty from kings to their supporters had created an aristocracy based in the palace, the temple, and the landed estates. On the new urban scene there were large palace-temple complexes, rich landholders, and elaborate tables of law. A certain class of women—the aristocracy—became visible and would remain so until the industrial revolution. Women in the scribal and small-merchant class, on the contrary, became invisible, working-class women (artisans, construction workers, petty traders, servants) somewhat less so. Thus, while the emergence of early trading towns began to tip the scales against recognition of the productive role of the mass of women, the first urban civilizations finished the process.

The Role of Law in Redefinition of Women's Work

The emergence of law contains the emergence of the concept of the male-headed household and of the administration of property by the male. The earlier, more fluid, clan rights to land and property that left resources available to the women and men who were prepared to work with them were transformed into rigidly spelled out male rights. This was no simple process: as late as 1751 B.C., the Code of Hammurabi contained sixty-eight sections on family and women, fifty on land and territory (dealing with clan rights), and seven on priestesses. While descent of the elites was usually recorded in government records through the male, a woman was sometimes named and descent traced through her. Women sometimes also appear in land deeds as heads of households and as donors and recipients of ritualized food offerings. They are recorded as doing long-distance trading under their own names. Ancient legal records show that the women of the elite often fought successfully to keep their rights to land under the new system that in principle recorded land only in the name of males.

No study has been made of the percentage of women holding land in their own names throughout history, but in Europe from A.D. 900 to 1200 it was sometimes as high as 18 percent. When land administered by women on behalf of children is included, the figures were as high as 25 percent (Herlihy, 1962: 89-120). The amount of attention given to women's rights in both Egyptian and Sumerian law (Wenig, 1970; Kramer, 1963), and the numerous references in contemporary documents to court battles fought by women in Greece and Rome, indicates that declaring the male the legal head of the household and building legal and administrative practices around him never fully covered the real-life economic and social exigencies with which women and men had to deal. What the device "male head of household" did do, however, was to make second-class citizens of the great mass of middle- and working-class women, who had no independent power base as did the women of the elite. By defining them as subsidiary household members, it became possible to avoid the issue of equal pay for equal work. This mainly affected working-class women, since members of the scribal and small-merchant class—the urban bourgeoisie of the ancient civilizations—were as apt to promote women as display objects as their brothers centuries later. Middle-class urbanites in the Mediterranean civilizations enclosed their women from the beginning. Europe, ancient and modern, followed suit.

There were two classes of "working women," then, from about 2000 B.C. on: the wealthy overseas merchants and the estate and temple administrators on the one hand and, on the other, the poor women who worked in textile workshops, ran the corner bakeries and breweries, and provided the upper classes with much the same range of domestic, health, and beauty services that working women do today. The occupational roles for women in the Age of Pericles can be classified in the following way.[4]

(1) Occupations for women slaves
   (a) Food processing: threshing grain, grinding flour
   (b) Mining: gold and silver mining; separating metal from slag, washing metal; transporting ore from underground corridors of mines to the surface
   (c) Textile workers: all operations connected with carding, spinning, and weaving carried on by women in workshops—no indication whether these were state- or privately owned. Weaving also carried on as cottage industry in private homes

(2) Occupations open to free women:
   (a) Agriculture, unspecified except for "field work"
   (b) Textile work as above
   (c) Trade: selling of vegetables, processed foods, baked goods, other home-manufacturer products, unspecified. Selling of cloth, garments, headdresses
   (d) Inn-keeping
   (e) Prostitution
   (f) Running schools for courtesans
   (g) Midwifery, nursing
   (h) Music
   (i) Dancing
   (j) Vase painting

(3) Occupations specifically forbidden to women:
   (a) Medicine (there are records of illegal practice and punishment of women practitioners)

(4) Occupations possible but not encouraged:
 (a) Scribe; schools for women rare (Sappho's school was an exception), but if a woman could write, she was not forbidden to exercise her skill

Poor working women had several disadvantages compared with men from the beginning. They had to compete with slave labor, for one thing.[5] Most of the textile workshops in Egypt and Greece were operated by female slave labor, and many services were tendered by slave women in the Mediterranean cities. Since slaves were only given subsistence, a double force operated to give free women pittance wages: (1) the availability of slave labor and (2) the fiction of male head of household. The free woman supposedly had someone to support her, and so her wages needed to be only supplemental.

CHARACTERISTIC CONSTRAINTS ON THE WOMAN WORKER

In the foregoing analysis, I have traced the work settings for women in hunting and gathering societies, the early agrovillages, the trading towns, and the first urban civilizations. From the first urbanism until the industrial revolution, there were in my view no substantial differences in the work situation for women. The following discussion of the social, legal, and familial constraints on women will apply primarily but not exclusively to the Western world from Greek and Roman times onward.

The Male Head of Household Fiction

One of the most enduring constraints is the male head of household concept. I have labelled the term a fiction for, while a careful study still needs to be done, it appears that in any setting—urban or rural—in any period of history for which data are available, one-fifth to one-half of the heads of households were women. (It will be remembered from Chapter 1 that the current world figure is 38 percent.) Many of these women were rearing children without male partners because of widowhood, desertion, divorce, or because they were plural wives infrequently visited by the husband and with full responsibility for the care and feeding of their children.[6] They may be never-married women who have been driven by poverty to sell sexual services and who have raised children with minimal resources; they may be not-yet-married women who will later assume domestic roles; or they may be never-married women who have chosen an independent way of life as entertainers, intellectuals, or merchants (variously labelled hetaira, courtesans, and prostitutes); they might or might not have chosen to raise children of their own. Most of these women, except for the wealthy and the independent entrepreneurs, had to struggle to make a living. They had to accept the low wages established through the fiction of male support and the reality of the competition with slave labor.

What family arrangements did women heads of household make for the care of their children while they were at work? Women in great poverty had to leave children without care to run about the streets or locked in airless rooms.[7] Probably the institution of the neighbor who takes in children for a few pennies is as ancient as that of the urban working woman. For the most part, however, what care such children received throughout the Christian Era came from women who chose celibacy rather than motherhood, the women of the religious orders. They ran the soup kitchens, the orphanages, and the schools for the very poor. When many of the earlier religious orders declined and before the nineteenth-century growth in religious service orders began, the plight of children of the poor became desperate. In 1770 thousands of children of Parisian working mothers were rounded up from the streets by the "authorities" to be deported as labor for overseas settlements (Rúde, 1964). Only the mass exodus of their mothers from their places of work stopped this roundup. Indeed, it was around the problems of these "ragged children," as the British called them, that the nineteenth-century philanthropic and social service movements developed. For the women heads of household who were the mothers of these children, however, there was never much more than pious exhortation to "stop sinning." They were fallen women in the eyes of the middle and upper classes, not working women with family responsibilities. That notion continues even today.

Familial Division of Labor

Rural areas. The division of labor between women and men in rural areas throughout the world has varied depending on the scale of agriculture. With cash cropping and plantation agriculture comes the development of labor-saving machinery and the dominance of the male.[8] In developing countries, the growth of large-scale agriculture usually puts heavier workloads on women in terms of working hours because they are required to weed and carry water to the cash-crop fields while still growing food for the family in their own plots. Since the breeding-feeding activities are not counted as productive labor, the wages of third world women agriculturalists are often of some indeterminate minus quantity. That is, they subsidize, even more than other working women, the men of their households and of their community. In a society with large-scale urban migration, the women are usually left behind to do the farming. Rarely do they share the urban wages of male family members, although these wages may be invested in buying more land for the woman to farm. (See Chapter 5 for a further discussion of women in agriculture.)

In Europe during the Middle Ages the situation of farm women varied. There was the prosperous but hardworking peasant household where length of working hours was perhaps fairly equally divided. There were the widows who had an immense workload because they were compelled to render, unaided, feudal services that were shared in husband-wife households.[9] There was also the desperate situation of laboring women without partners who sometimes died, with their babies, of exhaustion and starvation in the very fields that were yielding unprecedented harvests (O'Faolain and Martines, 1973).

Wage and labor differentials in rural areas. With the decline of the feudal estates in the later Middle Ages, the new phenomenon of detached wage labor began in rural areas. Here the outlines of women's subservient economic situation as wage laborers became clear. The state tried to establish control over manpower movements but in effect controlled the movement of women. The 1563 Elizabethan Statute of Artifices, for example, stated: "By this Act [the Statute of Laborers] every woman free or bound, under 60, and not carrying on a trade or calling, provided she had no land, and was not in domestic or other service, was liable to be called upon to enter service either in the fields or otherwise, and if she refused, she was imprisoned until she complied; whilst all girls who for twelve years had been brought up to follow the plough, were not allowed to enter any other calling, but were forced to continue working in the fields" (Cleveland, 1896: 76).

Men continued to move to get jobs, but women with family responsibilities had to work in the fields and to take home piecework they could do while still caring for children. With the unity of capital and labor gone, the only limit set on the exploitation of the poorest class of laboring women was death by starvation. That grim scenario became more fully developed in the next century.

It is with the appearance of wage labor that the manifestations of wage differentials (which may in fact have existed all the time) became visible. Because of their immobility women had no bargaining power and thus suffered wage discrimination everywhere. In 1422 the scholars of Toulouse paid women grape pickers half what they paid the men who only had to carry the full baskets back to the college cellar. (The monks of Paris did the same [Thrupp, 1964: 240-241].) Women construction workers who worked side by side with men in building the College of Toulouse were paid far less than the men for the same labor (Thrupp, 1964: 244). Not even the labor shortage resulting from the Black Death improved women's wages; they remained substantially the same on the Continent for nearly 100 years (Perroy, quoted in Thrupp, 1964: 244). The supposed labor shortages from the Black Death did not help the laboring poor in England, either (Ziegler, 1970: 240-259). While this could be interpreted as reflecting widespread unemployment in the previous century, one could also say that laborers in that previous century had shorter hours, better working conditions. Fourteenth-century workers, especially women, had to work longer and harder for the same pay.

The opportunities for the woman of the rural upper class were limited only by her abilities; entrepreneurship was rewarded. With plenty of hands to help, the breeding-feeding role posed no problem to her. During the Middle Ages and as a result of the absence of men in crusades, there may have been an increase in the number of women in landholding and public roles, but the basic pre-Crusade participation level was already high, as the Herlihy study (1962) shows.

Urban areas. It is difficult to construct a clear picture of the situations of urban middle-class women. The enclosure concept that I have emphasized is only part of the picture. In addition to the unknown number of women who had no significant activities beyond supervision of children and servants, there were women who acted as partners in their husbands' enterprises, including trading. It is hard to determine how many of the women who became known as successful traders in their own right began as partners with their husbands and expanded the business after widowhood. The well-to-do middle-class woman trader was a familiar figure in all the port cities of the Mediterranean from Phoenician times on. Many of the first converts to Christianity were well-to-do women merchants who put their homes and their wealth at the disposal of the early Christian communities. The wealthiest Greek trader in Byzantium in the Middle Ages was a woman (Sherrard, 1966), and women traders were major figures in Bristol in the 1400s (Power and Postan, 1933). These were all middle-class women whose enterprise and ability enabled them to "earn" the help they needed to free themselves from the burdens of the breeder-feeder role.

Somewhere on this continuum of producer roles for the urban middle-class woman, which runs the gamut from the almost totally nonproductive display wife through the independent trader, there exists the craft partner, the woman who was jointly engaged with her spouse in home workshop production as a member of a craft guild. Where this kind of economic partnership existed, there may have been considerable sharing of the child care part of the breeder role with the spouse. The craft guild tradition, which began in the Mediterranean before the Christian Era, was one of husband-wife partnership which involved both more equality in the producer roles and more joint involvement with the children. The dividing line between teaching and nurturance faded away when both spouses were engaged in the craft role. In addition, every craft guild household had outside children age seven and up in an apprentice relationship. Even in non-craft-guild families it was common to send one's own children out to other households in the community and take other's children into one's home to rear. This practice seems to have been a combination of mutual boarding out, a way of getting extra household help, and a device for involving others in the education of one's children (Laslett, 1972). Because people were raising each other's children, men became more involved in the rearing process than they might have been had children stayed in their own homes.

The whole history of the craft guild movement in England and on the Continent (though more so in the former than the latter) is a history of the involvement of women in the productive process in partnership roles with men. (There is less information about the relative roles of father and mother in relation to children and production in rural settings.) It may well be that the small-scale craft guild enterprise that predated the industrial revolution provided the setting of a more egalitarian, less exploitative work and parenting partnership than any other kind of work setting.

Household Size and Familial Constraints

In the sixteenth century, the process of pushing women back inside their families, denying them economic and other extradomestic involvements, gained momentum. Household size became an important constraint and should be considered. Recent studies of local records in various parts of Europe reveal the surprising fact that household size has changed very little from the Middle Ages to the present (Laslett, 1972). Apart from the great manor houses of the nobility and the homes of rich merchants, most people lived in families with an average size of 4.75 persons per family, plus a servant.[10] Not only were families small, but the marriage age for women and men was beginning to rise. For European women in the 1500s the average age at marriage was about twenty-one, rising in succeeding centuries to twenty-five and twenty-eight. Furthermore, because multigenerational families were very much the exception, most women were confined to very small domestic spaces in small families before and after marriage. While women certainly had larger households during their child-bearing years, high infant death rates and the practice of older couples and widows maintaining separate quarters left women in increasing domestic isolation as they lost freedom of movement in other spheres.

The tension level between mothers and daughters was apparently very high in this period. There are many mentions of brutal child-rearing, and particularly of mothers beating daughters who resisted parental marriage plans. Even the gentle Queen Margaret of Navarre, known as an advocate of peace, beat her daughter daily for weeks on end to make her agree to a politically designated marriage. Agnes Paston of the lively Paston family, known for its voluminous intrafamily correspondence and numerous lawsuits, beat her daughter so badly that "her head was broke in 2 or 3 places." Lady Jane Gray's mother beat her. Since the records all refer to mothers, not fathers, beating their daughters, and this in the context of an otherwise "good" family life, it would seem that women of this period were subject to severe emotional pressure which they relieved by child abuse. Sending daughters out to other families as servants was one of the few available means of relieving the strain, but this required reciprocity and acceptance of someone else's daughter into the home. The disappearance of convents in England and in many places in Europe,[11] and the closing down of other occupational options for women, made marriage arrangements increasingly important and also made marriages harder to achieve. Mothers bore the brunt of these problems in terms of pressure to get their daughters out of their small households.

The effect of a lowering status of women on mother-daughter relations is a subject that needs much more attention. Obviously not all mothers beat their daughters, and when there were beatings they do not seem to have led to severed relations. There was, rather, some continued expression of affection between mothers and daughters in later life. Women seem to have fled from continuing extended family situations whenever possible. This is supported by the fact that in the 1500s, even with housing shortages, 16 percent of all English households in the 100 communities Laslett examined were headed by women (1972: 447). Of these, 12.9 percent were widows, 1.1 percent single females, and 2.3 percent "unspecified females" in humble households, as well as on estates. There are many references to the joy with which women set up their own households after widowhood and the vigor with which they resisted courting by amorous widowers. The extended family togetherness we nostalgically refer to as part of our golden past simply did not exist in the European heritage, and there is some evidence that it never really existed on a large scale anywhere. (See Chapter 4 for a discussion of household size in Morocco.)

More important, perhaps, the picture of women that emerges from this material is a useful corrective to the popular misconception that women throughout history have submissively endured everything. They have endured a great deal, but not necessarily submissively.

ALTERNATIVES TO FAMILIAL ROLES

During the entire historical period from 500 B.C. to the industrial revolution, there were important alternatives for women to being the wife/mother in a male-headed household or the family-burdened female head of a household. One alternative was celibacy. The nun role has existed from early times in Hinduism, in Buddhism, and finally in Christianity and Islam. Although religious orders for women took different forms in Asia, the Middle East, and Europe, the basic pattern of an alternative role that did not involve the breeder-feeder function was present in all these societies. Between A.D. 500

and 1400 there was an extraordinary flowering of convent culture in Europe. This culture produced science, art, and literature, and a social service infrastructure in the fields of health, education, and welfare unparalleled until the nineteenth century. While nuns were in one sense isolated within the male-dominant structure of the Catholic Church, in another sense they lived in protected niches within which they could be free. And if the price they paid for that freedom was celibacy, there is real evidence of the creativity and joy of convent life in those centuries (as well as before and since). The nineteenth and twentieth centuries have seen a second explosion of creativity through celibacy, partly within and partly outside religious orders. Today, there are approximately 2 million nuns in the world from all the major religious traditions.

In addition to the celibacy in the convent, there was the "beguinage"[1,2] — an urban secular commune for rural women migrants to the city during the major urban migrations of the thirteenth and fourteenth centuries. Invented by women, the beguinages were so successful that they were seen as serious threats to some of the existing craft guilds and their members were persecuted by members of the guild. Besides the beguines there were also hermitesses— solitary women who lived in huts by bridges, on the edges of towns, and in forest solitudes all over England and, to a lesser extent, in the rest of Europe. These were a special class of independents in the Middle Ages—able to support themselves through their knowledge of human nature and folk medicine. With no institutional protection of any kind, most of them were burned as witches during the height of the medieval witch mania. Last, there were vagabonds, the hard-working fun-loving women who moved partnerless through the Middle Ages, always able to pick up the pennies they needed at a fair or celebration of some kind. When they were willing to settle in a town, they were not infrequently supported by town councils, glad to have resident entertainers for their community. Besides being entertainers, they ran the soup kitchens and the first-aid stations in wars, including the Crusades. They were good soldiers when they were needed as fighters. Altogether, they were a social category for which we would have no labels today. Marriage was not on their agenda, and at times up to one-fourth of the women of Europe belonged in their company.

THE END OF AN ERA

During the late 1500s and 1600s many of the phenomena described above began to disappear. The craftwomen, the celibates, and the vagabonds all declined in numbers and status. In the guilds in particular there was a rapid loss of rights and status for women. Men were feeling the pressure of women as competitors in the labor market and successfully pressed for their expulsion from guild after guild. This transition era initiated the prolonged suffering of both rural and urban female laborers as they were squeezed out of secure medieval work statuses. The hermitess or vagabond of the fourteenth century became the work-deadened automaton of the seventeenth and eighteenth centuries. Rural laboring women went hungry, and the children of women in the factories were rounded up like cattle and placed in workhouses or shipped overseas to labor in the colonies. Married and single women alike were trapped by the formula of "supplemental" pittance wages for women.

This was also the period when the gentlewoman in straitened circumstances appeared—the middle-class woman without training or resources who could not enter domestic service because of her social status. She became a governess or a companion in homes of slightly better off middle-class people, working for little more than bread and board, often in a position close to that of the household slave of Greek and Roman times. Just below her in station was the domestic, even more of a household slave. By the 1700s, these women began to emigrate overseas to new hardships, but also to new opportunities.

It is this period that witnessed the emergence of the Marxist analysis of the situation of women. Woman and men alike, whether Saint-Simonians, anarchist socialists, or Marxist socialists, all saw the necessity for society to deal with the burden of the breeder-feeder role that entrapped women by providing child care and domestic maintenance for everyone. However, no one looked back to the time when men had shared part of the breeder-feeder role. Everything (except biological child-bearing) was to be taken over by the state. If this proposal asked nothing of men, it had the virtue of helping married and single women heads-of-household equally.

Since no socialist state could afford to duplicate the individualized breeder-feeder role of women as a public service, and no capitalist state wanted to, it was easy to turn this task back to women in the end. The famous Ellen Key "return to matriarchy movement" to restore full legal head of household rights to women independently of marital status has to be seen in that context (Key, 1911). Indeed, all the nineteenth-century utopian movements from Brook Farm to New Harmony left women's roles unchanged. Only the Shakers and the Mormons offered something different; the former the freedom of celibacy, the latter the freedom of co-wives with whom to share farm labor. Both attracted women in droves.

It was a hard century for working women, and it was an unsettling one for middle-class women who had been led to expect something different—some kind of equality. All the women-triggered social reform movements of the nineteenth century and all their concrete achievements—protective legislation and new types of social service institutions—could not take the edge off the bitterness of unacknowledged colleagueship. Women had worked side

Familial Constraints on Women's Work Roles

by side with men in civic roles—and remained unrecognized. Women were invited, welcomed, urged into the labor force—but at bargain prices. Civic work and industrial labor were both considered avocations. The breeder-feeder role was the unremitting background rhythm to all other activities of women. Even in the socialist countries, where women were the most needed and most welcomed into the labor force, they were expected to carry on the same breeder-feeder role at home after hours.

The Twentieth Century

The UNESCO Time Budget Series shows with startling clarity that every married woman who works today still bears the triple burdens of breeder-feeder-producer. The Szalai study (1972), from which Tables 3.1 and 3.2 are taken, includes twelve countries and shows remarkable consistency. I have selected four countries that represent four distinct types of "work culture." Because time budgets would differ for different groups within the same city, as well as between cities in the same country, and between countries, all figures must be treated as giving general indications only.

Table 3.1 gives the percentage of employed women and men participating in primary activities and Table 3.2 the number of minutes spent per day on these activities. Not surprisingly, more employed women than men do housework and child care, the differences range from 25 to 45 percent. Fewer women engage in study and participation, or in use of the mass media than

Table 3.1: Workday Time Budgets of Employed Women and Employed Men (percentage of each sex participating in primary activities)

	6 Cities, France		Torun, Poland		Jackson, USA		Pakov, USSR	
	Women	Men	Women	Men	Women	Men	Women	Men
Total Work (job)	98.9	99.8	97.2	99.6	98.8	100.0	99.1	99.8
Total Housework[a]	95.2	58.4	98.2	58.2	93.8	50.3	98.7	73.4
Other Household[b] Obligations	52.9	63.5	45.3	53.9	56.6	48.4	65.6	53.8
Total Child Care[c]	31.0	24.8	41.6	30.8	35.8	18.7	48.2	40.1
Total Personal Needs[d] (includes sleep)	100.0	100.0	100.0	100.0	100.0	100.0	100.0	100.0
Study and Participation[e]	8.8	9.7	18.0	19.2	13.6	18.9	19.8	34.3
Total Mass Media[f]	69.0	82.7	75.1	88.0	76.1	83.1	75.6	92.2
Total Leisure[g]	79.2	83.4	64.1	74.8	74.7	61.8	65.8	81.7
Total Travel[h]	88.8	95.0	99.1	98.5	100.0	100.0	99.8	99.5

SOURCE: From Szalai (1972): 584, 588; data are weighted to ensure equality of days of the week and number of eligible respondents per household.
   a. Includes cooking, home chores, laundry, marketing.
   b. Includes garden, animal care, errands, shopping, other household activities.
   c. Includes child care, other child-related activities.
   d. Includes personal care, eating, sleep.
   e. Includes study, religion, organization.
   f. Includes radio, TV (home), TV (away), reading papers, reading magazines, reading books movies.
   g. Includes social (home), social (away), conversation, active sports, outdoors, entertainment, cultural events, resting, other leisure.
   h. Includes travel to work, personal travel, leisure travel.

men. Everyone sleeps, has some free time, and travels (whether on foot or otherwise) to work and to do errands, so here any figures under 100 percent are artifacts of the enumeration procedures.

It is in Table 3.2 that we begin to get the concrete picture of daily life. In no country do employed men spend more than half an hour on housework, and employed women less than an hour and a half, even though women's working hours outside the home are sometimes longer than men's. In some, but not all, areas men spend a few more minutes on "other household obligations" than women. Time spent in child care alone as a primary activity is, according to these data, never more than half an hour, even for women. But this is somewhat misleading, since most child care runs concurrently with other activities—housework, use of media, and free time. In fact, child care is continuous for women during all hours they are not at work. Only in Pakov, USSR, do employed fathers give as much "primary care" to children as employed mothers do. Only in the United States do women spend more time on personal needs and sleep than men do.

The most consistent differences between women's and men's use of time, apart from housework, show up in the figures for study and participation, for use of mass media, and for leisure. Women have substantially fewer minutes to spend on each activity within these categories. Given the wide variations in the cultures represented, there is a remarkable overall consistency in the use

Table 3.2: Workday Time Budgets of Employed Women and Employed Men
(Time spent in primary activities, in average minutes per day)

	6 Cities, France		Torun, Poland		Jackson, USA		Pakov, USSR	
	Women	Men	Women	Men	Women	Men	Women	Men
Total Work (job)	492	583	490	563	482	570	478	506
Total Housework[a]	156	26	180	31	133	21	170	28
Other Household[b] Obligations	17	32	20	29	31	29	27	39
Total Child Care[c]	24	8	27	20	16	8	30	30
Total Personal Needs[d] (includes sleep)	621	621	543	560	590	572	546	573
Study and Participation[e]	7	9	23	25	17	27	27	52
Total Mass Media[f]	47	76	70	117	65	114	73	125
Total Leisure[g]	60	70	56	71	63	59	48	55
Total Travel[h]	57	75	86	91	73	85	81	20
Total Minutes	1440	1440	1440	1440	1440	1440	1440	1440

SOURCE: From Szalai (1972): 583, 587; data are weighted to ensure equality of days of the week and number of eligible respondents per household.
   a. Includes cooking, home chores, laundry, marketing.
   b. Includes garden, animal care, errands, shopping, other household activities.
   c. Includes child care, other child-related activities.
   d. Includes personal care, eating, sleep.
   e. Includes study, religion, organization.
   f. Includes radio, TV (home), TV (away), reading papers, reading magazines, reading books movies.
   g. Includes social (home), social (away), conversation, active sports, outdoors, entertainment, cultural events, resting, other leisure.
   h. Includes travel to work, personal travel, leisure travel.

of time by employed females as compared with employed males. Women's time is far more constrained than men's, as it has probably always been since settled life began. Household appliances and ready-to-use products or services for domestic maintenance or child care help somewhat, but the stubborn fact remains that the private spaces of the home and the private shapes of individual lives cannot be fully mass-serviced. Something remains that individuals must do. Must these individuals always be women?

If the private spaces of the home were closed down and everyone adopted communal living, home maintenance could be simplified. And if one simply stopped having children. . . . But there is no evidence that these things are happening. In the United States, for example, there has been a steady decrease in the number of married couples without their own households (see Figure 3.1). First marriages, and remarriages for the divorced, continue at a rate that makes American society much more "married" than the European society of the Middle Ages. And although families are decreasing in size in the West, there are no signs of children being given up as a project of the human race. Commune formation may be continuing at about the same rate as in the previous decade, but so is commune dissolution. Most young people in the United States who are attracted to communes evidently go through a commune initiation and then "go private." Private quarters, in socialist countries, in kibbutz-oriented Israel, and in commune—oriented China are valued as much as anywhere else.

In the Middle Ages there were beguinages, hermitages, and small family households. In the twentieth century there are communes, single-person households, and nuclear families. However we label them, these various types of social organization to meet human maintenance needs are probably all enduring features of the human landscape. The mix simply differs in different periods of history, depending on the ratio of single to attached women and on reproduction rates. Children are also enduring features of the human landscape. When women have too heavy a work burden with the triple breeder-feeder-producer role, the whole society suffers. Women suffer role overstrain, men suffer role deprivation, and children suffer from inadequate experiences of relating to the human community.

Marxist analysis failed to put its finger on one aspect of the oppression of women: the confining of breeder-feeder roles to them. Such analysts thought that by turning the state into the breeder-feeder all would be well. But human liberation depends on sharing breeder-feeder roles between women and men, as well as on having state-administered support services. The problems of scale in human nurturance are such that relatively small living units will always be required, no matter how closely integrated into larger communal sharing units. There is no way out for men but to confront parenthood, and no way out for women but to confront sharing their centuries-old monopoly on the breeder-feeder role. The biological aspect of breeding is a minute part of the total care that goes into the production of an autonomous human being; there is really very little that men need to be excluded from if one looks at the totality of the child-bearing process.

Another element missing in Marxist analysis is love. By failing to deal in theoretical terms with the special role of love and tenderness that enhances all other social interactions when present, and diminishes them when absent, Marx left love as women's work by default. It simply could not be taken over by the state.

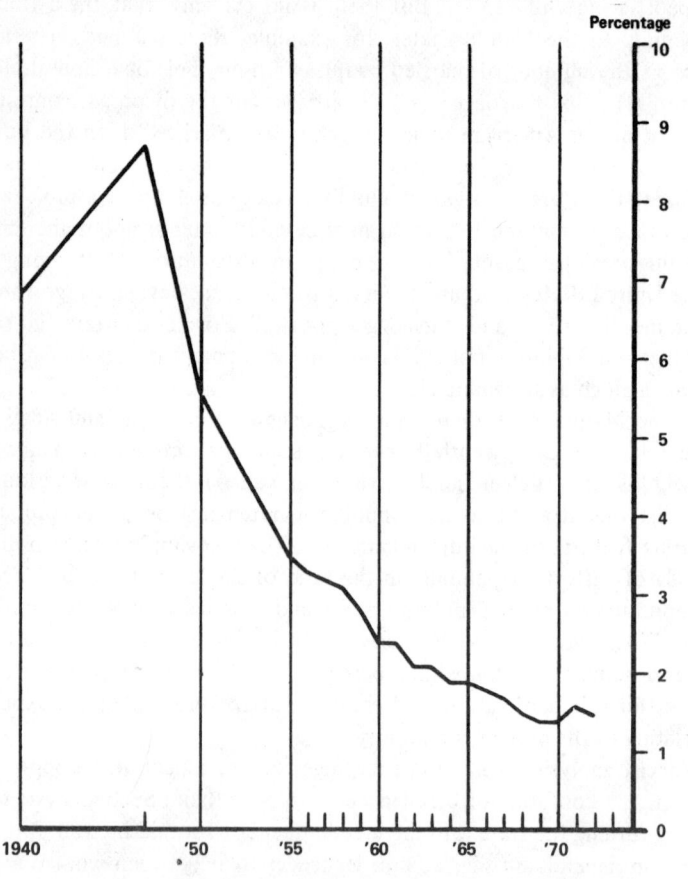

Figure 3.1: MARRIED COUPLES WITHOUT THEIR OWN HOUSEHOLDS: UNITED STATES, 1940-1972

SOURCE: From **Social Indicators** (1973), written and compiled by the Statistical Policy Division, Office of Management and Budget, and prepared for publication by the Social and Economic Statistics Administration, U.S. Department of Commerce (1973: 199).

One of the properties of love is that it acts to modify dominance relations. For this reason love has been rejected by some women's liberationists as one more element in a constellation of role expectations that has led to women's oppression. It has taken the twentieth century to produce the insight that the particular kind of reciprocity represented by love as *agape,* or caring, is a trait that is equally desirable in men and women. The men's liberation movement, in setting out to destroy both the image and the reality of sex-linked dominance behavior, may in the end be one of the most significant social movements of the twentieth century. By liberating the potential for tenderness in men, it undercuts much of the rationale for sex-based dominance and sets the stage for a new kind of involvement of men with children.

Equal involvement of women and men with children does not imply that every woman, or every man, must have a partner for parenting. Part of the new understanding of parenting is reflected in court decisions that allow sometimes men, sometimes women, sole custody of a child when single parenting becomes necessary. Single parenting involves extra burdens, but when it is not sex linked it becomes clearer that society should provide generalized "drawing rights" for persons of either sex who undertake the care of small children alone. A concept developed by Gösta Rehn, such a generalized set of rights "would make available to women in monetary form the help no longer available to them in the form of unpaid mutual aid" and would include income maintenance during time out for motherhood (as quoted in Jessie Bernard [1975: 273]). (The generalized drawing rights idea was developed in connection with the needs of women, but in a dual parenting society they should be available to any parent who needs them.)

The alternative to a new role sharing, supplemented with a variety of support services for single parents, is concentrating on producing a race of superwomen who can excel in the breeder-feeder role and also in the producer role. The research on role transcendence and the type of woman who excels in all of her human roles (Bernard, 1975: 51-54) suggests that what some women acquire by chance, through a biologically inherited metabolic pattern that ensures abundant physical energy, could be deliberately provided to all women by chemical intervention and genetic engineering. Is that the way we want to do it? Would men enjoy living in the shadow of a race of superwomen? A reversal of dominance patterns might be enjoyable for some in the short run, but in the long run it leaves us with all the limitations of the old male-dominance pattern.

What type of role patterning will emerge in the future to deal with social production and nurturance requirements is not yet clear. What is clear, as this chapter has demonstrated, is that women have always carried out the producer role as well as the breeder-feeder roles. The triple role has always been present and is no new phenomenon of the industrial revolution, or of the twentieth century; nor is the wage differential related to the triple-role handicap new. What is new is a vision of human potential which is being applied to women as well as to men, and which inevitably leads to the affirmation of equal rewards and equal opportunities for both sexes. The kind of creativity that we now see as possible for all human beings, and that needs to be fostered from earliest childhood, depends in a very direct sense on the exposure of men to breeder-feeder roles. This is where the male areas of freedom lie. This is where the male constraints, which were not discussed in this chapter,[13] but which are as punitive in their way as are the female constraints, must be broken. What is involved here is not the old battle of the sexes, which was a battle for dominance, but a process of mutual liberation on behalf of that gentler and more creative generation to come—our children's children.

NOTES

1. I include in the concept of breeding both bearing children and caring for them until they are self-sufficient. The biological aspect of child-bearing is only one component of breeding as defined here.

2. Men may prepare special feast foods, but in no society is the preparation of food for consumption in the home the regular daily work of men.

3. I agree with him that matriliny is not a general evolutionary stage but only arises under certain conditions. Not all agrovillage development would follow the pattern I am suggesting.

4. This listing represents a synthesis of information about Greek women from a great variety of sources, including material summarized in Sullerot (1968); from Boulding, (1977).

5. Free men had so many other advantages in ancient societies that the existence of male slaves did not affect their situation to the extent that female slaves affected the situation of free women (see Westermann, 1955).

6. A common situation in parts of Africa today (see Boserup, 1970).

7. There are African societies with far better settings for children of working mothers. See Chapter 4 for a description of this alternative model of urbanization.

8. See Boserup (1970).

9. For an incredible account of the workload under feudalism, see Duby (1968).

10. These "servants," it turns out, were not servants in the contemporary sense of the word but rather children of neighboring families in the same parish.

11. The pressure on mothers to get rid of daughters also existed in the Middle Ages at the height of convent life, and many daughters were beaten half to death by mothers who were trying to force them into convents against their wills. There are interesting records of lawsuits of nuns who claimed that they had been forced to take vows by their parents (see O'Faolain and Martines, 1973: 270-275).

12. This was a religiously based social movement, but the women were *not* in religious orders (see McDonnell, 1969).

13. The reader interested in the phenomenon of male liberation, highly relevant to this closing discussion, is referred to Farrell (1974).

PART II

WOMEN AND PRODUCTIVE SYSTEMS

In this section we shift from the broad overview of role patterns for women through time to an examination of the contemporary situation of woman as producer, breeder, and feeder with special emphasis on the third world. Since women's work sites and production are often in the subsistence sector and therefore overlooked in development studies, a special effort is made here to build up a picture of these worksites and this production and to link the world of barter, which makes the subsistence sector a far more complex economic phenomenon than it is usually described as, to the market economy that economists are more at home with. In addition to a general analysis of economic dualism as it affects the productivity of women, the crucial role of women in the agricultural sector in particular, and in food systems in general is dealt with in this section. Policy implications for development planning are pointed out wherever possible.[1] Since Chapter 4 is highly technical, readers unfamiliar with the concepts used, may prefer to skip this chapter and get the general ideas about women and productive systems from Chapters 5 and 6.

NOTE

1. The Irene Tinker and Michele Bo Bramsen book on *Women and World Development* (1976) has been published since this Section was written and adds valuable policy relevant material to what appears here, as does the Buvinić bibliography (1976) published as a companion volume.

Chapter 4

ECONOMIC DUALISM: Women's Roles and Poverty Traps

Recent work in development research suggests that industrializing countries may enter a prolonged state of economic dualism (Adelman and Morris, 1967, 1973). This dualism is characterized by the coexistence of a low-productivity subsistence agriculture sector and high-productivity agribusiness and industrial sector in the developing society. This compartmentalization generates income inequalities of such magnitude that many persons in the developing society are worse off during "development" than they were in the preindustrial stage. The capital-intensive character of the industrial sector, including industrialized agriculture, coupled with the complex knowledge and skill structures that join the human being to the machine, push a society that does not already have powerful mechanisms for guaranteeing free flow of information and skills to every corner of that society, into enclave development. The faster development takes place within the enclave, the harder it is to cross the information barrier for those on the outside. This leaves a mass of subsistence farmers for whom enclave technology is useless, since it cannot be utilized to increase their productivity. Neither can it be used to draw them into the industrial sector, because of the latter's small labor requirements. The industrial sector thus has nothing to offer them, since they cannot afford to consume its products either. Programs designed in the enclave to improve the agricultural productivity of the small farmers on the outside are preempted by the middle-sized farmers who expand their holdings at the expense

Author's Note: Paper prepared for the Conference on Economic Development and Income Distribution, sponsored by the Institute of Behavioral Science, University of Colorado, Estes Park, Colorado, April 23-24, 1976; an abbreviated, revised version of this chapter will appear in the Conference Volume, Income Distribution in Developing Countries, William Loehr and John Powelson, editors (Boulder, Colorado: Westview Press, 1977).

of small peasants. Such programs leave previously self-sufficient subsistence farmers landless and poverty-stricken, with no new source of income in sight.

The coexistence of a low-productivity subsistence sector and a high-productivity market-oriented enclave is not a new phenomenon of industrialization, however. From the time of the earliest clustering of towns in the Middle East and Mesoamerica (9000 B.C. or earlier) such dualism has existed. To a considerable extent it has been based on another type of dualism, a gender-linked division of labor that left women with the subsistence tasks of growing and processing food, caring for babies, and engaging in domestic manufacture for home consumption, while men entered the market economy of the new city-based production, trade, and service networks. While women have never been totally confined to the subsistence sector in any society, they have always been far more active in it than men once urbanism developed. Because the resultant income inequalities operated within family units rather than between economic or class interest groups, they were socially invisible. These inequalities have also been partially mitigated by intrafamily grants (men sharing some of their earnings with the women of their households). At the same time, the partial, private, and voluntary nature of the within-family income transfers and the lack of alternative economic opportunities for women contributed to the crystallization of a lower social and political status for women in relation to men both within families and in society generally.

One way to conceptualize the traditional gender-based dualism is to think of the women's sector as a labor-intensive subsistence sector with minimal access to the knowledge, skills, and technology of the preindustrial town and city. Once the economic egalitarianism of the hunting and gathering existence and of the earliest forms of slash-and-burn agriculture have been left behind, we find that women everywhere have fewer and poorer tools than men, and must draw more on their body power for work than men at comparable tasks. Boserup has effectively demonstrated this for women farmers (Boserup, 1970). Two other dualisms are superimposed on the gender-based dualism. One is suggested by the term "third world," produced by the most recent, late second-millennium wave of modernization that swept over the temperate zone of the planet and left the third world as the labor-intensive sector of the world economy. The second is the phenomenon to which dualism usually refers, modernization within third world countries, which leaves a large subsistence sector untouched by industrial development.

It will be argued in this chapter that it is the cumulative impact of this triple dualism that creates the poverty trap for so many third world countries, and that development policies that do not take account of primary, gender-based dualism are doomed to failure. The declining productivity of women in the subsistence sector has to do with disproportionately fewer and fewer resources being available to them. This is part of the general process of resource deprivation which also affects the poorer 40 percent of the male peasantry once the industrial sector begins to develop. It hits both men and women, but it hits women harder. While such sectoral imbalance also accompanied the earlier phase of industrialization in Europe, it was not so extreme because the prior resource depletion by the early medieval colonial exploiters, the Vikings, was probably modest compared to the resource depletion of the third world by the most recent European colonialism, particularly in Africa and Asia. Third world countries began modernization in an already "squeezed" condition.

The condition of triple dualism just described puts such a heavy weight on the part of the labor force least equipped in terms of skill and resources—that is, on women—that their daily labor cannot produce enough food and other home craft products to support an intersectoral flow of goods and services that can improve the standard of life of the total society.

The dualism created in the international economy by colonialism, and the problems of how to trigger the dynamics of a new international economic order, will not be dealt with in this chapter. It should be understood, however, that third world countries cannot effectively deal with the problems of internal dualism unless progress is also made at the international level. In fact, the extreme of economic dualism found in developing countries in this century has usually been introduced by a dominant expatriate colonial elite. That same elite stands in the way of the emergence of an indigenous middle class that will provide leadership for the breaking down of the barriers to the free flow of information, skill, and resources among sectors. It also stands in the way of the reconstruction of participatory mechanisms that join the best of traditional values and communications skills with newer organizational and communication technologies, because of the elite's scorn for the traditions on which that reconstruction needs to be based. Even after the expatriate elite has been replaced by an indigenous middle class, it is not necessarily easy for that class to throw off elitist attitudes and identity itself with populist interests.

Adelman and Morris state the problem clearly enough when they suggest that it will be necessary to develop "new political institutions and policies that will ensure development of the people, by the people, and for the people" (1973: 202). However, the likelihood of the emergence of such institutions and policies on the basis of prevailing modes of analysis of the problem is nil. Expatriate elites, development experts, and indigenous middle class leadership alike maintain an incomplete if not faulty view of the actual processes of capital formation, productivity, and economic decision-making on the part of up to 90 percent of a society's population, including the 50 percent which is female. The political consciousness that must be developed before more equitable social policies can take shape depends on a recognition of the resources, productivity, and needs of a hidden sector of society. While the understanding of the day-to-day functioning of the male peasant farmer and landless laborer is faulty enough, these groups are at least recognized as theoretical targets for economic policy. The female peasant farmer and landless laborer do not exist for the policy maker. Third world women are seen only as breeders and feeders, not as producers, traders, or performers of a variety of community services in the peasant village and the town. Part of the problem of adequate economic analysis lies in the necessity of assigning monetary values to the productive labor and the exchange activities of women who do not enter the cash economy. It is equally important to identify and count the monetary transactions of women at the village level, which have stayed hidden because economists have not looked for them.

The purpose of this chapter is to examine these hidden components of third world economies and to suggest their policy implications if permanent dualistic structures of poverty are to be avoided. To begin with, I will examine the more accessible and routinely enumerated economic activities of women in the framework offered by Adelman and Morris, grouping countries according to the progression delineated by them, from traditional to dualistic, to successfully modernizing societies. A further examination of the more hidden activities will supplement the statistical survey, with a view to uncovering the relationship between gender-based dualism and economic dualism in developing societies.

The analysis will be divided into two parts. In the first I have chosen twenty-one countries in various stages of modernization from the Adelman-Morris list of seventy-four countries. The twenty-one countries were selected to represent each developmental stage and a variety of religious and cultural patterns and geographic regions, and also chosen on the basis of availability of data on women in the labor force. The countries are grouped according to the Adelman formulation, as traditional subsistence, dualistic, and rapidly modernizing, on the basis of the data presented in Adelman and Morris (1967). Data on the participation of women in each society comes from a study initially undertaken for the UN (Boulding et al., 1976). Other country characteristics utilized in the tables that follow are also derived from UN sources. The Adelman and Morris data on income inequality (1973) are also used. Unavoidably, there are blank spaces in the tables where data are missing for a given country.

The data for the twenty-one countries are arranged in a series of tables to enable inspection of cultural and economic characteristics associated with the Adelman-Morris typology, with particular emphasis on occupations and education of women. No statistical analysis is attempted in this exploratory study.

In the second part, I draw on the analyses of capital formation and productivity of women in the traditional sector of third world societies as undertaken by Maher (1974), Hill (1969), Vreede-De Stuers (1968), Ward (1963a) and Boserup (1970), supplemented by the comparative studies of agricultural productivity in the United States, Japan, and India by Nair (1962, 1969), and Firth and Yamey's (1964) study of capital, saving, and credit in peasant societies. The closing discussion will evaluate the relevance of the two kinds of data on the participation of women for development policy, particularly with reference to the maintenance of dualistic structures that create differential economic, social, and political opportunities for different sectors of modernizing societies.

THE STATISTICS OF DUALISM

The countries chosen for an analysis of women's participation in societies with varying degrees of dualism are shown in Table 4.1. The indicators utilized in the typology—percentage of the population in traditional subsistence agriculture, extent of sectoral cleavage between modern and traditional economic sectors, extent of bureaucratic efficiency, and extent of development of a significant indigenous middle class, not expatriate-dominated, all come from Adelman and Morris (1967: 9-128). Each of these indicators is judgmental, based on country studies and evaluations by country experts (1967: 12-13).[1] All judgments refer to the state of a country as of about 1960, and the countries themselves were chosen as representative of societies "which, as of 1950, were underdeveloped with respect to social and economic structure" (1967: 9). By 1968, the year to which the UN data on women used in this analysis refer, some of these countries could no longer be characterized as "underdeveloped." This makes possible an examination of the dynamics of change for these countries, particularly for the period 1960 to 1968.

In order to keep the typology as simple as possible, I have collapsed various distinctions made by Adelman and Morris to produce three types of societies, and have left out entirely the completely traditional society in which "modernizing" sectoral cleavages have not yet taken place.[2] The societies that will be referred to as "high dualism" societies are those with over 55 percent of the population in traditional subsistence agriculture, with sharp sectoral or geographic cleavage, moderate to low bureaucratic efficiency, and a weak indigenous middle class, frequently expatriate-dominated. The "moderate dualism" societies are those with from 25 to 54 percent of the population in traditional subsistence agriculture with moderate to low sectoral or geographic efficiency and a significant indigenous middle class. The "low dualism" societies are those with less than 25 percent of the population in traditional subsistence agriculture, with minimal sectoral or geographic cleavage, high bureaucratic efficiency and a strong indigenous middle class.

Table 4.2 gives a picture of the participation of women in the traditional and modern sectors with contextual information about the majority religions

Table 4.1: The Data Base for Analysis of Women's Participation in Development: Country Listing, By Extent of Dualism[a]

High Dualism Countries[b]	*Black Africa*	*West Asia*
	Gabon	Iran
	Rhodesia	*Asia*
	Sierra Leone	Indonesia
	North Africa	
	Morocco	
	Tunisia	
Moderate Dualism Countries[c]	*Black Africa*	*Asia*
	Ghana	India
	Nigeria	Pakistan
	North Africa	*Latin America*
	UAR	Argentina
	West Asia	Colombia
	Cyprus	Mexico
	Syria	
	Turkey	
Low Dualism Countries[d]	*West Asia*	*Latin America*
	Israel	Chile
	Asia	
	Japan	

a. Dualism refers to sharp sectoral or geographic cleavages; based on classification in Adelman and Morris (1967: Chapter II), for the time period 1957-1962. The related concepts of bureaucratic efficiency and significance of indigenous middle class are also based on classifications in Adelman and Morris (1967: Chapter II). See definitions in notes b, c, and d.

b. Countries with over 55 percent of the population in traditional subsistence agriculture, with sharp sectoral or geographic cleavage, moderate to low bureaucratic efficiency, and a weak indigenous middle class.

c. Countries with from 25 to 54 percent of the population in traditional subsistence agriculture, with moderate to low sectoral or geographic cleavage and moderate to high bureaucratic efficiency, and a significant indigenous middle class.

d. Countries with less than 25 percent of the population in traditional subsistence agriculture, with minimal sectoral or geographic cleavage, high bureaucratic efficiency, and a strong indigenous middle class.

for each group of countries. The figures come from 1968 UN data converted into participation units (Boulding et al., 1976). Each participation unit indicates the female proportion of the total population engaged in the activity in question. There are as many problems with these supposedly "hard" data on the participation of women as there are with the "soft" data on dualism, though for different reasons. It is extremely unlikely that any country at any stage of development is accurately counting its women farmers or its traders, as we shall see later. While I have placed agricultural and own-account workers in the traditional sector, when we get to the low dualism countries this is no longer an appropriate classification. In these countries farmer women and self-employed women may well be integrated in the modern sector. In any society, women in the industrial sector are more easily counted, since that sector is urban-based. To what extent third world village women who are engaged in sales, services, and technical work are counted is hard to say. For all these weaknesses, the UN figures represent first approximations of the economic participation of women as seen by a country's bureaucrats.

What is striking in comparing women's participation rates for differing degrees of dualism is that the highs and lows of participation in agriculture are the same in all groups of countries. High dualism countries have as few as 2 and as many as 51 percent of women in agriculture. Moderate dualism countries have as few as 3 and as many as 54 percent, and low dualism countries as few as 3 and as high as 53 percent. If we look at cultural regions, there are wide divergences in black Africa, Asia, and West Asia. North Africa and Latin America are more homogeneous.

Looking at the religion column, we see that religious tradition no more determines participation in agriculture for women than does cultural region, since while the predominantly Muslim countries of Morocco, Tunisia, and Iran have few women farmers, the predominantly Muslim countries of Indonesia, Syria, and Turkey all have high proportions of women farmers. The only thing all Muslim countries have in common is that they have few women in sales. They may have quite a few women in professional, service, and clerical work—or very few. Catholicism, also considered a restraining influence on women in the labor force, is consistently associated with few women in farming (at least in Latin America; all the Catholic countries in our list are also Latin American), but puts them in very high numbers indeed in professional, clerical, and service work. It would appear that religion acts as a constraining factor on the participation of women in the labor force insofar as it affects the settings in which work is carried out (for example, whether work is carried out under conditions of seclusion) rather than the absolute numbers of women employed. This will discussed further later.

Variation in the number of women working on their own account is almost as great as variation in the number of agricultural workers, but the mean of own-account workers is higher for the low dualism countries than for the high dualism, less industrialized societies.

If we read the figures across for the traditional and modern sectors of individual countries in each development category, we find a great unevenness in extent of participation in various occupational categories, in both the high and moderate dualism countries. Only in the low dualism countries is there a tendency toward evenly high participation in all categories (except for the administrative field, from which women are uniformly excluded in most countries of the world). Only two categories have high participation of

(Text continued on page 87)

Table 4.2: Women's Participation in Traditional and Modern Occupation Sectors, by Extent of Dualism of the Economy[a] and Predominant Religion

Country	% Women Employed in Traditional Sector[b]		% Women Employed in "Modern" Sector[c]						Majority Religion Percentage
	Agriculture	Own Account Workers	Professional & Technical	Administrative & Managerial	Clerical & Related	Sales Workers	Service Workers	Production Transportation Laborers	
HIGH DUALISM COUNTRIES									
Black Africa									
Gabon	51	35	—	—	—	—	—	12	50 Cath/ 42 Anim
Rhodesia[d]	7	16	38	5	56	36	63	4	85 Anim
Sierra Leone	42	13	27	9	16	47	6	—	62 Anim
North Africa									
Morocco	8	6	15	3	26	4	27	—	98 Musl
Tunisia[e]	2	6	17	4	18	2	19	7	95 Musl
West Asia									
Iran	6	7	26	3	7	1	22	25	98 Musl
Asia									
Indonesia	31	23	36	10	11	49	38	31	80 Musl
MEAN	24	15.14	26.5	5.67	22.33	23.17	29.17	15.8	
MODERATE DUALISM COUNTRIES									
Black Africa									
Ghana	37	45	20	3	7	80	29	—	42 Xian/ 46 Anim
Nigeria	10	—	15	7	10	60	26	21	38 Musl / 43 Anim
North Africa									
UAR	3	3	24	4	10	6	14	—	92 Musl
West Asia									
Cyprus	54	18	33	5	21	13	31	—	80 Cath/ 20 Musl[f]
Syria	49	3	27	8	8	0	8	—	87 Musl
Turkey	48	4	21	13	13	1	7	10	98 Musl
Asia									
India	36	27	16	3	3	11	25	—	84 Hindu
Pakistan	14	5	10	1	1	2	15	—	98 Musl

Table 4.2: (Continued)

Country	% Women Employed in Traditional Sector[b]			% Women Employed in "Modern" Sector[c]						Majority Religion Percentage
	Agriculture	Own Account Workers	Professional & Technical	Administrative & Managerial	Clerical & Related	Sales Workers	Service Workers	Production Transportation, Laborers		
MODERATE DUALISM COUNTRIES (Continued)										
Latin America										
Argentina	5	13	59	7	29	17	62	—		95 Cath
Colombia	4	15	47	15	24	26	75	18		96 Cath
Mexico	5	15	38	12	30	29	66	17		96 Cath
MEAN	24.09	14.8	28.18	7.09	14.18	32.27	32.55	16.5		
LOW DUALISM COUNTRIES[g]										
West Africa										
Israel	23	19	49	39	39	29	52	—		Judaism
Asia										
Japan	53	30	37	5	49	42	58	27		(Buddhist/ Shinto)
Latin America										
Chile	3	21	48	9	38	38	73	14		98 Cath
MEAN	26.33	23.33	44.67	17.67	42.0	36.33	61.0	20.5		

a. Participation figures are in terms of the ratio of women to the total labor force employed in a given occupation. —— means information not available. See definitions in Table 1 regarding dualism.

b. See Boulding, Nuss, Carson, and Greenstein (1976), for further discussion of these variables which are derived from UN data for 1968 or the closest year to that date; both agriculture and own account work **may** be in the modern sector.

c. See Boulding, Nuss, Carson, and Greenstein (1976).

d. The figures for Rhodesia, as an expatriate-dominated society, are suspect, particularly on participation of women in agriculture. They have probably done little counting of black women.

e. Tunisia, unlike the other countries in this group, is classified by Adelman and Morris as having a moderately significant indigenous middle class and a high bureaucratic efficiency.

f. Cypriot Christians are Greek Orthodox, not Catholic.

g. There is very little subsistence agriculture in these countries, and most of the women employed in agriculture are using some modernized techniques. Many own account workers in these countries may be in the modern sector.

Table 4.3: Women in Agriculture, Trade and Industry: Family Workers, Own Account, and Employees[a]

	Agriculture		Trade[c]	Home and Factory Industry[d]	
	% Female of All Agricultural Workers	% Female Wage[b] Laborers of All Agricultural Wage Laborers	% Female Who Are Own Account Workers of All Female Traders	% Female in Family Labor Force	% Female Among Employees
High Dualism					
Sierra Leone	42	5	75	15	2
Morocco	8	5	48	25	15
Tunisia	2	2	—	—	—
Iran	6	4	59	36	18
Moderate Dualism					
Ghana	37	6	94	39	3
UAR	3	4	81	7	2
Syria	49	8	48	14	6
Turkey	48	23	56	17	10
India	36	44	—	35	12
Pakistan	14	6	83	11	2
Mexico	5	16	—	—	—
Colombia	4	3	26	33	13
Low Dualism					
Chile	3	2	27	35	12

a. The dates to which the figures for each country refer are as follows: Sierra Leone, 1963; Ghana, 1960; Morocco, 1960; UAR, 1960; Turkey, 1965; Syria, 1960; Iran, 1956; Pakistan, 1961; India, 1961; Colombia, 1964; Chile, 1960; Mexico, not given.
b. After Boserup (1970: 68).
c. After Boserup (1970: 88).
d. After Boserup (1970: 109), includes home industries, manufacturing industries and construction activities.

women in all countries at all levels of dualism: professional workers (which means every country uses women as teachers) and production workers. Production workers is an interesting category which includes craftsmen, production-process workers, and laborers not elsewhere classified. Thus it covers both traditional and modern forms of wage labor, from road and construction work to factory work.

Apart from the category of administration, there is no occupation that does not have a substantial number of women in it in *some* countries at each level of dualism. It would appear that the extent of dualistic structure in a society does not directly affect the frequencies of participation of women in the labor force, except in the case of low dualism societies, where participation is more uniformly high than elsewhere.

Table 4.3 offers a more detailed examination of patterns of participation by women in the agricultural, own-account, and production sectors reported in Table 4.2, and does so in a way that breaks down Table 4.2's oversimplified categorization of labor as being either traditional or modern sector. The data in Table 4.3 have been compiled by Boserup (1970) from country studies. Figures are available for only thirteen of the twenty-one countries we are studying, but what is available is highly suggestive. The figures on female wage laborers as a percentage of all agricultural wage laborers are higher in moderate dualism than in high dualism countries. Further study might indicate that wage labor employment for women farmers is a transition phenomenon accompanying industrialization in some countries. Agricultural employment for women will be discussed again later. The percentage of women traders who are self-employed probably represents traditional sector employment, as opposed to hired salespersons, who are more likely to be in the modern sector. The figures for own-account traders do not differ between high and moderate dualism countries—or rather, the highest figures for self-employed traders are in the moderate dualism countries. Small-scale trading is a highly adaptive activity and can be carried on under a variety of conditions and degrees of modernization, so we should perhaps not expect to see shifts in extent of self-employment in trade during the middle stages of development.

The Boserup data on home and factory industry are particularly interesting in that they help us get behind the single aggregate figure on women production workers generally used, and thereby to uncover a much larger participation by women in industry than has been recognized. Table 4.4 contains a list of the countries from our study for which there is Boserup data, with the UN data and the Boserup data compared. The UN figures for women in production include other categories of labor besides manufacturing and construction, so we would expect it to be larger than the Boserup figure for women employees in industry, but the differences are not great. What is

Table 4.4: Comparison of UN and Boserup Data on Women in Production*

Country	% Female Production, Transportation, Laborers (UN)	% Female in Home and Factory Industry (Boserup)	
		% Female in Family Labor Force	% Female Employees
Iran	25	36	18
Turkey	10	17	10
Colombia	18	33	13
Chile	14	35	12

*All figures in this table taken from Tables 4.2 and 4.3.

striking is the large number of women in home industries. These home industries are not to be confused with the production of simple craft items that women make on their own to sell. Rather, they should be compared to the home industrial workshops of Europe during the fourteenth to sixteenth centuries, before the industrial revolution. The bulk of the labor in these workshops came from family members, but there were usually one or more paid workers present, too, as well as apprentices. (See Boulding, 1977: chs. 10 and 11 for a discussion of preindustrial workshops in Europe.) Home industry is an important factor in the utilization of the productive capacities of women in the development process. It will be noted that among the four countries for which we have data, two are Muslim and two are Catholic. These countries represent the entire range of dualism, from the high dualism of Iran to the low dualism of Chile, but only Turkey, in the moderate dualism category, has less than one-third of its women in the home industrial labor force.

In Table 4.5 we shift to a focus on the dynamics of dualism, by examining GNP and population growth rates for 1961-1968 and 1963-1968 respectively, and extent of income inequality, for countries at each level of dualism. The growth rates come from the Boulding Global Data Bank, the 1961 figures for GNP per capita come from the 1967 Adelman and Morris study, and columns 4 and 5 on income inequalities are computed from estimates of income inequalities in the 1973 Adelman and Morris study. The shrinkage in number of countries for which there are income inequality data is due to the fact that the Adelman-Morris estimates only cover forty-three of the seventy-four countries treated in their original study. Column 6 on percentage share of income for the poorest 40 percent comes directly from the Adelman-Morris estimates.

While extent of dualism has not affected proportions of women in the labor force, we would expect it to show up in relation to growth rates and income inequalities. Both GNP growth rates and population growth rates have been used for each country, since unless the GNP is growing faster than the population, a country is not improving its economic situation. The countries with an asterisk (*) have GNP growth rates that exceed their population growth rate. The countries marked with a dagger (†) are those in which the poorest 40 percent have less than 10 percent of the total income. Large income inequalities are found in both moderate and high dualism societies, but not in low dualism societies. This is what we would expect from the Adelman-Morris theses, that dualism creates a poverty trap. However, we find rapid growth countries, where GNP is outstripping population growth, at all three dualism levels. Unfortunately, income inequality measures are not available for four of the seven rapid-growth countries, so we can say nothing about whether high-growth countries tend to have lesser or greater income inequalities than countries that are doing less well economically. It happens that in Israel, Japan, and Pakistan, the three countries for which we have data, the poorest 40 percent have a larger share of the income—15 to 17 percent—than in most of the other countries in the list. On the other hand, no one could argue that 15 to 17 percent of the total income for the poorest 40 percent is a very impressive figure. We can only say these nations are not the worst on income inequality. Of the seven rapid growth countries, four are predominantly Muslim (Iran, Syria, Turkey, and Pakistan), one is Catholic/Muslim (Cyprus), one is Judaic (Israel), and one is Buddhist/Shinto (Japan). It would not seem that Islam is holding back economic development, family planning, or the participation of women in the economy to the extent of which it is often accused. Iran and Syria, it must be said, have very high population growth rates. Iran gets away with growth only because of its abundance of natural resources. Syria is just barely outstripping its population with its economic growth, and may not be able to maintain that growth over time. Only Catholic-Muslim Cyprus and Buddhist/Shinto Japan have anything like population equilibrium.

Now that we have identified the countries where GNP is outstripping population, we can turn to an examination of the participation of women in these seven countries, grouped by level of dualism (Table 4.6). It will be seen that women are important in the agricultural labor force in five of the seven countries; Iran and Pakistan are the exceptions. (They are also important in the wage labor sector of agriculture in several of these countries. See Table 4.3.) This role of women in agriculture, which has been mentioned in connection with earlier tables, requires further discussion and will be taken up later. It should be noted now, however, as a factor of possibly substantial importance to economic development. Own-account workers are not particularly evident in the growth countries, but professional and service roles are important in the modern sector. In general, except for the two countries in the low dualism group, however, the pattern of women's participation in the labor force is spotty by category for any one country.

(Text continued on page 93)

Table 4.5: Relative Rates of Growth of GNP and Population, and Extent of Income Inequalities by Extent of Income Inequalities by Extent of Dualism[a]

Country	Relative Rates of Growth of GNP and Population		GNP Per Capita in U.S. $[d] 1961	Income Inequalities		
	GNP Growth Rate, 1961-1968[b]	Population Growth Rate, 1963-1970[c]		GNP Per[e] Capita for Lowest 40%	GNP Per[f] Capita for Highest 5%	Percentage Share[g] of Income for Poorest 40%
A. HIGH DUALISM						
Black Africa						
Gabon	.7	1.3	200	40†	1880.00	8.
Rhodesia	.1	3.2	215	14.5	1720.00	12.
Sierra Leone	1.5	1.5	70	17.68†	473.20	10.10
North Africa						
Morocco	.4	3.0	150	21.75	618.00	14.50
Tunisia	2.7	—	161	42.75†	722.59	10.62
West Asia						
Iran	5.0*	3.3	211	—	—	12.50
Asia						
Indonesia	.8	2.8	83	—	—	—
B. MODERATE DUALISM						
Black Africa						
Ghana	−.7	3.0	199			
Nigeria	−.3	2.5	82	28.7	629.43	14.00
North Africa						
UAR	1.5	2.5	120	—	—	—
West Asia						
Cyprus	5.9*	1.0	416	—	—	—
Syria	3.5*	3.3	152	—	—	—
Turkey	3.2*	2.5	193	—	—	—
Asia						
India	1.0	2.1	80	40.00	320.00	20.00
Pakistan	3.1*	2.1	79	34.56	316.00	17.50

Table 4.5: (Continued)

Country	Relative Rates of Growth of GNP and Population		GNP Per Capita in U.S. $[d] 1961	Income Inequalities		
	GNP Growth Rate, 1961-1968[b]	Population Growth Rate, 1963-1970[c]		GNP Per[e] Capita for Lowest 40%	GNP Per[f] Capita for Highest 5%	Percentage Share[g] of Income for Poorest 40%
B. MODERATE DUALISM (Continued)						
Latin America						
Argentina	1.0	1.5	379	163.92	2228.52	17.30
Colombia	1.4	3.2	283	51.64†	2284.38	7.30
Mexico	3.4	3.5	313	82.16†	1785.35	10.50
C. LOW DUALISM						
West Asia						
Israel	4.7*	2.9	814	325.60	2735.04	16.00
Asia						
Japan	9.9*	1.1	502	192.02	1485.32	15.30
Latin America						
Chile	1.8	2.4	453	169.88	2047.56	15.00

*Countries where GNP growth is outstripping population growth.
†Poorest 40 percent have 10 percent or less of total income.
a. See definitions in Table 4.1 of dualism.
b. From Boulding Global Data Bank.
c. From Boulding Global Data Bank.
d. From Adelman and Morris (1967: 88), taken from AID sources.
e. These figures are computed from estimates in Adelman and Morris (1973: 152) on percentage shares by population groups for selected countries, utilizing 1961 GNP per capita data taken from Adelman and Morris (1967: 98).
f. Taken directly from Adelman and Morris (1973: 152).
g. Refers to 1968. From Table 37 in **1974 Report of the World Social Situation** (United Nations, 1975a) based on M. S. Ahlvivalia.

Table 4.6: Participation of Women in the Labor Force[a] in Seven Countries with Growth in GNP of 3.1 and Above, Where GNP Growth Rate Exceeds Population Growth Rate[b]

Country	Agri-culture	Own Account Workers	Profes-sional & Technical	Adminis-trative & Managerial	Clerical & Related	Sales Workers	Service Workers	Production Transportation Laborers
HIGH DUALISM COUNTRIES[c]								
Iran	6	7	26	3	7	1	22	25
MODERATE DUALISM COUNTRIES[c]								
Cyprus	54	18	33	5	21	13	31	—
Syria	49	3	27	8	8	0	8	—
Turkey	48	4	21	13	13	1	7	10
Pakistan	14	5	10	1	1	2	15	—
LOW DUALISM COUNTRIES[c]								
Israel	23	19	49	39	39	29	52	—
Japan	53	30	37	5	49	42	58	27

a. For sources of variables, see footnotes to Table 4.2.
b. See Table 4.4 for the data on which this classification is based.
c. See definitions in Table 4.1 of dualism.

Table 4.7 compares the growth countries with the nongrowth countries in terms of their investment in education in general, and investment in the education of women in particular. Column 1 represents human resources improvement ratings, taken from Adelman and Morris' (1967: 123-126) adaptation of the Harbison and Myers weighted average of second and third level enrollment ratios for the total population. The figures on enrollment of women (in participation units) in higher education in 1968 in the fields of education, law, social science, engineering, and agriculture, and the first and second level school enrollment ratio for women, showing how many women of the relevant age groups were enrolled, come from the UN women's data project at the Institute of Behavioral Science. While it is clear that the growth countries have on the whole invested well in education in general and for women in particular, there really is not a great deal of difference between the low growth countries in the moderate and low dualism categories and the high growth countries in these categories in terms of investment in education. If one looks at estimates of natural resources available to countries, it becomes evident that countries with fewer natural resources (Cyprus, Syria, Pakistan, Israel, Japan) invest more heavily in education, and countries high in natural resources (Iran, Turkey) invest less heavily in education. If we look at countries high in natural resources like Argentina and Chile that have also invested heavily in education in general, and in the education of women in particular, we might ask why they are not doing better economically. Egypt has similarly invested in education, but compensatory investment, with a low resource base, has not produced for it the effects the Israeli and Japanese investments have produced in their respective countries.

It has been recognized for some time that it is the type (rather than the amount) of available education in a society that relates to economic growth. For example, the ratio of vocational education to general secondary education provides a much better predictor of economic development than does the availability of secondary education alone (Bennet, 1967). Adequate vocational education is scarce in most third world countries, since this type of education has been seen as leading to lower status employment; policy makers do not provide it, and students do not seek it. Both have been acting on an equally false image of relevant skills in creating a productive society. This is changing now, and there are increasing numbers of vocational schools giving specific technological skill training for men. The same is not true for women. While many are trained as teachers, they are trained even in dealing with very young children, to perpetuate a type of colonial learning orientation that does not foster problem-solving capabilities in children. Vocational training specifically designed and labelled "for women" is usually thought of in terms of courses in nutrition, child care, and family planning. While this kind of training is useful, it is equally useful for men and ought to be part

Table 4.7: Comparison of Countries Where GNP Outstrips Population Growth and Countries Where Population Growth Outstrips GNP Growth,[a] the 1960s, by Ratings on Human Resource Improvement Practices, School Enrollment Ratios for First and Second Level Education, Women Graduates in Higher Education, and Availability of Natural Resources

Country	Human Resources Improvement 1961[b]	School Enrollment Ratios, First and Second Level[c]	% Women Graduates in Higher Education[d]					Natural[e] Resources
			Education	Law	Social Science	Engineering	Agriculture	

A. GNP OUTSTRIPS POPULATION GROWTH

Country	HRI	SER	Edu	Law	SocSci	Eng	Agr	NatRes
High Dualism Countries[f]								
Iran	M-L	31	27	13	24	2	7	H
Moderate Dualism Countries[f]								
Cyprus	H	67	77	—	55	—	—	M
Syria	H	36	27	11	21	2	6	M
Turkey	M	42	44	17	13	8	10	H
Pakistan	M	18	36	1	3	0	0	L
Low Dualism Countries[f]								
Israel	H	82	22	31	37	6	5	M-L
Japan	H	91	74	—	36	1	5	M-L

B. POPULATION GROWTH OUTSTRIPS GNP, OR HOLDS EVEN

Country	HRI	SER	Edu	Law	SocSci	Eng	Agr	NatRes
High Dualism Countries[f]								
Gabon	M-L	72	—	—	—	—	—	M
Rhodesia	L	—	47	—	7	—	0	H
Sierra Leone	L	14	—	—	—	—	—	M
Morocco	M-L	20	21	7	7	0	0	H
Tunisia	M-L	49	20	9	14	0	—	M
Indonesia	M-L	—	—	—	—	—	—	M

Table 4.7: (Continued)

Country	Human Resources Improvement 1961[b]	School Enrollment Ratios, First and Second Level[c]	% Women Graduates in Higher Education[d]				
			Education	Law	Social Science	Engineering	Agriculture	Natural[e] Resources

B. POPULATION GROWTH OUTSTRIPTS GNP, OR HOLDS EVEN (Continued)

Country	Human Resources Improvement 1961[b]	School Enrollment Ratios, First and Second Level[c]	Education	Law	Social Science	Engineering	Agriculture	Natural[e] Resources
Moderate Dualism Countries[f]								
Ghana	M	43	—	—	—	—	—	M
Nigeria	L	14	18	11	5	0	1	M
UAR	H	39	32	12	32	8	16	M-L
India	M	28	33	4	2	1	1	M-L
Argentina	H	78	90	30	39	2	8	H
Colombia	M	61	—	11	54	5	4	M
Mexico	M	64	70	13	9	2	4	H
Low Dualism Countries[f]								
Chile	H	83	68	25	53	2	10	H

a. See Table 4.4 for the data on which the classification is based.
b. Human Resource Improvement Ratings from Adelman and Morris, (1967: 123-126) adaptation of Harbison and Myers weighted average of second and third level enrollment ratios.
c. Percentage girls enrolled in first and second level of all girls of school age, from Boulding, Nuss, Carson, and Greenstein (1976).
d. Based on UN data on the ratio of women to all graduates in fields listed (Boulding, Nuss, Carson, and Greenstein, 1976).
e. From Adelman and Morris (1967: 90-93).
f. See Table 4.1 definitions of dualism.

of the general elementary school curriculum rather than being treated as women's special vocational preparation for their economic roles. Women need the same range of vocational training as men, since on the whole they enter the same range of jobs, whether in agriculture or industry (although they work at lower status and wage levels).

The data on employment and education of women that we have examined in this section—related to economies with growth rates, degrees of dualism, natural resources, and religious traditions—suggest that there is a substantial economic involvement of women in every society that may remain relatively untouched by modernization in terms of increased allocation of skill training, resources, wages, and status to the female labor force. That this picture should emerge with existing data, which we know undercounts female labor, is surprising. It is not unlikely that the female work force, particularly the own-account workers, home-industry workers, and agricultural workers, are providing a significant amount of the total productivity of the economy, much of it uncounted. A cushion for modernization could thus be created enabling planners and policy makers to make poor allocation decisions and yet not have the society collapse economically. More recognition of the actual productivity of female labor, and more allocation of resources to female labor, particularly in agriculture, might well be the decisive factor for a country in determining whether economic growth can ever outstrip population growth,[3] and whether the trap of economic dualism can be sprung.

None of the data presented in this section can be treated as more than suggestive. Too few countries have been analyzed, and too little data have been available even for the few countries chosen. Two things will be required to present a more conclusive case:

(1) At the macro level, systematic attention must be given to the collection of complete and cross-national comparative data on women in agriculture, as unpaid family workers, as women farmers on their own account, and as wage labor. At present no data are collected on women farmers on their own account, although up to 50 percent and more of women farmers in some areas are de facto and sometimes de jure heads of households (Chapter 5). In addition, similar attention to home industry of all kinds is needed.

(2) At the micro level, country studies are needed to investigate the culture-specific patterns of women's labor within individual countries, going beyond existing census data to a more refined classification of types of work and work sites; individual case history studies are needed of women workers in local communities that will include detailed time budgets for women as well as for men, on the model so well developed by the Economic Commission for Africa (United Nations, 1974d).

In the next section we will look at some of the information on the activities of women that comes out of studies undertaken in Morocco and Indonesia, high dualism countries; Nigeria and India, moderate dualism countries; and Japan, a low dualism country. None of these studies was undertaken with the notion of economic dualism in mind, but all throw some light on the relationship between the economic roles of women and the economic development of the society in question.

HOUSEHOLD PRODUCTIVITY AND DUALISM

Pre-Transition Societies

In considering the economic roles of women in modernizing societies, it may be useful to step back and look at "baseline" levels of economic participation of women in countries that have not yet experienced the industrial enclave development that accompanies the early stages of modernization. Firth and Yamey (1964) should provide a useful nonquantitative source for such baseline information, but unfortunately the authors who have contributed to this compendium have noticed very little of women's economic roles and mention them only casually. Firth himself mentions women primarily as custodians of men's earnings. However, a careful reading of the fourteen studies in their book makes it clear that in each of these societies women are engaged in the following activities: (1) farming; (2) trade; (3) craft work; and (4) handling of money, credit transactions, savings, and investment activity. In none of these societies do women fail to accumulate and invest capital, whether in the form of land, livestock, gold, or other commodities. Some of the capital is in the form of dowry, or brideprice. While a woman does not necessarily have control over all of the bridal fund, in no case is she left without the possibility of accumulating capital over which she does have exclusive control.

Marguerite Dupire's (1963) study of the nomadic Fulani women distinguishes between cattle owned jointly by husband and wife, and cattle owned exclusively by the woman. Women have their own cash income from trade in cattle and dairy products, and all ownership of clothes, tools, and furniture is separate for husbands and wives. The dowry, which "belongs" to the wife and is "cared for" by the husband, is a separate item from her private capital. The dowry is considered as the children's inheritance, held by the husband.

Marilyn Strathern's study of New Guinean women analyzes how money flows in that society revolves around the movements of women, and the life cycle events of families. The wife becomes the instrument of the flow of wealth between groups. "Women are like tradestores," and "Women walk about and bring in plenty of valuables" are revealing folk sayings (1972: 99).

Interestingly, though the men regard themselves as the decision makers and the controllers of all the significant transactions in the society, with the women as their servant-producers, Strathern discovered that the women think of themselves as independent transactors. A complete analysis of this New Guinean economy from the women's perspective would be very interesting to compare with existing anthropological documentation.

H. J. Simons' book on the legal status of African women in South Africa documents the loss of rights to land and capital that can take place for women once economic dualism becomes strongly established in a country. Women cannot now assert inheritance rights they had under tribal law, yet "many tens of thousands of widows officiate in practice as the heads of their households" (1968: 254).

This very cursory examination of women's economic roles in pre-modernizing societies provides evidence that women have not only been a key part of the traditional production activities, but that they have also been independently active in capital accumulation and investment. The capacity of a modernizing society to attract into the modernizing sector the capital of the traditional sector is clearly relevant to the rate of development. Failure to note women's traditional economic activities has led to a failure by planners to consider this investment potential of women.

A High Dualism Society: Morocco

Morocco would appear to be a good candidate for the poverty trap, with an economic growth rate of .4, a population growth rate of 3.0 in the sixties, and a baseline GNP per capita of $150 in 1961. The poorest 40 percent of the population have 14.5 percent of the income, representing an extent of income inequality somewhere between the least and the most unequal, among the countries of this study. Ninety-eight percent Muslim, Morocco has few women in agriculture, and fewer own-account workers and professionals than most other countries, including many Moslem countries. The women who are in the labor force are mainly in clerical work and services. Only 20 percent of the girls of school age are enrolled in school, among the lowest figures in the high dualism group of countries. It would appear that Moroccan planners would be well advised to get more of their women educated and into the labor force. But on what basis could such a policy be developed, when there would appear to be such strong cultural sanctions against economic roles for women?

A study of non-market activities of Moroccan women by Vanessa Maher (1974) uncovers a vast network of economic activities neither visible to nor countable by economists. An accurate delineation of these non-market activities would be crucial to the development of policies that could break down both the sex dualism and the economic dualism of the Moroccan economy. It appears that there are many non-market modes of relationship available to those who cannot sell their labor in the marketplace. Vertical links of interdependence, both those of kinship and of simulated kinship (patron-client relations), provide the opportunity for poorer women to render services to women who are better off and have access to the market economy through their own activities or those of their husbands. These kin and pseudo-kin networks become the channels for market wealth to enter the traditional economy. Sometimes the vertical relationships are temporary, as when migrant women seek to gain a foothold in the town. Others are more or less permanent, feudal-type relationships. Maher gives examples of poor but enterprising women who provide a variety of home services, from nursing to cooking and party-arranging, for richer women who are either relatives or who originate in the same rural district. Their payment would be goods in kind, sometimes gifts of money, sometimes jobs for husbands or sons. A particularly enterprising poor women could utilize this service network to find wives for the men of her family, and husbands, education, and perhaps even job opportunities for her daughters.

The fact that women so frequently need help both in the recurring life-cycle circumstances of birth, marriage, and death, and in family crises of illness, unemployment, or movement of a household from one location to another (all of which events place on the women additional labor burdens not shared by the men of a family), has something to do with the ease with which women outside the market economy can enter the margins of the market world via service to its households and carry needed goods and cash back to their own subsistence sector. If we add to this patron-client relationship the opportunities that women have to interact and match skills and needs around the public oven, the water tap, and the bathhouse, we can see that the redistribution of resources outside the market economy is substantial even in a strongly purdah-keeping society.

It is a myth that societies maintaining the seclusion of women have such large extended family households that all needs can be met within the household. Maher (1974) reports the average household size for Morocco in 1961 was 5.1 members in the urban household, 4.9 members in the rural. Then there are a sizable number of widows who live alone and own their own houses. The small households and the number of live-alones create a continuous demand for services which in a modernized society are met by a whole army of specialists, but in Morocco are met by women who "earn their living" outside the market economy.

While the range of income-producing activities for Moroccan women is unusually narrow, even for a purdah-keeping society, full recognition of the economic roles women do play will assist in developing policies that will enable resources and opportunities to flow more freely across sectoral barriers.

A High Dualism Society: Indonesia

Indonesia, though with a totally different style of Muslim culture (and with a 20 percent non-Muslim minority), nevertheless has many of the problems that Morocco has. Its economic growth rate is only .8, and its population growth rate is 2.8. Its GNP per capita in 1961 was $83. It appears to utilize women in the labor force much more effectively than other high dualism countries, having the highest average rates of participation of women in each sector of the labor force of any high dualism country except Rhodesia (which we noted in Table 4.2 as probably reporting primarily on the white female labor force). There are no figures reported on school enrollment for girls. While I do not have available studies of women in the Indonesian labor force, Indonesia is discussed here with other Southeast Asian societies because of the suggestion in general studies on Southeast Asian women of an apparent reversal of traditional economic roles for women with development, and because of the possible relationship between such a reversal and the slow growth of the Indonesian economy.

Indonesia shares with other Southeast Asian societies a situation of active participation by women as farmers and traders in the premodern society. For example, Halpern (1964) points out that a Laotian family business is very likely to be registered in the wife's name. Swift (1964) notes in the Malay peninsula, since women are not expected to use their earnings to support the family, they are free to invest in land, gold, and business enterprises. Topley (1964) reports that Hakka tribal women in the Hong Kong New Territories form their own credit associations and often keep the accounts for the family business. Writing about the women of Asia in the early sixties, Barbara Ward (1963b) warned that Western economic experts, by ignoring women's traditional economic roles, were in effect reducing their property rights and opportunities to make money, which could have deleterious effects on the economies involved. Her warnings went unheeded.

While a direct study of Indonesian women's loss of economic opportunity to my knowledge has not been made, Lev (1972), in his study of Islamic courts in Indonesia, does point to the centralizing developments in that country both under colonial rule and after independence. The orientation of Sukarno, as well as that of the subsequent modernizing leadership of Indonesia, has been centralist and also very repressive of local Islamic movements. One consequence of this orientation has been a whittling away of the local entrepreneurial opportunities for women who are thus placed in dependency roles they did not formerly have. Reducing the productivity of women by depriving them of capital and investment opportunities would certainly contribute to an exaggerated economic dualism. Recent efforts of Indonesian women themselves to create a policy turnaround in regard to the participation of women in the economy and in society may generate changes (Ihromi et al., 1973: 32-47; Papenek, 1975).

A Moderate Dualism Society: Nigeria

Nigeria is a highly diverse society made up of tribes speaking 250 different languages and dialects. Forty-three percent of its population is animist, 38 percent Muslim, and 19 percent Christian. Nigeria would also appear to be headed for the poverty trap, with an economic growth rate of −.3, a population growth rate of 2.5, and a GNP per capita in 1961 of $82. A disastrous civil war in the 1960s has something to do with these low figures for a large country with fairly substantial resources and the traditions of precolonial kingdoms. Income inequalities in Nigeria are about at the level of Morocco, with 14 percent of the income going to the poorest 40 percent of the population. Only 10 percent of the agricultural labor force is reported to be female, and own-account workers are not reported at all (although, as we will see below, there is substantial own-account trading by Nigerian women). Nigeria has a large proportion of women in sales: 60 percent of all sales workers are reported to be female. The country does very poorly in educating its women, however. Only 14 percent of girls of school age were enrolled in 1968, a figure even lower than for Morocco. Nigeria's figures for women in higher education are consistently lower than for other moderate dualism countries.

Nigeria would appear to be a classic example of a country that has ignored the economic roles of women during the modernizing process, since the country has moved past an initially high sectoral cleavage and has developed a well-trained indigenous bureaucracy and an active indigenous middle class; yet there are no comparable showings for the participation of women in the modern sector.

Sudarkasa's (1973) study of Yoruba women's work in the marketplace and the home, and Hill's (1969) study of "hidden trade in Hausaland," would seem to bear out this proposition. Among the Yoruba, the largest population group numerically in Nigeria (thirteen million), all women are traders. This is part of their life role as wife-mother in a polygamous society. From ancient times on, Yoruban culture has been an urban one, and women have always considered themselves citizens of the towns. Work on the outlying farms is usually done by the most junior wife in a family, together with the husband—who spends more time on the farm than in town. Husbands and wives keep their incomes separate, buy and sell to each other, and contribute well-defined shares to the maintenance and education of the children. While children are spaced two and one-half to three years apart, birth involves no diminution of the mother's economic activity. Babies are simply carried on mother's backs until they can walk. By the age of three they are sent to do simple errands and chores in the compound (an area which in a western city might be comparable to a city block), and any handy adult in the area will supervise and assist any child. By the age of eight, girls are helping their mothers with trade.

Because all women work, housekeeping is a series of specialized occupations—sewing, washing, ironing, cooking, hairdressing—that women do for each other for pay. Everyone buys breakfast "out" from women who set up roadside breakfast stands, and children from the age of five on are sent out to buy their own breakfasts. There is no custom of household preparation and eating of meals, though the evening meal *may* be prepared and eaten at home. This way of life is only possible because of the design of Yoruba towns. They consist of a series of interlocking compounds, actually neighborhoods, whose alleys and workshop spaces are all safe play areas for children. It has been said that children are far safer in these urban compounds in the crowded cities of Yorubaland than is any child in a western city or suburb. It is as if the entire town were a twenty-four-hour day care center. Most of the household responsibilities that western working women struggle with have been dealt with by Yoruban women through specialization.

The third largest tribal group in Nigeria, the Hausa (6.8 million) follow an entirely different set of customs, and yet the women are equally involved in the labor force. Hausa women live in full seclusion, but as Hill's 1969 study of the Batagarawa shows, the women may engage in trade at a level comparable to that of the Yoruba women and the West African trading women, all from the privacy of the husband's compound. Children and older women (not secluded after menopause) act as intermediaries for transactions outside the compound. The experience young girls get as intermediaries before they enter seclusion at puberty stands them in good stead as they continue trading from seclusion during child-bearing years.

So strong is this compound trading network that frequent attempts over a forty-year period to establish a public market in the area have failed (Hill, 1969: 394). Women have resisted it because it would deprive them of their business—they could not trade in the marketplace and keep purdah. Men have resisted it because they have found the existing system convenient and efficient. Hill points out that competitive forces operate as effectively here as in a regular market, in the following ways:

(1) the market is in constant session, rather than being open only once a week;
(2) people can shop around;
(3) short-term competitiveness is enhanced by the opportunities of women to engage in special deals and undercut other women;

(4) short-term demand is steadier in the "buy-local" situation;

(5) the wholesalers do not operate in collusion to fix prices—their sources are too numerous.

Women have a great deal of economic independence in this sytem. The only service they are obliged to render their husbands is cooking. All other services a husband must pay for, such as threshing groundnuts. In fact, a woman may buy the groundnuts from her husband, make oil, and sell it for her own profit. A woman's economic autonomy may thus insulate her from a husband's poverty: there are prominent women house-traders whose husbands are poverty stricken.

The following is a list of women's occupations, most of which are conducted from seclusion, and all of which are paid for in money: grain-selling for her husband; house-trading on her own account including the selling of hot cooked food (two-thirds of all women do this); agricultural labor, including winnowing, pounding, grinding grain (50 percent of women do this); spinning (done by 85 percent of women); market trading in regular markets (done by older women); selling of other products for her husband; midwifery; hairdressing; and farming. Four-fifths of all married and widowed women are members of female-initiated and female-administered rotating credit associations. With their earnings they invest in sheep and goats, household trading stock, cloth, household utensils, and loans to husbands.

Despite all of this activity, Nigerian economic planning not only does not take account of the economic productivity of its women, both hidden and visible, but it also actually tries to decrease that productivity by substituting apparently more modern methods of trade and production, methods which would lower productivity by excluding the economic contribution of substantial numbers of the female labor force. If it is desirable to shift some economic activities from private courtyards to a more public domain—and that may be desirable—such a shift could only be economically successful if experienced women traders helped design the new pattern and the transition mechanism.

A Moderate Dualism Society: India

India is another country headed for a poverty trap. Its economic growth rate is 1 percent, its population growth rate 2.1 percent, and the 1961 GNP per capita was $80. Eighty-four percent of the society follows the Hindu religion. The country has been the seat of one of the great empires of the ancient world, and it also has experienced the modernizing infrastructure of a long-time colonial occupier. It has not been a fortunate country: since independence it has experienced disastrous civil wars and partitions, and it is currently operating under an authoritarian rule geared to emergency conditions. Only 28 percent of girls of school age are enrolled in school, but India does give a more diversified graduate training to women than most third world countries. Since India is larger and more diverse than Nigeria, it is difficult to select specific materials on the role of women that will throw direct light on the general problem of Indian development. From the overall figures in Table 4.2 we see that over one-third of Indian women are counted as agricultural workers. From Table 4.3, using the Boserup data, we note that 44 percent of all agricultural wage labor is female, a very high figure. Participation of women in other sectors is uneven. India shows neither the highest nor the lowest participation figures in the various occupational categories, for moderate dualism societies.

While under some conditions women as wage laborers might be a promising sign of transition from the subsistence sector to the market economy, under Indian conditions as described by Nair (1973), this would appear to be a regressive situation. Men's agricultural wages are already tending to be less than subsistence level, and women's wages even below that. Policies to increase the agricultural productivity of women would need to give a lot of attention to the work situation of women on family farms and women-headed farm households, as well as to the situation of wage laborers. One of the major problems of Indian development seems to lie in the agricultural sector, and in an inappropriate level of protection to comparatively unproductive middle-level farmers at the expense of the subsistence farmer. If male subsistence farmers are being pushed into ever more precarious situations, the position of agricultural women is desperate.

In Kerala, where we find highly educated, politically aware and technically sophisticated owner-operator farmers, women have a much higher status and more participatory role than elsewhere in India. Whereas in the rest of India only 20 percent of girls of school age are enrolled in school, in Kerala 55 percent of all women are literate. Yet I do not have the impression from Nair's study that women's agricultural roles receive any attention, even in Kerala. Nair herself rarely seems to be aware of women farmers; in her otherwise excellent study, all the interviews are with men. Nair does note that when male farmers in Myore prosper from rising prices, they start spending time in the city hotels, drinking coffee and eating their meals there, leaving the women behind to work in the fields. (The women are forbidden to drink coffee or handle cash, so there is no danger of their wasting their time in hotels.) Needless to say, agricultural productivity does not increase under such conditions. On a visit in 1974 to a model village and agricultural school near Varanasi, India, I noted that all the students in the school were boys, but that most of the workers in the surrounding fields were women. When I asked the young principal of the school why there were no girls in the school, he explained apologetically that his teachers were all too young. Only the gray haired could teach women students with propriety. The complex of changes in social structure and values required to admit women to these village schools appears to be slow in coming. Meanwhile, the young men who graduate from these schools go to the city to become government officials. In no way does this system allow for the translation of all the fine new technical agricultural know-how from the brain to the hand to the seed in the ground.

Although the problems that are driving India into the poverty trap are more complex than those which most countries face, one wonders what would happen if it were possible to link the energies of the poorest of Indian women farmers to even modest amounts of agricultural knowledge and the tools of intermediate technology.

The Camilla project during the early 1960s in Pakistan carried out precisely such a program (McCarthy, 1976). The project also involved the development of a women's credit union that enabled village women to accumulate and invest modest capital of their own, as women of traditional peasant societies are generally free to do. The results of the Camilla project, in a purdah-keeping society, were spectacular in the changes in economic behavior of women that it brought about. It has not been replicated because the productivity of women is not a policy priority of any planning agency.

The institution of purdah is a challenge to the planner. The extent of purdah varies widely from one Muslim country to another, and may be the most fervently practiced in countries where Muslims are a minority group, as in India. More studies comparable to the Hill study of the Hausa in Nigeria, and the Maher study of Moroccan women, are needed. Vreede-De Stuers' (1968) study of Muslim women in Northern India emphasizes a type of development that she calls zenana modernization ("zenana" is the Indian word for the women's quarters in the purdah-keeping home). She argues that the emanicipation of Muslim women is going on inside the zenana. Zenana hospitals and parks, social-welfare clubs, days at public exhibitions, and boxes at the theatre are rapidly multiplying. The Muslim women who were forcibly ejected from zenanas during the bloody struggles that preceded the partition of India re-entered purdah as soon as conditions returned to normal. This was true of all classes and ages of women. The tendency for the women of upwardly mobile families eager to adopt seclusion and the veil as a sign of increasing prosperity has been noted in many Muslim countries. Many of the more sophisticated among purdah-keeping women take the position that purdah is their symbol of cultural autonomy, of modernization without westernization. Education and entry into the labor force can all take place within segregated settings.

On the face of it, this approach to modernization would seem to be no more viable than the apartheid practices of South Africa, which are intended to foster separate development of the white and black communities. There is one big difference, of course, in that zenana modernization is promoted at least in part by women. What percentage of educated women support the concept of zenana modernization I do not know. Westerners should probably suspend judgment on this issue until cultural consensus is clearer in countries where this concept exists, and concentrate on analysis of the level of productive activities that go on within purdah, and the effectiveness of channels of communication and resource redistribution between the women's sector and the men's sector in regions where zenana modernization is consciously chosen by women.

A Low Dualism Society: Japan

Now at last we shift to a success story, to a country that has managed to move beyond rigid sectoral cleavage to a relatively fluid society with high social mobility. Japan had the highest economic growth rate in the world in the 1960s, 9.9 percent, and one of the lowest population growth rates, 1.1. In 1961 it had a per capita GNP of $502, and the poorest 40 percent had 15.30 percent of the income. The religion is Buddhist/Shinto. Looking at the participation of women, we see that Japan has a high percentage of women in all sectors, *including* the agricultural. Fifty-three percent of Japanese farmers are women. Only one other country in our group, Cyprus, has that high a figure. It rates among the highest in the number of own-account workers, and has the highest percentage of women in clerical and related work, 49 percent. Excluding African "women trader" countries, Japan has the highest percentage of women in sales, and is among the highest in percentage of women service workers. It also has the second highest percentage of women production workers. Only in percentage of women among the professions does it fall into the intermediate rank.

Clearly, women have played a unique role in the economic development of Japan. Japan's agriculture is the most productive in the world, in terms of yield per hectare, and this productivity is due in substantial measure to the fact that Japanese women have worked side by side with their men in the fields, using the same tools, applying the same level of skill and knowledge. In recent years, the percentage of women farmers has gone even higher than the 1968 figure, as men have migrated to the cities and women have stayed behind to continue working the farms. This is a very unstable condition, of course, because the hard physical labor is now unevenly distributed between women and men, and agricultural productivity is certain to decline if more assistance is not given to women. The secret of Japanese agricultural productivity to date, according to Nair, is that development assistance has been geared to small farmers. They have been able to increase productivity at their existing scale of operation, rather than having been forced to give way to larger scale operators. If this could be considered a general principle in Japanese society—enabling individuals to be maximally productive at their existing scale of operation—it may help to explain the mystery of why Japanese society has been able to utilize so fully the productive labor of its women.

The statement that Japanese women (known to have a traditionally subservient status in relation to men) have been exploited and oppressed in the modernization process would be a great oversimplification, though a tempting one to make. While it is true that they have always worked hard on the farms, have put in many additional hours raising silkworms in the famous household silk industry, and have worked diligently in textile factories to make Japanese textiles the best buys in the world market, it is also true that Japanese men have worked the same long hours. The Japanese family workshop has equalled if not exceeded the productivity of the European family workshops of the preindustrial era, and certainly in the past hundred years. While European and North American women were withdrawing from the labor force in large numbers, Japanese women were staying in, and working harder than ever. It may indeed be that technological adaptations within existing scales of operation are part of the secret. Japan has always operated on the "small is beautiful" principle recently discovered in the West.

Despite all of the material written about status inequalities of Japanese women, the fact remains that Japan has made a substantial investment in the education of its women. Ninety-one percent of Japanese girls of elementary and secondary school age are in school; the next highest percentage among our countries is for Israel, with 82 percent. While it does not rank highest in percentage of women in graduate-level enrollments, Japan is, like Israel, consistently enrolling women in all categories of training. Since Japan is a country with few natural resources, it has cultivated all its human resources, women and men, carefully.

On the other hand, it cannot be denied that Japan has systematically excluded its women from administrative and policy-making positions, both traditionally and in the twentieth century. Given the fact that Japanese women have probably been more important to the economic development of Japan than women have been to any other society in the past two centuries, this fact must be recognized; current economic policy must be geared to that realization before Japan runs out of the advantages derived from its earlier superior utilization of its female labor force. Other countries are now becoming more aware of the importance of their female labor forces, and may follow Japan's pattern of employing women in work settings which optimize their skills. Japan now needs a more sophisticated analysis of its own productivity patterns, and this cannot be achieved without admitting women as colleagues into planning circles, where they are now notably absent. Until this decade, Japan has been able to evade the price that must inevitably be paid for allocating inferior status to its women in the planning and decision-making process. Now the bill will come due for Japan, as it is coming due for countries everywhere.

CONCLUDING REFLECTIONS

Our examination of special studies on women's economic roles in societies at various levels of modernization, including pre-transition societies, has thrown some light on how gender-based dualism operates to reinforce economic dualism once sectoral cleavages are established in modernizing societies. Both production and redistribution of goods for the society as a whole are impeded by this double dualism. The studies of women in premodern societies are suggestive of the extent to which women accumulate and invest capital in traditional societies where there are few barriers to a free flow of what limited resources exist.

In Morocco, a high dualism society, we saw that women found ways to continue productive activity outside the market economy, penetrating the economy to the extent that they found jobs for male relatives through the operation of the patron-client system. Given the low economic growth and high population growth of Morocco, it is at least worth exploring whether a freer movement of women's activities across sectoral barriers might not increase overall economic productivity. In Indonesia, modernizing centralization was seen to remove traditional economic roles from women. In two moderately dualistic and "anciently developed" societies, Nigeria and India,[4] we saw high levels of economic activity for women, both in purdah and in public settings, but in either case largely segregated in the subsistence sector. In none of these four countries was there a free flow of women's capital into the modern sector, and in none of them were women agriculturalists operating with equipment or credit facilities that made improvement in productivity possible. In Japan, a low dualism society with the most successful development story of the twentieth century, we saw high levels of economic activity for women unimpeded by sectoral barriers, both in agriculture and industry. Gender-based dualism, while strong in the society's symbol system, has not impeded the development of more equal working partnerships among the agricultural and urban laboring folk. Neither has it impeded the education of Japanese women. Only at the professional level does the symbol system seem to operate to prevent full participation of women in the work force.

In all these countries, women are excluded from the very roles, in policy-making and planning, which would enable them to promote the integration of the labor and capital resources of the women's sector into the larger society.

Generalizations based on very limited data from a very few countries would rightly be suspect. My intentions in choosing the twenty-one third world countries from the Adelman and Morris studies of economic dualism were to try to bring their data to bear on the problems of gender-based dualism, and to place the two phenomena in a common conceptual framework. As long as "women in the labor force" remains a special category, the economists' afterthought, the basic economic partnership between women and men that has existed from earliest *Mulier* and *homo erectus*[5] times will be distorted in a way that impedes the full economic, social, and political development of any society engaging in that type of categorization of women.

It is clear that women have during every period in history been food producers, craft workers, laborers, construction workers, and traders. Some social structures have required more elaborate arrangements than others to carry out their economic roles. The activity itself, however, has been a constant, though the formats have varied. As societies have become more complex and more centralized, the women's sector has become progressively less visible, particularly as urbanization has created a class of male clerics and decision makers out of touch with the production system of their own economies. The imbalance between perceptions and reality has now gone very far, and it is dangerous to the future of the human community. All kinds of international hostilities pile on top of basic failures of perception regarding primary production processes. The problems of the new international economic order are not only problems for all states—first, second, third, and fifth worlds equally—of bringing domestic planning into line with a realistic assessment of world needs, in a way that will break down have/have-not dualism. They are also the problems of recognizing who the producers are in every society, and bringing the excluded partners into the planning process. The excluded partners are not only women; they are also the poverty sector, the subsistence sector, of every society at every level of industrialization. To emphasize women is not to downgrade the importance of the larger problem of the participation of the poor in societal development. It is rather to point to the peculiar multiplier effects of gender-based dualism once an economy leaves the subsistence pattern and moves to urbanism and industrialization, and to the importance of developing policies that will short-circuit the dynamics of that dualism and release into the total economy the productivity of women and men alike.

NOTES

1. These judgments have been sharply questioned by others, and by Adelman and Morris themselves. I believe they are valuable as first approximations. Recognizing the limitations of the judging procedure, I have nevertheless used their classification in each case, even where my own judgment would differ, for the sake of consistency.

2. While for our purposes this is a most interesting group, statistical data on the participation of women is rarely available for these largely subsistence societies, and therefore they had to be omitted.

3. I have pointed out in Chapter 5 that women breed the help they need in the absence of other kinds of help, such as tools. The higher the infant death rate, the longer they have to go on breeding to get the necessary help. This is one of the many vicious cycles that results from the phenomenon of triple dualism, and keeps the subsistence sector of an economy from accumulating the surpluses that will enable its members to enter the modern sector.

4. India and Nigeria are not, of couse, historically comparable. India had an ancient imperial structure, while Nigeria had small kingdoms, but no large-scale empire.

5. The use of *Mulier* here follows the practice indicated in Boulding (1977) of indicating the female as well as the male of the species when referring either to pre-sapien forerunners or to early sapiens.

Chapter 5

WOMEN, BREAD, AND BABIES: Directing Aid to Fifth World Farmers

It has been strongly suggested in the previous chapter how important women farmers are to development. This chapter will focus entirely on the woman farmer. The subtitle, "Directing Aid to Fifth World Farmers," is a reference to that special set of spaces in every society where women carry out their productive roles. The fifth world[1] is the product of gender-based dualism. It can be found on every continent: in the family farms and kitchen gardens, the nursery and the kitchen. The fifth world also sends its fingers out to the least paid work spaces of business, industry, and the service sector. Within the rural and nonindustrialized parts of that fifth world women breed babies, produce milk to feed them, grow food and process it, provide water, fuel, and clothing, build houses, make and repair roads, serve as the beasts of burden, and sit in the markets to sell the surpluses.

The ancient myth that woman's only place is in the home, by the side of a man, and caring for children with the means he brings to her is so persistent that western development experts have been able to go into the third (and the oil-poor fourth) world countries to give development aid without noticing the fifth world at all, as was suggested in the previous chapter. Because the changes associated with modernization and urbanization have put unbearable stresses on women in many developing countries, their productivity is breaking down. Declining food production and increasing numbers of babies are the concomitants of the failure of that stressed 50 percent of the active labor force in these countries to receive aid. In the absence of help from male partners in the provision of food for their families, and from development experts with intermediate technology labor-moderating innovations, the only source

Author's Note: A background paper prepared for the Conference on the World Food and Population Crisis: A Role for the Private Sector, Dallas, Texas, April 3, 1975.

of aid for a farm woman is her children. The producer must breed her own help. It has taken the fiasco of the first development decade to raise the questions which led to the declaration of International Women's Year and the placing on the world agenda of the situation of women as producers and breeders.

The very nature of the fifth world almost precludes effective work with this agenda item, since much of the knowledge and expertise required to deal with the problems lie in the fifth world, with women, and the agenda-setters, who are men, do not recognize either their expertise or reservoir of skilled labor. One crucial problem is how to create an effective set of communication linkages and a basis for recognizing and pooling the separate knowledge stocks of women and men before it is too late. "Running out of women" is far more serious than running out of oil, or other natural resources. Eventually decision makers will recognize this fact.

THE FIFTH WORLD ON THE FARM

This study will focus on the uncovering of the fifth world in Africa, as a demonstration of the urgency of more effective allocation of resources in dealing with hunger and overpopulation. Africa is today bearing the cruelest load of suffering in the current food supply crisis, though the manifestations of the crisis are to be felt on all continents. However, the African woman, in her person and in her capabilities, holds the key to the solution of both the food and the population crises. It is particularly appropriate to begin uncovering the fifth world on the continent where women do on the average of 70 percent of the agricultural work, and where practically 100 percent of agricultural aid has gone to men.

The reason for the preponderance of women in agriculture south of the Sahara is that these are areas where farming follows the pattern of shifting cultivation. Small pieces of land are cultivated for a few years until productivity declines, then new land is cleared and the old is left fallow. The only role for men in this system of farming is tree felling. Up to forty years ago this type of farming predominated "in the whole of the Congo region, in large parts of Northeast and East Africa and in parts of West Africa" (Boserup, 1970: 17).

As development programs have introduced cash crops and the plough, the newly mechanized work has been taken over by men. Women are left with the unmechanized parts of the new type of farming—weeding and carrying water—as well as with continued work on the subsistence plot (with the old primitive tools) to feed the family. Cash from cash crops rarely goes to the women to use for feeding the family.[2] As a result, "modernization" has meant even longer working hours for women than before, including more hours of weeding and water carrying. Not only do larger fields need more water, but also new poultry and livestock projects need it as well. The subsistence farm woman as a result is exhausted and ill from work and childbearing, yet continues to bear children in the hope that some will survive to help her with her labor in the fields. Since in general men and boys take priority in being fed when food is short, and in getting meat and special foods, the women and girls have the added burden of being undernourished as well as overworked. Babies, both male and female, suffer from the poor quality of the breast milk that comes from a malnourished mother. Courses in nutrition will not solve her problem, even if she had the time and energy to attend them. It is in her role as food producer that she most desperately needs help.

Yet it is in this role that help is most consistently denied. It is to men that agricultural training programs are offered, men who are given access to loans and credit. It is they who are brought into cooperative development schemes and encouraged in the use of improved seeds, fertilizers, insecticides, and tools. Finally, men are brought into the cash-crop cultivation and also given priority in employment in the industrial sector.

Rural Women's Time Budgets

To give an overall idea of the relative amounts of time spent by women and men on agriculture in the traditional rural and early modernizing economy in Africa, the following estimates are reproduced from an Economic Commission for Africa (ECA) Report (United Nations, 1974a). The estimates are given in terms of the unit of participation for women's labor based on available data on the percentage of labor associated with a particular task which may be attributed to women. To make clear the meaning of the unit of participation, I will cite the ECA example for Bukoba in Tanzania, where "it is estimated that men work 1,800 hours per year in agriculture and women work 2,600 hours. This totals 4,400 hours, of which 60 percent is women's work. Women's 'unit of participation' is thus 0.60" (United Nations, 1974a: 9; also see Table 5.1).

In order to translate this into a sample of a working day for a woman, we turn to an example from Zambia (Table 5.2). Not only is the agricultural working day of the African woman usually longer than that of the man, but also the female begins her agricultural labors much earlier in life than the male, at the age of five or so, contrasted with age ten for boys, and continues them much longer. Women over fifty-five are still working in the fields, men hardly at all. Table 5.3 showing the division of labor in one area of Zaire cannot be taken as typical of Africa as a whole—division of labor varies from area to area even within a country—but it is reflective of the general picture

Table 5.1: Participation by Women in the Traditional Rural and Modernizing Economy in Africa

Responsibility	Unit of Participation*
A. Production/Supply/Distribution	
1. Food Production	0.70
2. Domestic Food Storage	0.50
3. Food Processing	1.00
4. Animal Husbandry	0.50
5. Marketing	0.60
6. Brewing	0.90
7. Water Supply	0.90
8. Fuel Supply	0.80
B. Household/Community	
1. *Household*	
a. Bearing, rearing, initial education of children	1.00
b. Cooking for husband, children, elders	1.00
c. Cleaning, washing, etc.	1.00
d. Housebuilding	0.30
e. House Repair	0.50
2. *Community*	
Self-help projects	0.70

SOURCE: Data based from The Changing and Contemporary Role of Women in African Development, UNECA (United Nations, 1974b); Country Reports on Vocational and Technical Training for Girls and Women, UNECA (United Nations, 1972-1974); studies, mission reports, discussions, as cited in United Nations (1974a: 7).

*Estimates are given in terms of the unit of participation for women's labor, i.e., women as a percentage of the total population in a given activity.

of much heavier involvement in agriculture for women than for men in Africa. Information is given in units of participation, as in Table 5.1.

Contrast the involvement in agricultural productivity delineated in Tables 5.1-5.3 with the access to agricultural training indicated in Table 5.4. "Nonformal" education means all the extension programs and community development programs that are mounted outside the regular elementary and secondary school system.

Among the major exceptions to this pattern are the market women's associations and cooperatives, projects for support of small entrepreneurs, and social cooperative training courses for women.

The imbalance between the participation of women in agriculture and their opportunities for training in it would be ludicrous if it were not so tragic in its consequences for agricultural productivity. How is it possible that decision makers have overlooked this imbalance? I suggest that this "overlooking" is a by-product of modernization itself.

One of the effects of modernization on any society, including the old

Table 5.2: A Zambian Women's Day During the Planting Season

Activity	Time Spent (hours)
Waking up in the morning at 05.00 hours	——
Walking to the field with baby on her back (1-2 km)	0.50
Ploughing, planting, hoeing until about 15.00 hours (eats snack in field)	9.50
Collecting firewood and carrying it home	1.00
Pounding or grinding grain or legumes	1.50
Fetching water (1 to 2 km or more each way)	0.75
Lighting fire and cooking meal for family	1.00
Dishing out food—eating	1.00
Washing children, herself, clothes	0.75
Going to bed at about 21.00 hours	——
Total	16.00
Summary: Hours of work 15	
Hours of rest/eating 1	
Hours of sleep 8	
Total 24	

SOURCE: Report on five workshops in Home Economics and Other Family-Oriented Fields, UNECA (United Nations, 1973, as cited in United Nations [1974a: 6]).

Table 5.3: Division of Rural Labor in Kivu Province, Zaire

		Unit of Production	Work
Women		1.00	Ploughing, sowing, upkeep of plantation, transport of produce, carrying of water, preparation and transport of firewood, marketing, beermaking.
Men (in the rural areas all the time)		0.30	Care of banana trees, clearing land when necessary and help with the cultivation of new fields; certain other jobs.
Children aged 5-9:	Boys	0.00	No contribution.
	Girls	0.05	Help with weeding and carrying water.
Children aged 10-14:	Boys	0.15	Looking after cattle; help with weeding.
	Girls	0.55	Help mother with all agricultural work.
Old people over 55:	Men	0.05	Very little work; some jobs in banana groves.
	Women	0.20	Help with light work in the fields.

SOURCE: **Analyse de la malnutrition au Bushi,** published by **Oeuvre pour la lutte centre le bwaki et la protection de l'enfance,** as quoted by David Mitchnik in **The Role of Women in Rural Development in Zaire, Oxfam,** Oxford, 1972. Reproduced here from United Nations (1974a: 4).

Table 5.4: Participation of Women in Nonformal Rural Education in Africa

Area of Access	Unit of Participation*
Agriculture	0.15
Animal Husbandry	0.20
Trade and Commerce	?**
Cooperatives	0.10
Arts and Crafts	0.50
Nutrition	0.90
Home Economics	1.00

*Units given are extremely rough estimates due to lack of data. Estimates are based on ECA Country Reports (United Nations, 1972-1974), and informal knowledge, as cited in United Nations (1974a: 41). Ideal units in most of these areas might be 0.50, indicating that both men and women have access to the nonformal training.
**Very little training in trade and commerce is known to exist at the nonformal level.

industrialized societies of Euro-North America, is to insulate the managers, the intellectuals, and the teachers from producing sectors both in agriculture and in industry. The decision makers whose function it is to redistribute societal resources do not have access to the knowledge and competence of women and men in the lower ranks of the producing sectors. They therefore make serious mistakes in allocation of resources.[3]

The Decision Makers Discover Women

There has been a tiny crack in that insulation barrier in the West as a consequence of the liberation movements, including the women's liberation movement. The attention of decision makers has been drawn to massive amounts of excluded competence. The Percy Amendment, one of the fruits of the women's liberation movement in the United States, adds to the U.S. Foreign Assistance Act of 1973 the stipulation that all assistance given in the areas of (1) food and nutrition, (2) population planning and health, (3) education and human resources development, and (4) any other selected development problems

> shall be administered so as to give particular attention to those programs, projects, and activities which tend to integrate women into the national economies of foreign countries, thus improving their status and assisting the total development effort [Public Law 93-189, 93rd Congress, s. 1443, December 17, 1973; Sections 103-107 and Percy Amendment Section 113].

As a result of the Percy Amendment, AID did for the first time what it should have done at its inception; it sent women out to look and listen in the field—to watch what farmer women actually did and to listen to them talk about what they did (AID, 1974). In Africa they observed women farmers in Ghana, Kenya, Lesotho, and Nigeria; in Latin America, women farmers in Bolivia, Paraguay, and Peru. While there were substantial differences in practices from one country to another both within and between continents, the basic findings were the same in every case:

> Women today appear to play active roles, both as decision-makers and participants in most rural development-related activities. More specifically... (except in northern Nigeria), *women have complete equality, regarding participation in basic agricultural production* [AID, 1974: 132; italics added].

The activity imbalance between women and men lay in the area of decision-making, not in the production process (where in fact the imbalance went the other way). Even in the decision area, many more decisions were the product of joint consultation than had ever been suspected. In trading activities, particularly in marketing the crops the woman has grown, she was usually the sole decision maker. Her economic interests as marketer have a profound effect on a whole range of decisions made jointly by wife and husband regarding development improvements in poultry, cattle, new crops, etc. The reason she can appear to be an obstacle to innovation is that the majority of development innovations have not taken account of her interests, adding extra work without extra benefits. Besides, these innovations often have reduced the income over which she personally has disposal.

Another recent study that has given separate attention to women farmers (Moock, 1973), undertaken in Vihiga Division of Kenya, highlights the performance of women farmers when they are sole heads of household, or sole managers with migrant husbands living and working elsewhere. In this region, 6 percent of the women were heads of their own farms, and 32 percent were managers with absent husbands, making a total of 38 percent of the farms being operated by women. The study focused on the managerial ability of farmers. The dependent variable was bags of maize per acre, and twenty variables ranging from seed genotype, plant density, and fertilizer use through worker characteristics, hours worked, and contact with extension workers were carefully studied in a sample of seventy-two farms and a control group of eighty-eight farms. Contrary to all expectations, the women who farmed alone turned out to be better managers than the men, "producing an additional bag and a half of maize with a given package of physical inputs" (1973: 341). This productivity only emerged with regression analysis, since the first round of analysis seemed to indicate that the women were less productive. It was when additional factors were taken into account, including the quality of seed, amount of fertilizer, and kinds of help made available through the extension agent, that it became clear that women got more from their inputs.

As might be expected, less help of every kind was available to them. Moock suggests that they made up in commitment and hard work for what they lacked in resources.

The seven country survey cited earlier (AID, 1974) focused on women farmers with partners living at home, the Moock study on women farming alone. In both cases the role and performance of the woman farmer appears as far more significant than has ever been realized. It would seem at first glance that the kinds of problems these two sets of women face are very different, and that the outcomes in terms of agricultural productivity and number of children born might be very different for the two groups, at any given level of assistance. However, the need for better seed, better tools, and more recognition by extension agents is the same for both, as is the incentive to have more children to help with the work. Annual or more frequent visits home by migrant husbands living elsewhere ensure the possibility of annual pregnancy for married women farming on their own. Women farm owners are either widows who already have children and possibly grandchildren to help, or they are enterprising women with sufficient resources to command labor. Probably 99 percent of women who farm depend on their own breeding activity to generate additional help. While the patterns for giving aid to these two categories of women may differ slightly, the need for aid is pressing in both groups.

INDICATORS OF THE SITUATION OF RURAL WOMEN

In order to give a comprehensive overall picture of the situation of women agriculturalists in Africa and of the associated facts about economic and social productivity, adequacy of food supply, and rate of population increase, I have constructed a series of tables describing three different groups of countries. The first is a group of seventeen countries with substantial numbers of women-headed households; the second is a group of eight countries not particularly known for large numbers of women-headed households, but in which the majority of women are engaged in agriculture. The third is a group of eight countries known to have substantial nomad populations.

The following characteristics are included in each table:

(1) Percentage of total population engaged in agriculture and herding. This gives a picture of the overall importance of agriculture in the society's economy.

(2) Percentage of all women engaged in agriculture and herding. This is a most difficult figure to arrive at, and my estimates here are bound to be controversial. Reporting practices on women in agriculture vary enormously from country to country, with women often only being reported if they happen to be wage laborers in agriculture. Women farming on their own account or as

unpaid family labor are frequently not included, nor is subsistence farming. Since subsistence farming is "full-time" farming in terms of the woman's work day (see Tables 5.1 and 5.2) and we know that women do on the average 70 percent of the agricultural work, I have revised upward all UN reports that clearly do not include the bulk of the agricultural labor of women. For each country I drew on three sets of figures: (1) the *1972 ILO Yearbook of Labour Statistics* figures on total population engaged in agriculture, (2) supplemental figures on women in agriculture published by the Economic Commission for Africa (United Nations, 1974a) based on country reports, and (3) the computations of women in the labor force prepared for the *Handbook of International Data on Women* (Boulding et al., 1976) based on raw ILO figures of women in the labor force and women in agriculture. Based on inspection of each of the above sets of figures, and giving particular weight to estimates of the total population engaged in agriculture, the size of the urban population, and country-by-country case studies of the role of women in agriculture, I arrived at the figures given in the second column of the table. Table A.1 (Appendix) gives all the possible different figures for each country side by side, with notes, so that the reader can discern the basis for the final estimate of the percentage of women in agriculture in Tables 5.5-5.7.

(3) Percentage of women rural heads of household through polygamy. Estimates of polygamous households come from Boserup (1970). It is clear from her work and other studies that a frequent pattern in polygamous households is for each wife to have her own dwelling, subsistence garden, and associated enterprises. The husband visits each wife in turn, but provides very little if any contribution toward her subsistence. She is thus in effect a farm manager with an "absent husband," though she sees that husband more frequently than the women in the next category to be described, and may have frequent decision inputs from her husband.

(4) Percentage of women rural heads of household through migration, widowhood, or divorce. The husbands of these women who are not divorced or widowed may be living in a nearby town or may be migrant workers in mines or on plantations elsewhere in the country or in another country. These women are farm managers whose husbands (or other family members for husbandless women) may have more or less input into major decisions regarding crops to be planted, development plans, etc.

(5) Presence in urban areas. While not directly related to rural productivity, the number of women living in towns and the number of women who are heads of urban households affect to some extent the marketing strength of rural women, and therefore the resources at their disposal. Information for this column is sparse, and I indicate the urban sex ratio when this represents a substantial surplus of women over men, or percentage of women-headed urban households when this figure is available.

(6) Percentage of women of appropriate age group enrolled in secondary school. This figure gives us general information about women's access to the modern knowledge stock in a society and tells us indirectly how many women are available for modern sector positions. University education is not considered here because the fraction of the population attending a university is so small in many of these countries that it does not give significant information on the skill potentials of either women or men.

(7) Percentage of women receiving vocational education. Vocational training is usually at the secondary level and includes agricultural as well as craft training. It has more direct significance for rural women than general secondary education, since it is aimed at increasing their productivity in a way that general education is not.

(8) Agricultural training programs for women. Information on numbers of women receiving agricultural training is not usually available, but the existence of any such training opportunity at all for women is significant, given a general absence of such agricultural training and of women extension agents in most countries. Only presence or absence of such training opportunities is indicated.

(9) Community development programs for women. Again, numbers are not available, but the presence or absence of community development programs which provide for the participation of women is another important indicator of the possibility for rural women to increase their productivity. Self-help road and building construction programs, when these consist mainly of women participants, are mentioned here in notes for the appropriate countries.

(10) Percentage of women married by the age of nineteen. In societies where 50 percent or more of the women are married by the age of nineteen, women begin the double load of farming and breeding earlier than in countries where women marry later. We already know that in agricultural societies, girls are doing agricultural work from the time they are five years old. In societies with later marriage they usually[4] have a longer period of productive activity in their youth unencumbered by constant pregnancy.

(11) Number of women's NGOs represented. There is a total of forty-seven nongovernmental organizations for women out of the approximately 2,500 NGOs reported in the 1973 and 1974 *Yearbooks of International Associations.* These are transnational organizations organized around particular interests ranging from religious to occupational, educational, and political associations. Nongovernmental organizations are private citizen initiatives with international headquarters serving sections in as few as three and as many as over a hundred countries. While NGOs are essentially urban-based, several of the women's NGOs have taken a particular interest in rural women,

and support community development programs for them. These organizations therefore represent a kind of opportunity structure for rural women.

(12) GNP per capita. This is the conventional measure of the economic productivity of a country. It does not take account of most of the productivity of women, which is in subsistence agriculture and household craft, but it is a measure of the development of the "modernized" sector of a country. It provides a valuable context within which to view the situation of women.

(13) The rate of growth in GNP from 1961 to 1968. These figures give a picture of the rate of development of a country and are similarly a useful contextual indicator of the potential resources which may become available to women.

(14) The population growth rate from 1963 to 1970. This is particularly useful viewed in conjunction with the GNP growth rate. For many of the countries under study, as we will see, negative economic growth accompanies a strongly positive population growth rate.

(15) The comparison of food unit production in 1969 and 1973. This comparison is the third indicator of rates and directions of change in productivity. Not surprisingly, countries with declining economic growth and rapidly increasing populations are growing less and less food for more and more babies. The double producing-breeding burden for women shows up most sharply here.

(16) Percentage of the population living in urban centers. This figure gives some indication of the communication infrastructure of a society and the possibility of pumping new resources into the countryside. When combined with the rather meager information on women in cities, it can give a clue as to how much help urban women could give rural women.

(17) Major religion. Information on major religion is included to explore the possible relationship between religious tradition and women's roles. We see that producer roles for rural women exist under each type of religion. When no one religion includes a clear majority of the population, the second largest is listed. If "other" is entered, this means there are two or three other religions all present in significant numbers.

(18) Historical tradition. The entries in this column, based on information in the country historical capsules included in the *Associated Press Almanac of 1973,* indicate whether the geographical territory of a given country was the site of old imperial kingdoms such as the Ghanian, Malian, Songhaian, Egyptian, or Ethiopian empires, or of ancient trade ports, local kingdoms, or less stratified tribal cultures. As in the case of the major religious tradition, we see that there is no strong relationship between the presence of older imperial structures and the number of women in agriculture, though some former empire areas have an urban tradition that has reduced the numbers of both women and men in agriculture.

Table 5.5A: Countries with Substantial Numbers of Women-Headed Households: Participation of Women

Country	% Total Population in Agriculture and Herding	Estimated % of All Economically Active Women in Agriculture and Herding[a]	% Rural Women-Headed Households Based on Polygamy[b]	% Rural Women-Headed Households Through Migration Widowhood Divorce[c]	Presence of Women in Urban Areas	% Women of Appropriate Age Group Receiving Secondary Education	% Women of All Those Receiving Vocational Education	Presence of Agriculture Training Programs for Women	Number Women's NGOs Present	Presence of Community Development Programs for Women	% Women Married By Age 19
COUNTRIES WITH SUBSTANTIAL NUMBERS OF WOMEN-HEADED HOUSEHOLDS											
Botswana	90	95	---	33	---	4	---	---	6	---	---
Central African Republic	90	90	---[d]	---	---	1	17	---	4	---	57.5
Congo	60	60	11-17	---	---[h]	8	7.5	---	10	---	58.4
Gambia	90	90	---[d]	---	---	4	10	yes	4	yes	---
Ghana	56	55	---	50[e]	---[i]	8	10	yes	16	yes	---
Ivory Coast	86	80	27	"many"	---[j]	3	33	yes	7	yes	35.6
Kenya	88	85	---	50	10[f,n]	4	---	yes	16	yes[o]	22.3
Lesotho	98	98	---	33[f]	---	5	24.5	---	5	---	---
Malawi	90	90	---	33	---	1	15	---	1	---	79.1
Mali	90	90	---	16	---	2	4	yes	0	yes	---
Nigeria	80	60	63	---	---[k]	4	30	yes	23	yes	62.8
Senegal	85	80	21-24	---	---	2	---	yes	7	yes	---
Sierra Leone	90	89	51	---	---	4	---	yes	16	yes	49.5
Uganda	90	90	45	---	---	2	---	yes	10	yes	---
COUNTRIES WITH WOMEN-HEADED URBAN HOUSEHOLDS											
Benin	84	84	---	---	30[l]	2	37.5	---	8	---	66.7
Malagasy Republic	90	41	---	75[g]	---[m]	8	---	---	13	yes	38.5
Tanzania	95	95	---	---	---[m]	1	---	yes	6	yes	---

a. E. Boulding estimate (See Appendix Tables A.1 and A.2).
b. Estimates from Boserup (1970).
c. Estimates from United Nations (1974a).
d. Present, no figures.
e. In South Only.
f. Estimates based on Seven Country Survey (AID, 1974).
g. That is, 75 percent of women are rated "economically independent."
h. Sixty-six percent of Congo's markets conducted by women.
i. Eighty-four percent of Ghana's markets conducted by women.
j. "Many" women-headed households in urban areas.
k. Sixty percent of Senegal's markets conducted by women.
l. Thirty percent women-headed households in urban areas.
m. Urban Sex Ratio is 90.
n. Ten percent women-headed households in urban areas (AID, 1974).
o. Eighty to 90 percent of road construction under Food-for-Work Program done by women.

COUNTRIES WITH MANY WOMEN-HEADED HOUSEHOLDS

The countries in Table 5.5 have from 15 to 50 percent women-headed rural households. (Three countries are included with no specific figures, but other evidence of substantial numbers of women-headed households.) Whether households are woman-headed due to visitor-status of husband in polygamous households and migrant-husband households, or due to widowhood or divorce, they all represent situations where women do the bulk of the agricultural work and make all the daily decisions. The extent to which major decisions about crops and innovations are made by absent spouses or other family members varies from region to region, but it is clear that the workload and much of the decision-making fall on women, as well as the breeding and rearing of children. In most of these countries between 1 and 4 percent of girls of school age receive secondary education. Where vocational training is available, in nine out of the seventeen countries,[5] the opportunities range more widely. From 4 to 40 percent of all persons receiving vocational education in a country are women. The vocational training figure is in units of participation of women compared to men; women's education is not, due to problems of immediate data availability. What this relatively high vocational training figure represents for the most part is a series of programs in nutrition, child care, and other "domestic arts," and *not* training for nondomestic production of any kind. Nine of the seventeen countries now have some possibility of agricultural training for women. Mostly this has developed in the past three years. The same is true of community development programs: even recently instituted programs have tended to emphasize nutrition and domestic life styles rather than production activities.

Of the nine countries that report on the number of women married by age nineteen, seven report 39 to 79 percent of women married by nineteen. Five of these seven countries have 80 percent or more of the women in agriculture, and most of them have been working in the fields in varying degrees since they were five years old. For the six of those seven early-marriage countries that provide statistics on both GNP and population growth rates, all but one have declining GNP, that one barely holding its own. Populations are growing at the rate of from 2.1 to 2.5, and food production per capita is declining to as low as 61 units of food per capita on the base of 100 units of food produced in 1965.

Countries like Ghana and Lesotho, with less than a third of women married by age nineteen, also have a similar picture of increased population and declining productivity. The only countries with increased agricultural productivity are Botswana and Tanzania, both with 90 percent or more of their women in agriculture. While drought and other natural catastrophes have played their part in the problem of declining productivity, a lot of it can

Table 5.5B: Countries with Substantial Numbers of Women-Headed Households: Country Characteristics

	GNP Per Capita	GNP Growth Rate 1961-1968[a]	Population Growth Rate 1963-1970[b]	Changes in Units of Food Produced from 1969 to 1973	Percentage Population in Urban Areas	Major Religion	Historical Tradition
COUNTRIES WITH SUBSTANTIAL NUMBERS OF WOMEN-HEADED HOUSEHOLDS							
Botswana	100	0.80	2.7	97-113	20	Animist	Bantu Immigration Area
Central African Republic	120	−0.60	2.3	94-94	15	Animist	Bantu Immigration Area
Congo	230	2.20	2.1	78-62	35	Animist	Bantu Immigration Area
Gambia	100	−0.10	1.9	105-101	12	Islamic/Animist	GMS Empires[c]
Ghana	170	−0.70	3.0	95-99	34	Animist/Other	Ancient Kingdom
Ivory Coast	260	4.80	2.3	118-112	19	Animist	Tribal Culture
Kenya	130	1.40	2.9	105-103	16	Animist	Ancient Trade Port
Lesotho	80	1.20	4.0	93-78	1	Protestant/Other	Tribal Kingdom
Malawi	50	2.20	—	119-119	5	Christian/Other	Tribal
Mali	90	1.30	2.1	99-61	10	Islamic/Other	GMS Empires[c]
Nigeria	70	−0.30	2.5	95-83	19	Islamic/Other	Ancient Empire
Senegal	170	−1.40	2.4	89-68	27	Islamic/Other	Colonized Early No Empire
Sierra Leone	150	1.50	1.5	109-103	11	Animist	Ancient Kingdom
Uganda	110	1.10	—	109-99	2	Christian/Other	Powerful Chiefdoms
COUNTRIES WITH WOMEN-HEADED URBAN HOUSEHOLDS							
Dahomey	80	1.10	2.5	106-95	16	Animist	Ancient Kingdom
Malagasy Republic	100	−0.20	2.3	101-92	12	Animist/Other	Indonesian Origin
Tanzania	80	1.20	2.6	119-133	5	Animist/Other	Colonized Early No Empire

a. From Boulding Global Data Bank.
b. From Boulding Global Data Bank.
c. GMS Empires are Ghana, Mali, and Songnhay Empires.

surely be traced to the incredible load placed on women to continue to provide subsistence through agriculture while modernization practices are being aimed at men. The breeder-producer load is very heavy here, particularly for women-headed households. The countries are poor to begin with, six having a GNP per capita of under $100 and only two with a GNP per capita of over $200. Eight of the countries have less than 15 percent of the population living in urban areas. There is certainly some interaction effect here between poverty and women-headed households. We find all degrees of urbanization among the declining-productivity countries (1 to 34 percent urban), all varieties of religion, and all varieties of historical tradition. Agricultural and community development programs are too recent and probably too inadequate in coverage of agricultural skills to make much difference. The countries in which marketing is predominantly controlled by women (Congo, Dahomey, Ghana, and Senegal) and the other countries where there is a substantial urban presence of women (Kenya, Lesotho, Madagascar, and Tanzania) do not show any urban-to-rural effects with regard to GNP-population rate imbalance or food productivity (Congo and Tanzania do the "least worst"). Neither is there any apparent association between number of women's NGOs and such imbalances, nor between women's NGOs and lower population growth rate. In other words, urban-based organizational networks for women do not necessarily lighten the burden of rural women.

Table 5.6 describes a group of countries with equally high participation of women in agriculture, but with fewer women-headed households. The countries are richer than in the first group: four of the eight have GNPs of over $200. None of them is less than 15 percent urban. Possibly the workload is less extreme here for women, though in two countries women do 80 percent and more of the food-for-work and self-help programs of building roads, buildings, airports, etc. In five of the six countries reporting age of marriage, over 40 percent of the women are married by the age of nineteen. Yet here the imbalances between GNP and population growth do not seem so severe as in the first group of countries in Table 5.5. In three of the eight countries the GNP is growing faster than the population, and the drops in food production are less severe. These are countries that are giving more secondary education to women, and Egypt is implementing a major program of training women in agriculture. There is no particular preponderance of women's NGOs in the countries that are doing best economically, nor in countries with lower population growth rates.

There are overall differences between the two sets of countries in Tables 5.5 and 5.6 in wealth, extent of urbanization, number of women-headed households, and rate of population growth. Growth imbalances are present in the second set of countries, but they are not so extreme. While no conclusions can be drawn from this type of aggregate data, one might speculate

Table 5.6A: Other Countries with High Participation in Agriculture: Participation of Women

Country	% Total Population in Agriculture and Herding	Estimated % of All Economically Active Women in Agriculture and Herding[a]	Presence of Women in Urban Areas	% Women of Appropriate Age Group Receiving Secondary Education	% Women of All Those Receiving Vocational Education	Presence of Agriculture Training Programs for Women	Number Women's NGOs Present	Presence of Community Development Programs for Women	% Women Married By Age 19
Cameroon	90	90	---	4	28.5	---	10	yes	---
Egypt	51	50	---	20	---	yes[d]	15	yes	32.7
Gabon	85	94	---	6	---	---	3	yes[e]	62.7
Guinea	80	85	---	1	19.5	---	2	---	46.4
Liberia	85	93	90[b]	4	---	---	14	---	56.5
Swaziland	80	80	---	8	---	---	4	---	---
Zaire	70	95	---	4	21.0	---	7	yes[e]	46.4
Zambia	80	70	---[c]	8	---	yes	11	yes	40.8

a. E. Boulding estimate (See Appendix Table A.1).
b. Urban Sex Ratio.
c. Forty-one percent of Zambia's markets conducted by women.
d. One out of every six agricultural students in Egypt is a woman (Ford Foundation, 1973: 34).
e. In these countries women do 80 percent and more of the Food-for-Work and Self-Help program of building roads, airports.

[126]

Table 5.6B: Other Countries with High Participation in Agriculture: Country Characteristics

Country	GNP Per Capita	GNP Growth Rate	Population Growth Rate	Changes in Units of Food Produced from 1969 to 1973	Percentage Population in Urban Areas	Major Religion	Historical Tradition
Cameroon	140	1.1	2.2	110-109	15	Animist/Other	Bantu Immigration Area
Egypt	170	1.5	2.5	106-102	38	Coptic	Ancient Empire
Gabon	310	0.7	1.3	116-123	16	Animist/Other	Minor Chiefdoms
Guinea	90	2.7	2.2	105-98	15	Islamic/Other	GMS Empires[a]
Liberia	210	0.7	1.7	87-87	20	Animist	Coastal Migration Area
Swaziland	200	5.4	3.0	137-148	19	Animist/Other	Recent Migration
Zaire	90	−0.3	4.2	117-111	20	Christian/Other	Bantu Immigration Area
Zambia	220	3.6	3.0	101-83	19	Animist	Tribal Area

a. GMS Empires are Ghana, Mali, and Songnhay Empires.

on the possibility that women in the second group of countries have a lighter workload. The percentage of women involved in agriculture is roughly the same in the two groups, but there is a relative absence of women-headed households in the second group.

The chief common characteristic of the countries in Table 5.7 is that they all have up to 10 percent or more nomadic populations.[6] Countries vary in the extent to which they report their nomadic populations, but in general nomads are not included in country statistics. The women, in particular, are usually not counted. While nomadic populations have a clear-cut division of labor, as do settled people, the women have substantial herding and food-gathering responsibilities and should therefore be included in any agriculture-and-herding estimates. Half the countries are highly urbanized, half much less urbanized. Most are located in North Africa, most are Islamic, and most have participated in the traditions of an ancient empire. These nations represent the extremes of oil riches and desert poverty. My estimates of agricultural activity of women in these countries are substantially higher than ILO reports, partly based on my knowledge of nomadic practices, partly based on accounts of the extent of weeding and irrigation work that women are responsible for in North African countries when male heads of households are enumerated as farmers. The weeding and water carrying plus subsistence kitchen gardening may involve fewer work hours than subsistence farming in sub-Saharan Africa, yet these activities still justify the term "farm worker" for the women.

While levels of secondary and vocational education for women are low, community development programs are expanding rapidly. Interestingly, in three out of the seven Islamic countries for which age of marriage is reported, 20 percent or less of the women are married by age nineteen, reflecting general age of marriage for North Africa as being higher, not lower, than elsewhere. New oil production will change the economic growth rates in relation to population growth rates for this area, but it is interesting to note that prior to 1968, six of these eight countries were in serious trouble with regard to GNP-population growth imbalance, but not with regard to food. Algeria was in the worst straits of all, the only country in the group showing by 1973 serious decline in food production as well as in GNP-population imbalance. Tunisia, with relatively fewer farm women than most other countries (45%) is now showing the greatest activity with regard to giving women general education and agricultural training. One-fourth of all agricultural training is going to women.

No conclusions can be drawn from Table 5.7. The North African women, compared to women in the countries cited in Table 5.6, appear to have a lighter workload. The highest population growth is taking place in the more urban, not the more rural, countries. It has often been pointed out that

Table 5.7A: Women in Agriculture in Countries with Substantial Nomad Populations:[a] Participation of Women

Country	% Total Population in Agriculture and Herding	Estimated % of All Economically Active Women in Agriculture and Herding[b]	Presence of Women in Urban Areas	% Women of Appropriate Age Group Receiving Secondary Education	% Women of All Those Receiving Vocational Education	Presence of Agriculture Training Programs for Women	Number Women's NGOs Present	Presence of Community Development Programs for Women	% Women Married By Age 19[c]
Algeria	60	60	90[d]	5	---	---	5	yes	46.5
Ethiopia	96	80	---	1	---	---	10	yes	---
Libya	36	20	---	7	---	---	2	yes	73.5
Morocco	---	41	---	6	---	---	8	yes	54.1
Niger	95	96	---	0.4	---	---	2	---	86.3
Somalia	95	85	---	1	14.0	---	2	---	13.5
Sudan	80	80	---[e]	3	---	---	5	yes	20.1
Tunisia	47	45	---	11[f]	---	yes	8	yes	18.9

a. Estimates of nomadic population range from less than 10 percent in some countries to more than 60 percent in others, but exact figures are not available.
b. E. Boulding estimate (See Appendix Table A.1).
c. Sudan has an unknown rate of polygamy.
d. Urban Sex Ratio.
e. Labor force does not necessarily include nomads.
f. Twenty-five percent of all second level agricultural training is given to women (Ford Foundation, 1973: 34).

Table 5.7B: Women in Agriculture with Substantial Nomad Population: Country Characteristics

Country	GNP Per Capita	GNP Growth Rate	Population Growth Rate	Changes in Units of Food Produced from 1969 to 1973	Percentage Population in Urban Areas	Major Religion	Historical Tradition
Algeria	220	3.5	3.8	82-77	38	Islamic	Ancient Trade Center
Ethiopia	70	6.0	1.9	103-103	11	Coptic/Other	Ancient Empire
Libya	1020	19.4	3.7	119-98	21	Islamic	Ancient Trade Contact
Morocco	190	0.4	3.0	105-99	23	Islamic	Ruled by Carthage
Niger	70	1.6	2.7	100-85	3	Islamic	Ancient Kingdom
Somalia	60	0.2	2.2	103-95	11	Islamic	Ancient Punt
Sudan	100	−0.4	2.8	118-118	8	Islamic	Ancient Nubia
Tunisia	220	2.7	—	81-98	36	Islamic	Ancient Carthage

women in urban areas, with few production activities available to them, may bear more children under those conditions of "relative work-deprivation" than rural women. Thus, it may be that urban development programs will be more important for the women of North Africa than will rural development programs.

These tables demonstrate that the role of women in agricultural productivity is a major one, and that too much of their work is carried out unaided. This is true in countries with substantial numbers of women carrying agricultural workloads alone, but it is also true in the other two groups of countries where women possibly carry less of a workload. In the countries of Table 5.5 the situation is extreme, but it would be true to say that in no country do agricultural development programs adequately take account of the role of women in the productive process, nor do they channel enough aid in their direction.

THE RELATIONSHIP BETWEEN FERTILITY AND AGRICULTURAL PRODUCTIVITY

This chapter has emphasized the need of overworked women to bear children as additional field hands. It is too often assumed that women are too stupid to know when to stop bearing children, and that they will go on bearing children when health and nutrition improve and infant mortality declines, resulting in far greater overpopulation. Therefore intensive family planning programs are thought to be needed to persuade women to bear fewer children. Yet on the rare occasions when researchers set out to study the behavior of farm women, it becomes clear that they can be very skilled managers of scarce resources and can do a great deal with what little they find. Any program that affects their work as producers is bound also to affect their fertility. It has long been known that increasing levels of education for women reduces fertility, and urbanization reduces fertility *if* opportunities for productive labor are not removed (United Nations, 1974c).

> Repeated studies from various parts of the world show a clear correlation also on the individual level between productivity and the number of children in the family. These studies indicate that it is the mother's employment, education and status, not the father's, which are the major factors influencing fertility. There is thus a close connection between a woman's access to material and social resources and her ability to utilize those means that are available to plan and space her children.[7]

In other words, whenever women have an opportunity to increase their skill levels in ways relevant to the productive opportunities of their environment, they will respond by increasing the quality of life for their families.

WHAT FARM WOMEN NEED

Farm women need resources to help them shape better conditions of life for themselves and the families they support, resources to introduce some elements of planning and predictability into their lives. These resources may be grouped under the headings of:

(1) intermediate technology,
(2) family-oriented supporting services,
(3) formal education,
(4) nonformal education,
(5) extension and community service specialists who are women and/or trained to work with both women and men,
(6) local opportunities for paraprofessional training for able community women,
(7) credit and marketing facilities,
(8) legal protection of women's rights as family persons and producers,
(9) recognition of traditional women's organizations and support for their active participation in community planning, and
(10) programs of placing women in administrative and planning positions at all levels from local to national and international.[8]

Intermediate Technology

Women need simple technological aids to lighten the burdens of their heaviest daily tasks. Such aids are useful only when they are accompanied by the active participation of the women who will use them. There are many examples of labor-saving devices, including wells, being rejected by women because they were planned and installed without consultation with the local women, and therefore without regard to fitting the innovation into the total needs and work patterns of the women. Since many villages have some form of community organization among women already, however rudimentary, these should be utilized from the very beginning of any planning process. Examples of appropriate technology:[9]

(a) agricultural implements—low-cost ox-drawn ploughs for women, hand-operated inter-row cultivators, planters, winnowers, seed-cleaning sieves, chicken feeders, and waterers;

(b) food-processing implements—sun dryers, smoking drums for fish and meat, insect-, rodent-, and damp-proof farm food storage facilities, solar water heaters, improved stoves, maize-shellers, cassava grinders, community mills and wells;

(c) fuel and haulage—planting near villages of fast-growing trees that can be cut for firewood, promotion of acquisition of small portable mechanical saws, of wheelbarrows, bicycles, and tricycle carts, local building of donkey and ox carts for women, exploration of new patterns of village work organization for community preparation of charcoal and for water and wood collecting, utilizing brigades of young people, both boys and girls.

Family-Oriented Supporting Services

Child care programs are increasingly being initiated by rural women themselves, as in Kenya and Tanzania, and are best linked to traditional mutual help associations rather than as urban-designed programs.

Maternal, paternal, and child health services and family planning programs should be developed as basic community facilities in connection with traditional services of midwives, healers, and vendors of health and virility herbal compounds.[10] Family planning programs should be incorporated with "programmes to raise women's earning capacities, lessen their labours, improve health, and thus increase the chances of successful pregnancies and survival of infants and children" (Ford Foundation, 1973: 52).

Formal Education

School curricula should not differentiate between boys and girls. Both boys and girls should learn among other things, modern agriculture, village technology, science, trades and crafts, family decision-making, family planning, nutrition—and be trained and encouraged to take up activities in the modernized sector of the economy. Education campaigns (should) encourage parents to send daughters to school—to keep them there and to make clear that they can reach the top levels of responsibility.

Basic education . . . should not leave girls with unemployable skills such as embroidery and family cookery. This would necessitate local market research, and marketing assistance, and could be accomplished through rural youth clubs, where they exist [United Nations, 1974a: 85-86].

Help is needed in the development of self-employment or small-scale or cottage industries to enable rural women to have incomes, or to supplement the family income. Projects such as SEDCO [Small Enterprises Development Corporation] in Swaziland . . . might be in food production, processing or preparation, animal husbandry or in crafts or services. This may involve the establishment of training programmes in practical money-earning skills for teenage boys and girls such as the village polytechnics in Kenya [United Nations, 1974d].

Nonformal Education

Education for women outside formal schooling programs can bypass conventional schooling approaches. Using paraprofessionals, minimally trained peers, voluntary agencies, youth groups, religious organizations, as well as experienced educators, programs can be developed which combine literacy training with priority local skill needs through action programs in agricultural improvement (*not* just aimed at cash crops, but at food crops), development of cooperatives, new income-producing craft skills, training in small-scale processing industries skills in needed village technology, including home construction and road-building technology. Wherever possible there should be joint training opportunities for women and men, and all programs should aim at new concepts of work-sharing, re-evaluation of old patterns of division of labor. Traditional homecraft programs in nutrition, cooking, child-rearing, and sewing should be dismantled and reintroduced for both men and women in programs oriented to problems of agricultural productivity, of food preservation problems related to local spoilage, and to problems of community child care needs.

Extension and Community Service Programs
Specialists Who Are Women

There needs to be training for women specialists, but the training should be sufficiently linked to training for men so that men are also trained to work with women farmers and to accept women specialists as their colleagues. Wife-husband teams of extension agents have been proposed for areas where women have low status, to bolster the status of the woman specialist and make her services more acceptable, but this should be done with extreme care or it will undercut long-range goals of more autonomy for women. Incentive systems related to traditional cultural values need to be developed for male extension agents that will make it rewarding to them to work with women farmers and with women colleagues.

Local Opportunities for Paraprofessional Training for Women

Identifying the ablest women farmers in a community and giving them paraprofessional training to work with other women farmers in upgrading their use of labor-saving, productivity-enhancing technology may be the single most important rural program that a country could undertake. Giving additional training to women who are already rendering services to the community, such as midwives, healers, hairdressers (one of the oldest traditional occupations for women and usually ignored by development specialists), and other kinds of service specialists in the traditional sector, and to women who are already accepted community leaders, will make every kind of community program more effective. Paraprofessional as well as professional training programs always need to be carried out in consultation with local men as well as women leaders, in ways that reward men for support of the training programs.

Credit and Marketing Facilities

Changes in regulations and practice can be made to allow farm and business inputs, loans, credit and guidance on business management to women for their use in food production, cooperatives and for income-generating activities. Changes in farmers' cooperative rules can be made to allow women with no title to land to be members and to hold office in cooperative societies. This is already being done in some East African countries. Sometimes it is preferable to allow women to form their own societies before joining those of men.

Improved marketing facilities can be intensified to enable the male farmer and his wife and/or the women farmers to market goods without spoilage and to have a fairer share of the benefits in comparison to the middleman. Many countries are making great efforts to popularize cooperative societies for marketing agricultural products but more could be done to save women carrying produce many miles to market [United Nations, 1974d: 13].

Legal Protection of Women's Rights

Laws governing marriage, divorce, inheritance, and employment adopted by the modernizing elite of a society usually run counter to traditional attitudes and practices, and much attention needs to be given to bridging that gap. Cash cropping also tends to abrogate traditional land-use rights of women, denying needed resources in land to the subsistence woman farmer. Traditional ownership and credit rights of the woman trader may also be eroded by the modern sector, and need to be protected.

Recognition of Traditional Women's Organizations

Women's village organizations should always be identified and consulted in the development of any program for women. Existing traditional women's credit associations rarely benefit farm women, and a conscious effort to bring women traders and farm women into mutual self-help programs should be considered. Urban women are generally unfamiliar with the situation of rural women, and efforts to bring urban women into programs with rural women must be undertaken in full recognition that urban women have lots to learn from rural women. They cannot simply appear on the scene as teachers. The Economic Commission for Africa Women's Programme (United Nations, 1974a: 86) has proposed an All-African Women's Voluntary Task Force that would allow skilled women from one part of a region to serve in another part and work with women's voluntary organizations to help focus their concerns and activities through improved organizational techniques and specific attention to the economically productive roles of women. By working with traditional women's organizations, it will become clear where the optimum teaching sites for training programs are located. Training programs are usually held on traditionally "male" social terrain, so that even when women are permitted to be present it is difficult for them to utilize the opportunities offered. More use of village churches and schools and traditional gathering places already used by women is necessary.

Programs for Women as Administrators and Planners

Most policy decisions concerning women are made by men and ... more women must be included in the policy-making and higher administrative ranks of government. At present, where data are available for 14 countries on women's representation in administrative, executive and managerial levels, the median is a low 6.4% of all persons in these positions [United Nations, 1974d: 11].

The Ford Foundation Task Force report (1973: 54) recommends:

- *Courses for national planners,* on how to integrate planning for women into national development planning. This was proposed by the *UN Expert Group Meeting on Women in Development,* June 1972, under the chairmanship of Sir Arthur Lewis.
- *Internships for college men and women,* perhaps during the holidays preceding their final year on qualitative and quantitative data and its analysis, as basis for planning for women's integration in development. These internships may be at national and international institutions.
- *Training courses for women leaders,* on data, analysis and methods of integrating women in all sectors of the economy. These would preferably be held on the national level.

Integrating women into national program planning and key resource allocation positions at every level is a monumental task. Partly it will be done through establishing national commissions of experienced women and men who will systematically study and advise on necessary steps, partly through the establishment of special women's bureaus. There will always be the danger that the special local knowledge of women will be ignored as professional women become active at the national level, and that the current rural-urban split will be made even wider as more educated women are absorbed into government. This would work against the needs of the woman farmer and must be prevented by working directly with rural women, and incorporating rural women themselves into planning programs, as much as possible.

NOTES

1. The fourth world consists of the third world countries that have no resources such as oil to exploit.
2. It would be interesting to do some macro-level studies of imports of nations that export cash crops, as well as of local purchasing habits, to try to ascertain how this cash is spent.
3. The practice of rotating government bureaucrats into the field and factory in the People's Republic of China represents one major effort to overcome this insulation effect of modernization.
4. This would not be true in societies in which the practice of free unions is widespread, but in most of the countries under discussion marriage is associated with the beginning of child-bearing.
5. That is, nine countries report vocational training. It may exist, unreported, in other countries.
6. Countries included in this table are chosen on the basis of UNESCO reports on nomadism, summarized in Chapter 2.
7. From an "Informal Background Document" prepared in Norway for the December 1974 Conference on Women in Agriculture held at Princeton University. Reference cited for the statement is the Economic Commission for Africa Report (United Nations, 1974a: 72).
8. For further discussion of the kinds of proposals listed here, see Ford Foundation (1973) and United Nations (1974a).
9. These proposals all come from United Nations (1974d).
10. See, as an example of use of traditional networks for modern family planning, Piet and Hendrata (1974).

VARIABLE SOURCES LISTING

1. *Percentage of Total Population Engaged in Agriculture and Herding*
   Source: 1972 *Yearbook of Labor Statistics.*
2. *Percentage of All Women Engaged in Agriculture and Herding*
   Source: A) Elise Boulding estimates; see Appendix Table A.1
   B) Boulding, Nuss, Carson, and Greenstein (1976).
3. *Percentage Women Rural Heads of Household Through Polygamy*
   Source: Boserup (1970) estimates.
4. *Percentage Women Rural Heads of Household Through Migration, Widowhood, or Divorce*
   Source: Estimates based on Economic Commission for Africa (ECA) country studies and various other studies.

5. *Presence in Urban Areas*
   Source: Estimates from a variety of country studies.
6. *Percentage of Women of Appropriate Age Group Enrolled in Secondary School*
   Source: Boulding, Nuss, Carson, and Greenstein (1976).
7. *Percentage of Women Receiving Vocational Education*
   Source: From Table 10, Ford Foundation (1973: 32).
8. *Agricultural Training Programs for Women*
   Source: Economic Commission for Africa reports and other reports.
9. *Community Development Programs for Women*
   Source: Economic Commission for Africa reports and other reports.
10. *Percentage of Women Married by the Age of Nineteen*
    Source: Table 6, United Nations (1974a: 13).
11. *Number of Women's NGOs Represented*
    Source: Boulding, Nuss, Carson, and Greenstein (1976).
12. *GNP Per Capita*
    Source: Boulding Global Data Bank.
13. *The Rate of Growth in GNP from 1961 to 1970*
    Source: Boulding Global Data Bank.
14. *The Population Growth Rate from 1968 to 1970*
    Source: Boulding Global Data Bank.
15. *The Comparison of Food Unit Production in 1969 and 1973*
    Source: Table 18, United Nations (1974a: 67-68). See Source for Variable 10 above.
16. *Percentage of the Population Living in Urban Centers*
    Source: Boulding Global Data Bank.
17. *Major Religion*
    Source: Boulding Global Data Bank.
18. *Historical Tradition*
    Source: *Official Associated Press Almanac, 1973.*

Chapter 6

WOMEN AND FOOD SYSTEMS: An Alternative Approach to the World Food Crisis

MAPPING THE DIMENSIONS OF THE PROBLEM

In the previous chapter we focused on women farmers. While the woman as grower of food is of primary importance, the growing of food is only one part of the entire food system of a society. There are serious problems in every sector of that food system, and the female labor force is a relevant factor every step of the way. In the many hundreds of publications that have come out over the past decade analyzing the dimensions and structures of present and impending food catastrophes, women are usually not mentioned at all. If they are mentioned, it is in connection with their lactation role. The resolution on Women and Food at the Home World Food Conference 1974 is the first major statement of any relationship (other than lactation) between women's roles and the food crisis. Unfortunately, the statement is brief, and it has received very little attention. This chapter may be considered a spelling out of the points made in the Resolution (see Table 6.9 for Resolution VIII on Women and Food).

The disagreement about the extent of the crisis, or whether there is one at all, such as we see reflected in recent United States published symposia on food (*Science,* May 9, 1975; *Scientific American,* September 1976), prepared by prominent scholars in the American scientific community, stems at least partially from an ignorance of the extent to which all sectors of the world food system—from production through processing to distribution—depend on the labor of women. In many parts of that system they are working side by side with men. In the least acknowledged sectors, they are working unseen,

Author's Note: Developed from a paper prepared for the Conference on The World Food Crisis: Values and Alternatives, Pierre, South Dakota, June 6, 1975.

in the kitchen and the kitchen garden. There are in fact two sets of obstacles to an accurate estimate of the extent and nature of the world food problem, as well as to possible solutions to it. One lies in the conceptual inadequacies of the disciplines that deal with the problem, the other in the ignorance of decision makers and scholars about that invisible domain we have been describing, the fifth world of women.

The invisible domain of the food-related work world will be dealt with first, and the disciplinary knowledge gap second.

Women in Food Systems

By food systems I mean all food-related processes and their accompanying institutional mechanisms as found in (1) production, (2) intermediate processing, (3) distribution, and (4) processing for final consumption and serving of food, whether these processes are exclusively local or are part of an international exchange system. Three other food-related processes I also include are (5) research on food, agriculture, and nutrition, (6) policy-making and planning in food-related areas, and (7) all educational programs aimed at persons involved in the food system.

We will examine the extent of participation, insofar as it can be determined, of women in each of these parts of the food system and note particularly the extent of their participation in policy-making as compared with their participation in the rest of the food system. United Nations data will be used to suggest participation rates, though in most cases UN data do not refer to food-related occupations alone. Participation rates are therefore to be taken as possible indicators of magnitude of participation in the food-related sector of the occupational categories indicated. The data, compiled for countries and territorial units reporting to the UN, are reported as regional means.[1] The percentages for the high and low reporting unit for each region are given, to indicate the range of participation rates. Except where otherwise indicated, the figures given are an *index of femaleness;* this means females as a proportion of the total population in that category. A world index of femaleness is also given for each category of participation.

Production

The problems of accurately estimating the involvement of women in food production have been discussed in Chapter 5. There are differences in reporting practices, particularly in the reporting of unpaid family labor and of the activities of herding and nomadic societies. Table A.2 (Appendix) summarizes information on the limitations of these data. We see that approximately half the countries and territories of each region report more or less severe data limitations. The countries *reporting* limitations tend to be the ones with the

Women and Food Systems

most conscientious and well-equipped statistical bureaus. Since many of the countries not reporting limitations are simply ignoring data deficiencies, it would not be unreasonable to suggest that there are inaccuracies in reporting women in agriculture, for example, for every country in the world. The data limitations are stressed here to remind the reader that underreporting of women's activities is one of the major problems in any analysis of women's roles.

Table 6.1 gives a regional overview of the reported participation of women in agriculture and manufacturing, along with the highs and lows reported for each region. (Table A.3, Appendix, provides a listing of countries included in each of the regions.)

It will be noted that the regional means for Africa, Asia, and Euro-North America all indicate more than one-fourth women in their agricultural labor force, while the regional means for North Africa/Middle East and Latin America are nearer one-seventh. The world mean for women in agriculture is 23 percent. In countries ranking highest in overall agricultural employment in

Table 6.1: Index of Femaleness in Agriculture and in Manufacturing Industries*

Regional Mean, High and Low	% Females in Agriculture	% Females in Manufacturing
Africa		
Mean	27	14
High	59 (Zaire)	42 (Ghana)
Low	01 (Uganda)	01 (Zaire)
North Africa and Middle East		
Mean	16	17
High	53 (Cyprus)	74 (Sudan)
Low	00 (Bahrein)	00 (Kuwait)
Asia		
Mean	29	30
High	53 (Japan)	54 (Philippines)
Low	01 (Fiji)	05 (Fiji)
Latin America		
Mean	13	30
High	59 (Bolivia)	56 (Haiti)
Low	01 (Honduras)	14 (Surinam)
Europe		
Mean	29	29
High	57 (Romania)	45 (Hungary)
Low	05 (Norway)	10 (Luxembourg)
World Mean	23	25

SOURCE: Boulding, Nuss, Carson, and Greenstein (1976).
*Females as a proportion of the total population in that industry, regardless of occupation.

their respective regions (Zaire, Cyprus, Japan, Bolivia, Romania), women are reported as providing more than half the labor force, ranging from 53 to 59 percent of the agricultural workers, across all regions. It is probable that the more agriculturally oriented a society is, the better the reporting on women in agriculture.

It is a hypothesis worth testing that in all but the most highly industrialized countries (and even there in the less mechanized production components), for every two men in agriculture there are between one and two women also in the farm sector. Systematic comparative *observation* of women working in the fields in countries with various levels of agricultural participation (not simply interviews of heads of households) will be required to test this hypothesis. Wherever such studies have been made, it is found that women are more involved in agriculture than anyone had expected. One particular feature of women's agricultural activities that is widely unreported is "kitchen gardening," the growing of food for the family table. This gardening is usually not estimated as part of agricultural production since the produce is not a cash crop and does not enter the market. Because many of the world's women feed their families almost entirely from these kitchen gardens, we must treat this kind of gardening as a significant agricultural activity.

Intermediate Processing

There are two types of sites for intermediate processing of food: the farm (or village or suburban) kitchen, and the factory. (Intermediate processing means the preserving of food by drying, salting, pickling, canning, freezing, or other techniques so that it can be eaten later.) There is no way to estimate at present the extent of involvement of women in factory processing of food. The figures in Table 6.1 on women in manufacturing include women in heavy industry as well as in textiles and foods. It will be seen that women provide from one-seventh to nearly one-third of the factory labor force on the average, depending on the region. The world mean is 25 percent. In countries where women's involvement in manufacturing is high, as in the Sudan (74 percent women), Philippines (54 percent), Haiti (56 percent), and Hungary (45 percent), this may represent more textile industries than food processing industries.

Domestic intermediate processing of food for later consumption is most likely to be carried out by two categories of women: farm women and "not economically active" homemakers. The former we have already discussed under the category of agricultural worker. Therefore, the figures on women in agriculture (Table 6.1), corrected upward, can also double as figures on one sector engaged in domestic intermediate food processing. The latter, the "not economically active" homemakers,[2] are reported in Table 6.2, along with the total of economically active women.

Table 6.2: Index of Femaleness of Total Labor Force, and Percentage Women Who Are Full-Time Homemakers

Regional Mean, High and Low	% Females of All Economically Active Persons	% of All Females Reported As Not Economically Active,* Who Are Listed As Homemakers
Africa		
Mean	29	39
High	48 (Tanzania)	43 (Rhodesia)
Low	09 (Angola)	30 (Swaziland)
North Africa and Middle East		
Mean	18	48**
High	43 (Cyprus)	— —
Low	04 (Algeria)	— —
Asia		
Mean	28	51
High	50 (Thailand)	86 (S. Korea)
Low	06 (Fiji)	34 (W. Samoa)
Latin America		
Mean	26	46
High	51 (Barbados)	63 (Guatemala)
Low	11 (Dom. Rep.)	25 (Bahamas)
Europe and North America		
Mean	38	53
High	54 (Austria)	62 (Monaco)
Low	18 (Portugal)	29 (Hungary)
World Mean	29	49

SOURCE: Data from Boulding, Nuss, Carson, and Greenstein (1976).
*All females includes children of all ages.
**Algeria is the only country providing data on homemakers, so the N for the region is 1.

Whatever the inadequacies of the category "not economically active homemaker," it represents an effort to identify that proportion of women outside the labor force with primary home responsibilities. For our purposes it throws light on the proportion of women outside the labor force who are likely to engage in intermediate food processing, whether with home-grown or purchased raw food materials. They are the women who would have the most time for this type of processing.

The femaleness of the total labor force (column 1, Table 6.2), ranging from 4 percent in Algeria to 50 percent in Thailand, with a world mean of 29 percent, is an indicator of the extent of need by working women for commercially available processed foods. In fact, however, an unknown number of working women also process food at home (in addition to preparing meals), in the well-established "dual role" phenomenon. In addition to this unquantifiable group of working females who do home processing of food, it would appear from column 2 in Table 6.2 that roughly half of all females not in the labor force are homemakers and could be labelled "available" for intermediate food processing. Some members of that available sector labelled homemakers do *not* process food, and some "non-homemakers" do process food as unlabelled family helpers, so the 50 percent figure may be a reasonable approximation. In countries with a high child-woman ratio the figure may be less, though in these same countries girl children begin domestic chores at about age five.

Sample studies need to be done in various parts of the world on the involvement of economically active women in intermediate food processing. There is no way of estimating what proportion of these women also have kitchen gardens (where labor may be shared with economically active men) and do food preserving. In all but major urban areas it may be that one-third or more of women who work outside the home also do food preserving. In short, a great deal of food preservation goes on in domestic settings, whether by women already in agriculture, by non-farm homemakers, or by women otherwise economically active. When employed women preserve food, this should properly be termed "moonlighting," although it is not directly remunerated.

Distribution

Certain parts of the food distribution system cannot be analyzed in terms of the participation of women. There is no way of knowing their full involvement in the commercial aspects of the food trade, domestic or international. Some part of that is captured in the figures on trade, linked with the restaurant and motel business, and is discussed in the next section. For this discussion of distribution I have chosen two sets of figures which cover other than food-related activities, but which as in the case of manufacturing give an idea of the extent of participation of women in the food-related aspects of the occupational categories in question. Transport and storage of food are important activities in any country, though more so in more highly industrialized areas, so the category of *transport, storage, and communication* has been chosen; the communication sector of that category is not likely to be involved in food handling. *Financial, community, social, and personal services* involve to a considerable extent the redistribution of goods, including food, through credit, welfare, and other social services. This category seems appropriate as an additional indicator of women's involvement in food-related distribution.

On the average, as Table 6.3 shows, women seem to handle between 5 and 15 percent of transport and storage work, activity that includes both skilled

Table 6.3: Index of Femaleness of Redistributive Industries and Occupations*

Regional Mean, High and Low	% Women in Transportation, Storage, and Communication Industries	% Women in Service Workers Occupations	% Women in Finance, Insurance, Real Estate, Business Services, and Community Social Services
Africa			
Mean	05	37	31
High	21 (Rhodesia)	68 (South Africa)	58 (South Africa)
Low	01 (Ghana)	06 (Sierra Leone)	04 (Mozambique)
North Africa and Middle East			
Mean	02	17	16
High	10 (Israel)	52 (Israel)	46 (Israel)
Low	00 (Libya)	06 (Libya)	06 (Libya)
Asia			
Mean	06	41	34
High	20 (Nepal)	88 (Western Samoa)	75 (Western Samoa)
Low	01 (Pakistan)	15 (Pakistan)	10 (Pakistan)
Latin America			
Mean	06	63	55
High	23 (Bahamas)	86 (Jamaica)	75 (Bolivia)
Low	01 (Dom. Rep.)	32 (Nicaragua)	34 (Surinam)
Europe and North America			
Mean	15	65	50
High	24 (Czechoslovakia)	81 (Finland)	65 (Denmark)
Low	05 (Malta)	37 (Greece)	33 (G. Fed. Rep.)
World Mean	08	50	41

SOURCE: Data from Boulding, Nuss, Carson, and Greenstein (1976).
*Females as a proportion of the total population in that industry or occupation.

and unskilled labor. In Czechoslovakia women's participation reaches 24 percent, and in Nepal, which generally has few women in the labor force, it is 20 percent. In Rhodesia and the Bahamas the figure is respectively 21 and 23 percent. The world mean is 8 percent. In studying these figures we should remember that women provide the human transport mechanism for food and other wares in much of the world, though the loads carried on their heads or backs do not usually get recorded in national statistics on transport. There would then be the same underrecording of women in transport as of women in agriculture. Water-carrying, a major occupation of women in much of the third world, does not enter the statistics either (White et al., 1972). The second column in Table 6.3 refers to women in domestic service and other types of services in the unskilled category. While the highs of 88 percent in Western Samoa, 86 percent in Jamaica, 81 percent in Finland, and 68 percent in South Africa indicate that females do the majority of these types of service work in many societies; the lows of 6 percent in Sierra Leone and Libya and the fact that the world mean is 50 percent tells us that for the world as a whole men hold 50 percent of service jobs in the *paid* labor force. (If we counted the unpaid service work of females the picture would be very different.) The last column lumps together a wide variety of professional service skills from finance to community and personal services. Since many countries collapse all these occupations into a single category for reporting purposes, we must do so, too. While these occupations are not as "female" as the service work in the previous column, the world mean of 41 percent indicates that females are very important in this cluster of skilled services. While many of these services have no direct relationship to food, they frequently determine the access of individuals and families to food.

Final Processing and Serving of Food

Since trade is linked with the restaurant and motel industries in the United Nations data, we must lump together the discussion of food sold over the counter to the householder, and food prepared and served in restaurants. Trade and restaurant activities will be discussed separately, however, from the activities of the householder preparing and serving food at home. Wholesale and retail trade and restaurant, hotel, and motel occupations (Table 6.4A)

Table 6.4A: From Processor to Consumer: Femaleness of Trade, Restaurant, Hotel and Motel Industries*

Regional Mean, High and Low	% Women of Total Labor Force in Wholesale and Retail Trade, Restaurant, Hotel and Motel Industries
Africa	
Mean	24
High	74 (Ghana)
Low	01 (Zaire)
North Africa and Middle East	
Mean	06
High	32 (Israel)
Low	01 (Syria)
Asia	
Mean	29
High	57 (Ryukus)
Low	02 (Iran)
Latin America	
Mean	34
High	88 (Haiti)
Low	09 (Cuba)
Europe and North America	
Mean	44
High	69 (Poland)
Low	15 (Portugal)
World Mean	31

SOURCE: Data from Boulding, Nuss, Carson, and Greenstein (1976).
*Females as a proportion of the total population in these industries, regardless of specific occupation.

draw from one-fourth to one-half or more of their workers from the female labor force, except in North Africa and the Middle East. In certain countries women have a near monopoly of trade and restaurant occupations (Ghana, Haiti, and Poland, for example).

What can be said about women's involvement in domestic processing and serving of food? Single (never-married) women will be excluded from this discussion, since while they may very well cook for themselves or have auxiliary responsibility in another household, they are not ordinarily carrying primary homemaking responsibility including cooking and feeding others. They may do so, however, if they have established an all-woman household, if they have adopted children, or if they are unmarried mothers. Most women in the household cooking-feeding sector, however, are the married and the once-married (widowed, divorced, separated) who are likely to have children and other adults (relatives or not) in their households (first 3 columns of Table 6.4B).

As we see from Table 6.4B, the married and the once-married generally constitute on the average 78 percent of the population of women over fifteen[3] in any society at any given time, ranging from only 64 percent in Latin America to 86 percent in Africa, with the remainder not yet married or headed for permanent singlehood.[4] Another way to look at the extent of feeding responsibilities of women in a society is to look at the child-woman ratio (last column of Table 6.4B), which is the number of children under five years of age per 1,000 women between the ages of fifteen and forty-nine. This figure says nothing about the distribution of the feeding responsibilities, but we note that European women carry by far the lightest load in terms of number of children to feed, and the women of North Africa and the Middle East the heaviest. It will also be noted, however, that there are very substantial differences between the highest and the lowest child-woman ratios in every region, including Europe. Regional foodbanks would make a lot of difference to the women of each region who carry the heaviest child-feeding load. Average household size (last column in Table 6.4B) is another way of looking at the feeding responsibilities of homemakers. Laslett's (1972) and Mayer's (1975) comments on household size being smaller than generally thought (see Chapters 3 and 4) are strongly borne out here. What must be remembered, however, is that in third world countries these small household sizes are accompanied by high infant mortality rates. Many babies have been fed partway through the first or second year of life only to die and be replaced by a new mouth to feed, perhaps again only for a year or two.

The feeding of children is an activity that must be treated separately from the feeding of adults, since for the first two years of a child's life it may be breast fed. The discovery that mother's milk has important nutritional components not available in other mammalian milk has been a big "find" of

Table 6.4B: From Processor to Consumer: Percentage of All Women with Household and Feeding Responsibilities

Regional Mean, High and Low	Marital Status of All Women				Total Ever Married	Child-Woman Ratio*	Average Household Size
	Married	Once-Married					
	% Married	% Widowed	% Divorced, Separated				
Africa							
Mean	67	12	07		86	688	4.4
High	77 (Liberia)	21 (Lesotho)	16 (Tanzania)			952 (Brunei)	4.9 (Kenya)
Low	47 (Somalia)	05 (Rhodesia)	02 (Lesotho)			398 (Gabon)	4.0 (Sierra Leone)
North Africa and Middle East							
Mean	70	13	02		85	800	5.7
High	78 (Libya)	17 (Algeria)	04 (Libya)			980 (Kuwait)	6.4 (Bahrein)
Low	65 (Bahrein)	11 (Kuwait)	01 (Iraq)			532 (Israel)	4.7 (Libya)
Asia							
Mean	64	12	02		78	682	5.3
High	78 (Indonesia)	16 (Indonesia)	06 (W. Samoa)			948 (Nauru)	6.9 (Tonga)
Low	52 (Ryukyus)	08 (Tonga)	00 (Hong Kong)			291 (Japan)	3.5 (Australia)
Latin America							
Mean	53	08	03		64	731	5.0
High	60 (Ecuador)	16 (Guatemala)	10 (Bahamas)			926 (Granada)	6.1 (Nicaragua)
Low	25 (Guatemala)	03 (Chile)	00 (Paraguay)			405 (Uruguay)	3.8 (Uruguay)
Europe and North America							
Mean	61	14	03		78	397	3.3
High	74 (Bulgaria)	20 (G. Dem. Rep.)	05 (Monaco)			830 (Albania)	4.0 (Malta)
Low	49 (Malta)	10 (Malta)	01 (Canada)			150 (Monaco)	2.5 (G. Dem. Rep.)
World Mean	62	11	03		78	635	4.3

SOURCE: Data from Boulding, Nuss, Carson, and Greenstein (1976).
*Number of children under 5 years of age per 1,000 females aged 15-49.

recent years in food research. One of the tragedies being played out in third world countries today revolves around the painful and costly campaign to undo the results of earlier western propaganda for bottle feeding and use of skim milk powder for infants, which has led many third world women to give up breast-feeding in order to be "modern."

The need for a woman to provide lactation, prepare for infants transition foods that ready the children for eating regular food, and at the same time to prepare the standard adult fare, puts her in the situation during her childbearing years of providing three types of meals concurrently. The amount of physical effort this requires in most parts of the world is much underestimated in industrial societies. In addition to this triple daily menu comes the extra work of preparing feast-day meals. No society is without relatively frequent occasions for feasting. Ironically, the food-preparing sex is also the sex that in every society follows a cultural mandate of placing more food on the plates of men and boys than on the plates of herself and her daughters. Women seem to be biologically programmed to endure a heavy workload, child-bearing, and lactation on a minimum of food, since it has been found that during times of famine fewer women die than men (Mayer, 1975: 572). Women's bodies evidently can utilize food more efficiently—probably a genetic feature that ensures successful procreation in times of food shortages.

This analysis, based chiefly on traditional role conceptions, does not take adequate account of variant households, communal or otherwise, and of slight increases in the involvement of men in the cooking and serving of food in some western countries. As yet these alternative patterns are carried out by only a very tiny minority even in the Western world, but it should be borne in mind that future food preparation and feeding roles may be patterned very differently from present ones.

The three-fourths or so of women in every society who are engaged in feeding its households is a critical percentage to bear in mind when considering the nutrition of any population. Decisions about diet, procurement of food and food preparation, manner of serving, and actual quantitative allocation of food (however culturally constrained) rest in the hands of these women. There are variations—in Muslim societies men buy the food, and in some industrialized societies they are beginning to. In the public sector in the West there has always been a tiny minority of high-status male food preparers. If we want to understand the food system as a whole, however, we must remember this great female army of gardeners, purchasers, preparers, and servers of food, the gatekeepers against many of the food utilization practices scholars would like to propose. The significance of this "army," which because of its generally low social and political status everywhere in the world is never thought of as making important decisions, is precisely that its "lowly and insignificant" members are the *policy makers* in this one area—they determine the food policies of their families. Men may control purse strings and have strongly voiced food preferences, but women have degrees of freedom within the kitchen that they command nowhere else. We will return to the issue of women as food policy makers later.

Food-Related Research

With the awareness that planetary resources are limited, the western world has turned increasingly to research for clues on the optimization of limited resources. The research has focused both on plant breeding and cultivation, and on our understanding of what the human body actually needs and how to prepare food to meet those needs. Every area of science is drawn on in this research, from social science and law to engineering, as we come to understand the interrelations of all parts of the food system including the human cultures within which they operate. Educational research becomes involved, too, as we seek to understand how people learn new techniques and new values. While there is no way to estimate the number of women engaged in food-related research, it is worth looking at the numbers of women graduates from institutions of higher education trained in some of the professions from which the new types of food-related research are emerging.

The figures in Table 6.5 tell us about these womanpower resources in terms of the percentage of female graduates in certain fields for the most recent year that graduation figures are available. Several categories very relevant for our purposes are missing. There are no figures on graduates in medicine and the biological sciences. What is available, however, is at least suggestive. The figures refer to percentages of women graduates in 1968. We see women are best represented in education, where they are roughly 50 percent or more of the graduates in all regions except Africa and the Middle East. In Argentina they are 90 percent of the graduates; in the Philippines, 82 percent; in Hungary, 79 percent; in Cyprus, 77 percent. Women provide only 5 percent of engineering resources (the world mean), but with higher numbers of graduates in Bulgaria (28 percent) and Cuba (15 percent). Eight percent of Egypt's engineering graduates are women. It will be noted that the United States does not appear among the "highs" in any of these fields, being relatively backward in the training of professional women. It has the distinction of being among the world's lowest-ranking producers of women engineers along with Lebanon, at 1 percent. (It should be said that Pakistan and Belgium do worse, with figures very close to zero.) Of particular interest for this study is the fact that women provide a world average of only 11 percent of the graduates in agriculture, with a high of 40 percent and a low of 1 percent, compared to the figure on women in the agricultural sector: a world mean of 23 percent, a high of 59 percent, and a low of 1 percent (see Table 6.1). By region, the highest ranking countries in graduate training of

Table 6.5: Femaleness of Graduate Training in Selected Fields*

Regional Mean, High and Low	% Women Graduates in		
	Education	Engineering	Agriculture
Africa			
Mean	26	00	18
High	54 (S. Africa)		40 (Mal. Rep.)
Low	07 (Cameroon)		01 (Nigeria)
North Africa and Middle East			
Mean	37	04	06
High	77 (Cyprus)	08 (Egypt)	16 (Egypt)
Low	14 (Sudan)	01 (Lebanon)	01 (Iraq)
Asia			
Mean	48	02	08
High	82 (Philippines)	05 (Philippines)	18 (Sri Lanka)
Low	07 (Nepal)	00 (Pakistan)	00 (Pakistan)
Latin America			
Mean	63	04	09
High	90 (Argentina)	15 (Cuba)	32 (Cuba)
Low	22 (Haiti)	01 (Puerto Rico)	00 (Ecuador)
Europe and North America			
Mean	56	07	13
High	79 (Hungary)	28 (Bulgaria)	38 (Bulgaria)
Low	17 (Norway)	00 (Belgium)	01 (Ireland)
World Mean	49	05	11

SOURCE: Data from Boulding, Nuss, Carson, and Greenstein (1976).
*Females as a proportion of the total population in graduate training.

women agriculturalists are the Malagasy Republic, 40 percent; Bulgaria, 38 percent; Cuba, 32 percent; Sri Lanka, 18 percent; and Egypt, 16 percent.

For most regions, the range from high to low in percentage of trained women is rather great. What is suggested, however, is that in every one of the world's regions there are trained women available as a resource for further research on various aspects of the world food system.

Policy-Making and Planning

Planning with regard to food-related activities is difficult because there are competing technologies to choose from, competing models for improving food production, and, in general, a great abundance of unrelated pieces of knowledge about food, from production to distribution, which are difficult to piece together into an overview of a very complex system. While people in administrative positions are usually there because they are supposed to have gained sufficient overview of whatever system they operate in to be useful to it, very few administrators have a broad view of food systems. Because women have a good deal of special food-related knowledge, one might expect a number of women administrators in food-related enterprises; but the

Table 6.6: Index of Femaleness of Professional and Administrative Status in the Labor Force

Regional Mean, High and Low	% Women in Professional and Technical Positions	% Women in Administrative and Managerial Positions
Africa		
Mean	30	07
High	51 (Swaziland)	10 (Zambia)
Low	14 (Angola)	03 (Ghana)
North Africa and Middle East		
Mean	26	03
High	49 (Israel)	07 (Bahrein)
Low	11 (Libya)	01 (Libya)
Asia		
Mean	33	07
High	57 (Philippines)	28 (Philippines)
Low	06 (Nepal)	01 (Pakistan)
Latin America		
Mean	49	13
High	64 (Jamaica)	43 (Granada)
Low	32 (Haiti)	05 (Surinam)
Europe and North America		
Mean	42	14
High	52 (Finland)	47 (Switzerland)
Low	32 (Switzerland)	04 (Netherlands)
World Mean	38	10

SOURCE: Boulding, Nuss, Carson, and Greenstein (1976).
*Females as a proportion of the total population in the professional and administrative status in the labor force.

general tendency against women being in significant policy-making positions works against this projection. Women may indeed arrive at the lower range of administration, but there they remain. The figures in Table 6.6 show the percentages of both professionally trained women and women administrators. The figures on women professionals consist for the most part of women teachers, but all the other professionally trained women are also lumped together in this category. The much lower figures in the second column, women administrators, must be even further qualified by pointing out that these figures are not reflective of high administrative posts for women, but of the extent to which they manage to get far enough up the ladder even to be classified as administrative and managerial workers. The record is not impressive, with regional means ranging from 3 to 14 percent, with a world mean of 10 percent. Of those women who are in administration, it is doubtful that more than a handful have anything to do with food policies.

General Community Education

Undergirding any kind of food policies must be a continuous process of community education that channels new perceptions and new behavioral alternatives to people in ways that will make possible modification of existing practices when they are wasteful or detrimental to productivity or health. Effective education and actual behavior change are always local. Regardless of what other community workers there are in a locality, the influence of the primary and secondary school teachers will always be very important in developing new attitudes (or resisting them). The first, and often the only, nontraditional information that children get about food habits is in primary school. This is also where attitudes, positive or negative, about farming as a way of life, are reinforced. It is therefore worth noting, as we see in Table 6.7, that women do a great deal of the world's education of small children, with regional means ranging from one-fourth to three-fourths women teachers in primary school, and a world mean of just under 50 percent. The tremendous involvement of women in primary level education recedes substantially at the secondary school level, with women teachers from 22 percent to 45 percent

Table 6.7: Index of Femaleness of the Teaching Profession at First and Second Levels of Education*

Regional Mean, High and Low	% Women of All First Level Teachers	% Women of All Second Level Teachers
Africa		
Mean	28.51	29.27
High	72 (Swaziland)	55 (Senegal)
Low	4 (Chad)	12 (Somalia)
North Africa and Middle East		
Mean	32.76	28.11
High	68 (Israel)	46 (Israel)
Low	2 (Yemen)	11 (Libya)
Asia		
Mean	42.96	22.55
High	79 (Philippines)	56 (Philippines)
Low	3 (Nepal)	4 (Nepal)
Latin America		
Mean	73.52	45.44
High	95 (Brazil)	62 (Bolivia)
Low	55 (Guyana)	24 (Guatemala)
Europe and North America		
Mean	63.06	41.89
High	89 (Portugal)	59 (Monaco)
Low	29 (Liechtenstein)	23 (Netherlands)
World Mean	48.31	35.19

SOURCE: Boulding, Nuss, Carson, and Greenstein (1976).
*Females as a proportion of the total population in teaching professions.

of all teachers, and with a world mean of just over one-third. Nevertheless, this is still very substantial participation by women in education. Although the status of teachers is not what it once was in the industrialized world, the role model effect of the teacher in most parts of the world is still an important one. This means that community change efforts relating to food production and consumption need consciously to include teachers—and these teachers are mostly women.

Summary of the Participation of Women in Food Systems

Table 6.8 summarizes the participation of women in the various food-related processes as identified in labor force statistics. The world means as well as the world highs and lows for the participation of women are given for each activity. If we look at the world means alone we see that women provide from one-quarter to one-half the labor force in each activity except transport at one extreme and administrative and decision-making roles at the other extreme. Looking at the "highs" we see up to 90 percent involvement in some countries in some of these productive functions. The "lows" appear to reflect as little as zero involvement. The general invisibility of women to administrators and enumerators insures the likelihood of underreporting rather than

Table 6.8: World Summary of The Femaleness of Food Systems-Related Occupations, Industries and Training*

Category	World Mean	World High	World Low
World Labor Force	29	54	04
Agriculture	23	59	00
Manufacturing	25	74	00
Transportation, Storage, and Communication Industry	08	24	00
Service Workers	50	88	06
Financing, Insurance, Real Estate and Business Services, and Community, Social, and Personal Services	41	75	04
Trade, Restaurant and Hotel Industries	31	88	01
Professional and Technical Work	38	64	06
Administrative and Managerial Work	10	47	01
Teachers: Elementary	51		
Secondary	37		
Women Graduates in: Education	49	90	07
Engineering	05	28	00
Agriculture	11	40	01

SOURCE: Boulding, Nuss, Carson, and Greenstein (1976).
*Females as a proportion of the total population in that industry, occupation or training.

overreporting of the participation of women, and most of the "lows," reflect underreporting, unpaid female family labor, or both.

The extent of participation of women in labor force activities outside the household is substantial. This is particularly striking in light of the fact that women workers generally carry an additional food-related workload at home after hours. Many of the resistances to innovation on the part of women, bemoaned by technical assistance people, stem from the sheer weight of this double workload. It takes extra energy to engage in an innovative practice, even if the innovation, once mastered, is labor-saving. A better use of women at administrative and policy-making levels in each of the activity sectors described in this section, and in government itself, would lead to a more realistic assessment of change programs. This would also lead to a more realistic analysis of the needs of women workers and householders that must be met as a precondition of change. Most technical assistance programs for women are aimed at changing their food preparation and housekeeping habits and completely ignore them as farmers and workers in every sector of the food system. In consequence these programs place additional burdens on women rather than helping increase their productivity.

We will now turn from the "invisible" facts about the participation of women in the food-related work force to another, interconnected set of invisibles, the conceptual gaps in the academic disciplines dealing with food systems. These conceptual gaps stem in part from the same source as the ignorance about the participation of women: the failure of observation.

CONCEPTUAL GAPS IN FOOD-RELATED DISCIPLINES

Agricultural economics suffers from a major conceptual gap in its definitions of food production. Because only food that enters the market system is taken account of, little attention has been given to the problem of counting production for subsistence. In the first world, failure to count backyard vegetable gardens is not so serious, because in the face of overall agricultural productivity the incremental yields from background gardens are insignificant (though not to poverty-level families for whom they mean the difference between eating and not eating). In the third world, the failure to count the productivity of kitchen gardens is far more serious, because it leads to a systematic underestimation of available food for the rural poor and to planning failures because potential productivity of backyard gardens is not taken into account in agricultural planning and aid programs. Planners generally give attention only to cash crops. This cash crop filter through which technical aid experts and planners tend to view agricultural productivity prevents them from dealing with some of the underlying facts of human productivity, and causes them to ignore significant food resources.[5]

One could of course go beyond kitchen gardens and count plant food resources available through gathering activities. The knowledge of plant foods among the 250 remaining hunting and gathering societies in the world is their protection against starvation in times of famine. Who knows what the noncultivated plant food resources of the world are? For all the rhetoric about the spaceship earth, and the overcrowded planet, we have really very spotty knowledge about planetary food reserves.

Nutritional science suffers from major conceptual gaps in the understanding of the interrelationship between physiological and cultural requirements for food intake for human beings at basic survival levels. Because the science of nutrition developed in the affluent West, standards for food requirements tend to be based on an overfed and protein-fixated population's view of the necessities of life. Each revision of nutritional requirements for the human body is down from the previous estimate, and the proportion of protein required per unit of caloric intake is also being revised downward. While it has long been understood that body type and size, physical activity, climate, culturally preferred food combinations, and preparation styles all interact in determining adequacy of nutrition, this knowledge has yet to be conceptualized in terms of minimum food needs (Poleman, 1975: 510-512). Also nutritionists have been slow to develop the concept of maximum nutritional tolerance, although the problems of obesity and alcoholism (another form of overeating) are increasingly well understood. Most overeating is cultural; people have no idea when they have exceeded the limits of the body's capacity to utilize food. When we have a more accurate picture of basic nutritional needs and of the extent of overeating in the West, we can deal more intelligently with problems of production, distribution, and consumption of food[6] in the first and second as well as the third worlds.

Another conceptual gap lies in the domain between nutrition and economics, since what nutritionists know about food needs does not exist in a form that can be taken account of by economists in planning for food distribution (Dwyer and Mayer, 1975: 568).

Medical science, a far more ancient discipline than nutrition, suffers from even more severe conceptual gaps in its understanding of basic requirements for health maintenance of the mind-body system, particularly insofar as nutrition affects such health maintenance. In fact, until recently medical schools gave no training in nutrition to their students. Although it is generally recognized that malnutrition renders a body more susceptible to all kinds of infection, there is still a tendency to pay more attention to prevention of diseases than to preventive nutrition. In general, the technical aid subculture operates in such a way that economists and planners turn to doctors rather than to nutritionists for information about third world diseases, although the nutritionists have the most knowledge about deficiency-related diseases

(Latham, 1975: 564-565; Dwyer and Mayer, 1975: 568). There is an urgent need for the development of medical research in the field of preventive nutrition.

Among notable conceptual gaps in *agricultural science* is the deep gulf between traditional knowledge in third world areas about treatment of soil, crop combinations, and long-run planting cycles (some so-called primitive agriculturalists work with ten-year planting cycles in precarious, difficult-to-work soils) and the soils laboratory knowledge of the West. This gap cannot be closed until western agricultural experts develop a pattern of "going to school," with local farmers as their teachers in areas where the experts have been called in to work.[7] I do not know whether the conceptual gap between the most sophisticated laboratory specialists and the intermediate technology proponents in agricultural planning is widening or narrowing at present (Brown and Pariser, 1975: 589-593, are inconclusive about this). Fossil fuel shortages may hasten the narrowing of the gap. It is not clear how much of a redefinition of development processes will be required to give priority to simple, nontechnical approaches to increasing agricultural productivity. What is clear is that western agricultural experts have been responsible for some serious agricultural disasters in the third world as a result of introduction of types of plants, fertilizers, irrigation techniques, and patterns of cultivation inappropriate to local conditions (see, for example, the case histories described in Borgstrom, 1973).

SEGREGATION OF WOMEN AS PART OF THE KNOWLEDGE GAP PROBLEM

Each of the knowledge gaps mentioned above points (to a greater or lesser extent) to the fifth world terrain—the terrain of women. At a very basic level, taking account of relevant observational material in order to improve production systems whether in the farmer's field, the human body, the factory, the laboratory, or the household, requires knowledgeable informants. Just as anthropology has taken a step forward in its understanding of social systems through the involvement in field work of women anthropologists who have been able to observe women's functioning in the social system on terrain closed to men, so development science will take a step forward when women sensitized to terrains not noticed by men (though not necessarily closed to them) work side by side with men as researchers, planners, technical assistance resource experts, and community developers. In third world and socialist countries, the recent increases in agricultural training for women represent a belated recognition of the long-ignored role of women in farming. Some women nutritionists are trying to break down the barriers between their field and the two related fields of agricultural economics and medicine, because their work experience leads them to see connections missed by male planners.

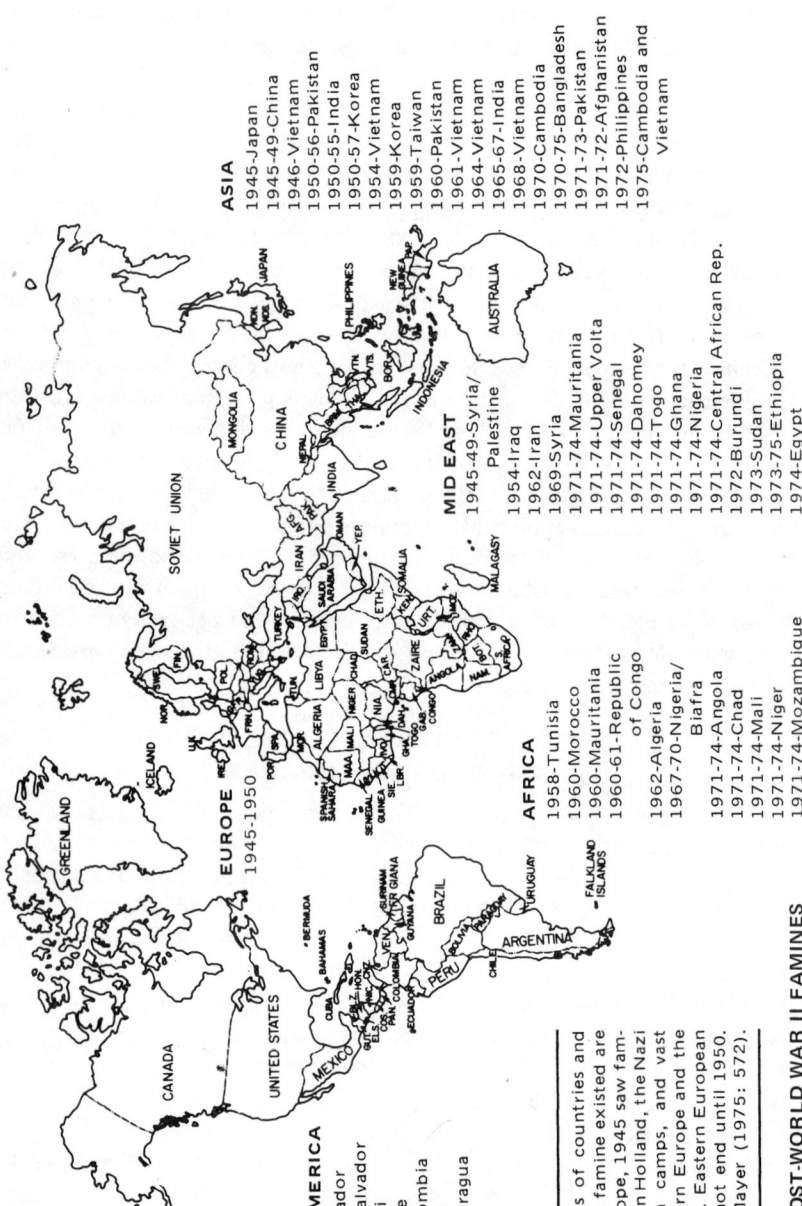

LATIN AMERICA

1949-Ecuador
1951-El Salvador
1954-Haiti
1960-Chile
1967-Colombia
1970-Peru
1972-Nicaragua

The names of countries and years where a famine existed are listed. In Europe, 1945 saw famines in western Holland, the Nazi concentration camps, and vast areas in eastern Europe and the Soviet Union. Eastern European famines did not end until 1950. Source: Mayer (1975: 572).

AFRICA

1958-Tunisia
1960-Morocco
1960-Mauritania
1960-61-Republic of Congo
1962-Algeria
1967-70-Nigeria/Biafra
1971-74-Angola
1971-74-Chad
1971-74-Mali
1971-74-Niger
1971-74-Mozambique
1971-74-Mauritania
1971-74-Upper Volta
1971-74-Senegal
1971-74-Dahomey
1971-74-Togo
1971-74-Ghana
1971-74-Nigeria
1971-74-Central African Rep.
1972-Burundi
1973-Sudan
1973-75-Ethiopia
1974-Egypt

MID EAST

1945-49-Syria/Palestine
1954-Iraq
1962-Iran
1969-Syria

ASIA

1945-Japan
1945-49-China
1946-Vietnam
1950-56-Pakistan
1950-55-India
1950-57-Korea
1954-Vietnam
1959-Korea
1959-Taiwan
1960-Pakistan
1961-Vietnam
1964-Vietnam
1965-67-India
1968-Vietnam
1970-Cambodia
1970-75-Bangladesh
1971-73-Pakistan
1971-72-Afghanistan
1972-Philippines
1975-Cambodia and Vietnam

Figure 6.1: POST-WORLD WAR II FAMINES

Because of the generally low status of women in planning systems, these efforts may not be recognized for a long time.

In the meantime, development experts project disaster or plenty, depending on their mode of analysis. The doomsday people see things too grimly, overestimating the problem because on the one hand they underestimate food resources available in the third world and on the other hand they overestimate human food requirements.

The optimists see problems as more manipulable than they are in reality. They overestimate what planning and new technologies can do, through ignorance of how poverty systems prevent redistribution of resources from rich to poor farmers, and they underestimate the obstacles of conservatism that stem from the severe work overload of women.

Both groups ignore the bulk of third world poverty-level food producers, because both live insulated from the realities of the systems of shortages which define third world existence. The euphoria of modernization theory has also insulated them from the historical perspectives that recognize recurring shortages as a regular feature of the human experience even in the twentieth century. Figure 6.1 reflects a much more recurrent picture of famine as a regular feature of the human experience over the past thirty-five years than most development experts acknowledge. Several authors in the *Science* "Food" issue (1975) comment on the short memories of both farmers and agricultural experts in the United States, whose lapses made a major disaster of the 1972-1974 crop failures. Thompson (1975: 535) claims that the weather was "discovered" in the United States in 1974. A memory reaching back no farther than the dust bowl era of the thirties, which occurred in the lifetime of many of today's planners, could have rendered accessible knowledge of weather cycle patterns that can produce planning to buffer crop failures. And even if human memory failed, information is all there in the records. As this is being rewritten in March 1976, local newspapers in the Rocky Mountain states are carrying warnings of a return to dust bowl conditions because of drought and of farmers' failure to continue preventive measures taught them during the thirties to hold soil down during drought periods.

Why have we developed such short memories in the 1970s? The institution of food bank for lean times, carefully practiced by the ancient Chinese, Egyptians, Sumerians, Aztecs, and countless other peoples, has been bitterly resisted by affluent Americans in the twentieth century just at the point at which it has become technically feasible to maintain a world food bank. Plans for such a bank have existed since World War II when Europe and the Americas shared a common food supply during war-incurred shortages. Misplaced nationalism and insulation from the realities of shortages on the part of male decision makers and the "haves" in the affluent countries have led to repeated rejections of these plans.[8]

The world as a common household is a necessary image to work with in developing any kind of world food sharing. The household is the source of the concepts economists have developed in the new subdiscipline of the Grants Economy. In more complex societies one-way transfers (which economists define as "grants") take place in all kinds of ways, but the prototype of the one-way transfer is the grant within the household to members of the kinship group. Because the term *grant* loses the sense of immediacy which the term *household* captures, and dulls the mind with thoughts of largesse from foundations, there is some value in keeping the household image in analysis of food systems. That image is unfortunately linked in people's minds with women, housework, and a general lack of sophistication about the "real" problems of the world. Admittedly, there are serious conceptual difficulties in translating that image into a decentralist world food sharing model. Grants economists should certainly help with that translation process. It would nevertheless be important to seat among the economists and planners a set of experts who work with that image in their daily lives and also have the technical knowledge required to do some experiments in translation at the international level: women with development training.[9]

The world food bank is not a panacea, any more than the green revolution was. It can, however, buy time while we work on the harder problems of how to divert unreasonable surpluses away from the rich and toward the poor in every country, in the form of resources the poor can use to make their own labor more productive. These are political and economic as well as technical problems, but more than that, they are *human* problems. Along with all the necessary macro level analysis, the household image will be needed—the image that humanizes social problem-solving.

The household image rules out among other things the strategy of triage—deciding in a disaster which victims could survive with help, and then throwing the others out to die.[10] Triage has been a very popular concept in some U.S. circles with regard to food policy, but it is based on an image of a planet that has large resource reserves roped off and marked FOR AMERICANS ONLY. The world food bank represents the household approach with a very careful examination of what is in the cupboard. We are very far from the point at which the first world would feel any severe pinching due to moderation of consumption patterns.[11]

The household image is out of fashion in contemporary radical analysis, especially in the women's movement, because of the association of the household with the concept of an exploitatively organized nuclear family that places excessive work burdens on women. Households can be organized in various ways. A commune is also a household. What is important about a household is that people take responsibility for each other over time, and that special individual needs are met for both children and adults in ways that no public institutional surrogates, important as they are, can manage. It is precisely this individuating aspect of the household image that is most urgently needed in systems planning, in order that we be continually reminded of human variation.

General systems analysis will become more adequate when a richer imagery enters into the modeling process. The societal food system needs to be seen as the frame for much of the ritual life of a society, and for its music, dance, and poetry. Every major symbolic act of a human community is patterned in part by local abundances and scarcities of food. Ritual eating and drinking based on food availability provide the cultural punctuation for all important events, whether in the public sphere of economic, political, and religious life, or in the personal spaces of family life. Art and ceremonials are inseparable from feasting in the human experience. Interestingly, in every society religious experience patterns both fasting and feasting, and self-denial, and celebration, thus unifying the experiences of deprivation and of abundance. It also patterns planting and harvesting, bringing together the experiences of giving and receiving. Techniques for dealing with food shortages are as much a part of the food system as are food production, preservation, and everyday and ceremonial consumption.

On a more mundane level, drawing on domestic household experience provides a good model for identifying wastage components of food systems. Women who are homemakers in industrialized societies are more conscious than men of the micro-food system that moves from garden or grocery store to table and mouth, and they can identify wastage points in preparation, serving, consumption, and storage. They can also identify idiosyncratic human habits, their own and those of their families, that lead to wastage. It would be interesting to see more women work on "seed to mouth" wastage systems on the micro level.

The miracle is that any food gets to human mouths at all. Tabulating various estimates on food wastage, from various sources, we note the following:

Sources of Food Wastage[1,2]

50%	Rodents	10%	Insects
15%	Milling process	15%	Storage and transit
15%	Cows, birds, monkeys		*Total = 105%*

All this before packaging! Estimate an additional 50 percent food loss through packaging for items commercially processed, and a minimum of 15 percent further loss from the moment of purchase to the moment of consumption, and we come up with the absurd figure of 175 percent food wastage, or a net loss of almost twice as much food as grows in the ground in the first place!

These figures are nonsense, of course, because I have taken wastage estimates from different culture regions, different environmental conditions, and different types of food products, and added them all together. But the very fact that food loss estimates of these dimensions in various settings and for various parts of the food system exist at all is a sobering reminder of the extent of the problem involved in minimizing food wastage. None of these wastage sources is completely eliminable, but all of them are amenable to substantial control. Each calls for a complex of suitable technologies and appropriate human habits in dealing with the source of waste. Macro-system analysis is only the beginning of dealing with the wastage problem. Classes in nutrition and food preparation are the tiniest of links in the waste chain. Who will put it all together?

The wastage chain is of course only a small part of the total food system. Each of the many occupations, industries, and types of training enumerated in Tables 6.1-6.8 of this chapter, and others not mentioned, make up parts of the food system. Any person experiences that system very selectively. Women, however, experience more parts of the system than is generally recognized, and therefore have insights about it that go unutilized because of their social invisibility.

Systems analysis tends to be chilly and abstract. I have suggested that women can assist in putting back into the world food model the dimensions of cultural richness, enhancing both its relevance and its analytic power. I have also suggested that women can assist with identifying isomorphisms between systems models and empirical features of real-life food systems, including work sites and wastage points. The fact, however, that women may help to humanize and concretize food systems analysis is a historical accident deriving from a long sequence of events dating back to the neolithic, and has nothing to do with feminine mystique or gender-linked capabilities.

Neither women nor men have gender-linked skills that uniquely qualify them to deal with the problems either of world hunger or of large-scale planning. They do have culturally differentiated life experiences—a phenomenon that may not continue into the twenty-first century, but one that we must consciously utilize as long as it exists. It is precisely in using these differentiated knowledge stocks by putting women and men into collaborative teams for social problem-solving that the absurd and useless aspects of that differentiation will gradually undergo erosion in the future. By the twenty-first century social problem-solving should no longer require elaborate identification of the sex composition of work teams. In the late twentieth century, however, conscious attention to this problem is an absolute necessity.

Table 6.9: Resolution VIII

Women and Food

The World Food Conference,

Considering that the major part of the required increase in food production must occur in the developing countries if the present tragedy of starvation and malnutrition for uncounted millions is not to continue,

Recognizing that rural women in the developing world account for at least fifty percent of food production,

Knowing that women everywhere generally play the major role in procurement and preparation of food consumed by their families,

Recognizing the important role of the mother in the health development of the future generation through proper lactation and furthermore that mothers in most cultures are the best source of food for their very young children,

Reaffirming the importance of the World Health Assembly resolution on lactation in May this year,

1. *Calls on* all governments to involve women fully in the decision-making machinery for food production and nutrition policies as part of total development strategy;

2. *Calls on* all governments to provide to women in law and fact the right to full access to all medical and social services, particularly special nutritious food for mothers and means to space their children to allow maximum lactation, as well as education and information essential to the nurture and growth of mentally and physically healthy children;

3. *Calls on* all governments to include in their plan provision for education and training for women on equal basis with men in food production and agriculture technology, marketing and distribution techniques, as well as consumer, credit and nutrition information;

4. *Calls on* all governments to promote equal rights and responsibilities for men and women in order that the energy, talent and ability of women can be fully utilized in pertnership with men in the battle against world hunger.

NOTE: Extracted from the Report of the World Food Conference (E/5587), 1974.

NOTES

1. Territorial units with a population of less than 500,000 have been excluded from the original UN listing of 216 countries and territorial units.

2. The percentage of not economically homemakers is a percentage of *all* females of all ages not counted in the labor force. The total N from which the percentage is derived thus includes babies and children. How the figure is arrived at for that percentage of women not in the labor force who are actually homemakers is not entirely clear. The non-homemakers include children, students, the elderly, the chronically ill, young women at home before entering marriage, and others in permanently dependent roles not seeking employment and also not taking primary responsibility for a home. Except for students, they may in fact be a very productive group domestically, given much of the household work to do without having the status of either homemaker or employed person.

3. Very few marriages are reported under age fifteen since the legal age for marriage is fifteen or above for most countries.

4. In Chapters 3 and 5, I have emphasized a different figure—the 35 to 40 percent of women who at any one time are unpartnered and may have household responsibilities without male assistance. The unpartnered figure comes from adding the singles and the once-married. The reason for adding the once-married to the married in this chapter is to arrive at an estimate of the number of women who are most likely to have children and other adults to care for.

5. The World Bank does now have under way a major program of identifying the problems and needs of the poorest third world farmers. Whether this will lead to better enumeration of existing food supplies remains to be seen.

6. Overconsumption of grain in the form of alcohol is in some ways a more serious problem because drinking habits are generally unrelated to food needs, particularly for the West, and not easily amenable to change.

7. It would be interesting to study the success in closing this gap among agricultural scientists and government planners in China, after several years of going from laboratory and office to tilling the soil according to the ideological mandate of going to the people.

8. The world food bank has never been conceived by planners as a first-world giveaway. This would be a poor approach from every point of view including that of the third world. Rather what is conceived is a series of national and regional food banks linked into a world system. Whether a given country is storing imported or homegrown crops in its banks is not so important as the fact that every country would take responsibility for holding buffer stocks, to be redistributed through the world system according to agreed upon priorities when acute food crises develop. Contributions of food-exporting countries to such a bank would naturally be far greater than contributions from food-importing countries, but responsibilities would be shared in appropriate ways. The Rome World Food Conference represents the most recent effort to gain acceptance for the world food bank idea and it remains to be seen whether political objections to the project can be overcome. The Programme of Action that came out of the conference is lamentably vague on details, but it does specify an 'International Undertaking on World Food Security' as the action arm of a World Food Authority (document adopted in Rome, November 16, 1974, approved by the General Assembly, December 17, 1974).

9. Unfortunately women can easily be trained to the same blindnesses that men have, so the same care is needed in identifying trained women who have retained their powers of observation of the fifth world as is needed in developing these powers in men.

10. The concept is somewhat more complicated than this, but not much. For a well-known application to food problems, read Paddock and Paddock (1967).

11. Borgstrom paints a vivid picture of how the third world exports its food, feed, and other agricultural products to the first world (up to nine-tenths of third world exports fall in these categories) while its own people go hungry. A well-fed United States and England are the two worlds' largest importers of protein (in the United States, much of this is fish protein for pet food), while the third world sends out its badly needed oilseeds, fats, and fish. The western world imports one-half of all beans and peas, more than one-half the wheat, three-fourths of the corn, three-fifths of the soybeans, nine-tenths of the peanuts, and three-fourths of the oilseed cake from the rest of the world market. Much of this comes from the third world (Borgstrom, 1973). At the same time nearly 80 percent of the grain produced in the United States is fed to animals, and non-food use of fertilizer in the United States alone is estimated by some to be enough to meet the fertilizer shortfall in a hundred developing countries (Planetary Citizens, 1975). Reversing these resource flows involves the politics as well as the economics of hunger. More than image-making will be required, and yet images are important.

12. These estimates are quoted in Brown (1970).

PART III

WOMEN AND THE INTERNATIONAL SYSTEM

If it is difficult to grasp the multidimensionality of women's roles in national development processes, hidden as they often are from the public eye, it is even more difficult to articulate and make visible the roles of women in developing and maintaining a just and peaceful world order, to capture their activities in the spheres of conflict regulation and resource distribution at the level of the international system. They do, however, play such roles, although this is the least well-developed aspect of women's participation in the twentieth century. In this section we will explore what the war-peace and redistribution roles of women actually are, how effectively they are able to function in these roles, and what needs to happen to enable women as individuals, as members and creators of all-women's groups, and as partners with male colleagues, to realize their full potential as citizens of the planet. This involves an examination both of the traditional roles of women as family and community peacemakers and breeders of soldiers, and of the new roles which women have created for themselves under the conditions of the past two centuries of increasing disparities between East and West, North and South. Their roles as professionals and volunteers in the world community, and the organizations which they have shaped to their purposes in the absence of adequate participatory opportunities in public international structures, will receive special attention. The policy implications of this section are not as clear-cut as those of the previous section, but they are nevertheless present and will be discerned by readers presently active in world affairs.

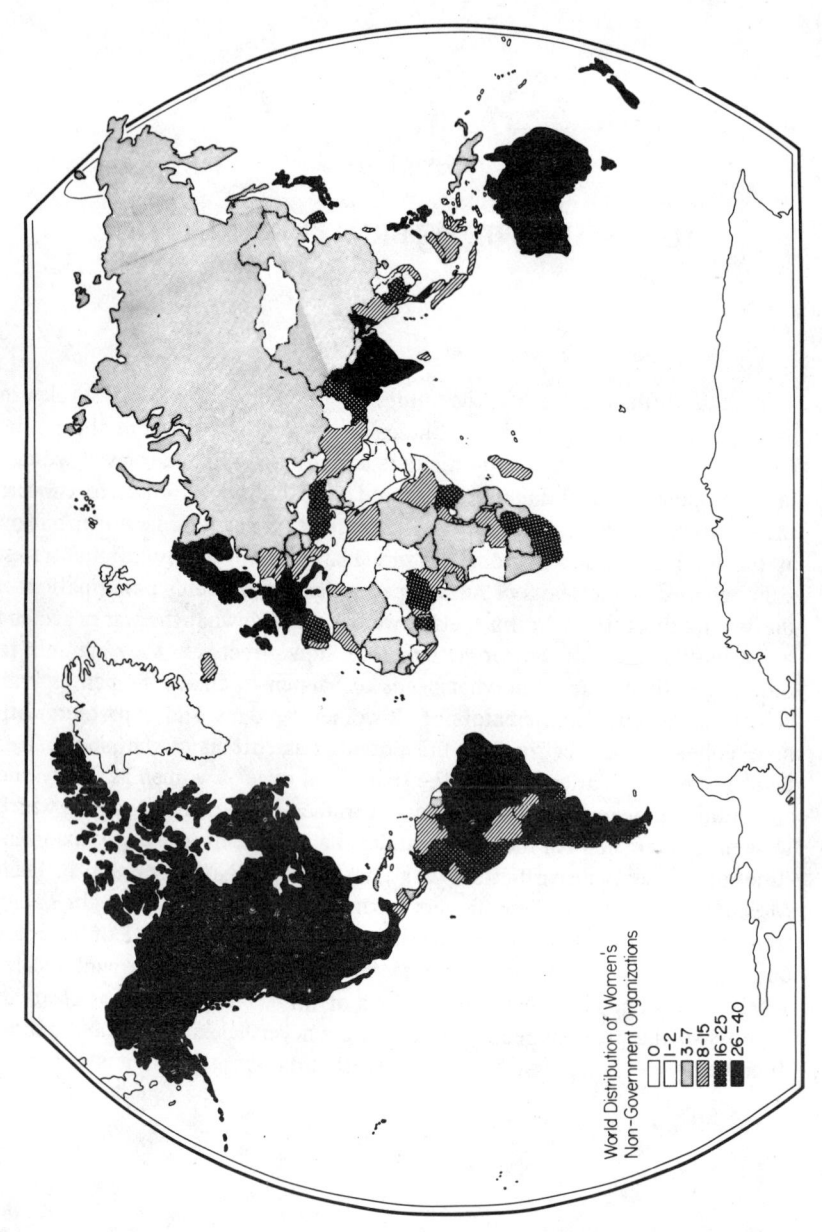

Chapter 7

WOMEN AND PEACE WORK

Women's peace and world order roles have traditionally been of two kinds. On the one hand it has been the woman's task to rear soldiers and to fight on the battlefield herself when needed. On the other hand she has symbolized the gentler arts of peace and nurturance and has struggled to counteract the effects of militarism in ways appropriate to her situation. Women have thus always been involved in both the defense systems and the nurturance systems of every society. The image of the fifth world—the invisible continent of women—as consisting of that set of spaces in society where the capacity for love, relationship, and wholeness is undividedly fostered in children and reinforced in adults, is in one sense profoundly false. Society has hung a distorting mirror over every hearth.

Because most treatments of "the woman as peacemaker" emphasize her nurturance roles in the family, it is necessary to point out the relationship between family life and militarism. Very rarely do women rear their sons to counteract militarism, except in deviant pacifist subcultures. A study of conscientious objectors in the United States during World War II showed that many of their mothers, particularly those outside the historic peace churches, opposed their taking the pacifist position. This means that a great deal of the nurturance practiced by women is an enabling device to make existing societal defense systems work. In one sense women prepare children and men for lifelong combat, whether in the occupational sphere, the civic arena, or the military battlefield.

The emphasis on peacemaking as inherent in the woman's familial role misleads us twice over. Not only is the role of mother two-edged, but also from one-third to one-half of women in any given historical era do not live

Author's Note: Paper prepared for the International Workshop on Changing Sex Roles in Family and Society, Dubrovnik, Yugoslavia, June 16-21, 1975.

out what we consider "typical" familial roles, as pointed out in previous chapters. While unpartnered women are also coopted into the general process of performing nurturance roles, they stand outside male-dominated systems to an extent that partnered women do not. They may be an important unrecognized resource for alternative approaches to peacemaking.

While I have emphasized the enabling role women generally play in relation to militarism, it is also true that women are far more subject than men to role conflict relating to peacemaking processes. Opposing functions are in fact required of them. This chapter will deal with the historical dilemma of women as they have struggled with their opposing roles, with a particular focus on how they have worked to redefine the nurturant role on behalf of a different and less combative social order. After a brief historical review we will look at the options for women today in dealing with the twentieth century versions of the old dilemma.

PEACE ROLES FOR WOMEN THROUGH HISTORY[1]

The Ancient Peace Roles

Women have dealt with the oppressiveness of combat structures in two ways: by noncompliance, as in the *Lysistrata* from ancient Greece, or by attempting to soften the edges of the social hurt by promoting public structures of nurturance. Noncompliance as in the women's protest movements, is recurrent but sporadic throughout history, and it rarely effects institutional change. The public-structures-of-nurturance approach has been continuous since the beginning of urban life. It involves the extension of the intimate services of the hearth into the public sphere through hospitals, orphanages, and food distribution centers. Women's involvement with schools originated as an extension of orphanage work. Working with and without men, women have provided the resources, the social organization, and the volunteer labor for "works of mercy." In the first great empires of the Mediterranean the princess-priestess operated from her base in the palace-temple compound, while the slave woman operated from her crowded dormitory quarters somewhere in the city. Both were part of a redistribution system which male administrators counted on.

One could argue that the whole blood and thunder saga of the human enterprise since, say, 4000 B.C. has depended on this type of redistribution system. Being operated by women, society's breeders, it operated from the underside of history. It operated in part from palaces, in part from the homes of the artisan and the quarters of the slave, in part from the convent networks created by women in Hindu, Buddhist, Christian, and Muslim societies. Every conquest empire depended heavily on the skills of its women in developing redistribution structures to prevent social collapse.

The Industrial Revolution and New Conceptions of Society

The work of creating and maintaining these public structures of nurturance and their private counterparts for most women paralleled their other responsibilities of domestic maintenance and economic production. Only for the aristocracy could public nurturance be a full-time activity. With the coming of the industrial revolution, the hitherto small group of underemployed middle class urban women expanded rapidly. As the new class of nonproductive women multiplied, a new view of the world took shape for them. From an attitude of open-mouthed wonder about faraway places, women rather quickly shifted to a comprehension of continents linked by trade routes and busy slave ships. As a result they were plunged into the challenges of internationalism about 150 years ago. While statesmen and revolutionaries were locked in struggles for national independence, and merchants mined Africa for the new gold—black human gold—and colonists staked out claims for God and king, women were feeling the pull of quite a different current. This other current was internationalism, which might be thought of as the undertow of nationalism and imperialist expansion. It pulled them in the opposite direction from the rest of society. Not only women, of course, felt this undertow. But because even the most imaginative of men were accustomed to leadership roles, and did not know how to accept women as collaborators, many of the women who felt this undertow were driven to seek each other out and form their own groups.

This phenomenon deserves a lot of attention because it represents a significant change in the scale and complexity of the social systems with which women were dealing. Their redistribution roles were no longer exclusively at the service of their own local or national society. Whether they were concerned with slavery, economic oppression of workers, or wars of conquest, they were beginning to think in terms of global systems rather than national welfare.

The new internationalism. Between 1820 and 1830, the first all-women national peace societies were founded in England and America, and by 1852 the Olive Leaf Circles were issuing the first international women's publication, *Sisterly Voices*. Women were also involved in the birth of the international labor movement. In 1840 the French-Peruvian Flora Tristan Moscosa, at home on two continents, traveled around the world promoting her plan for a world-wide workers' international. Her plan was spelled out in her book, *L'Union Ouvrière,* published in 1843. The first Voix des Femmes, predecessor of the Canadian peace organization of that name formed in the 1960s, was born as a socialist movement in Paris in the 1840s. By the time of the establishment of the short-lived Paris Commune in 1871 many women had apprenticed themselves to the new internationalism. When Louise Michel broke into the bakeries of Lyons in 1882 to redistribute bread to the poor, she was bridging the gap between the housewives who rioted for bread in the 1700s, and the creators of the new socialist-anarchist vision of a post-imperial society. By the 1880s and 1890s, the vision of an international socialist community based on nonviolence and the repudiation of nationalism was being articulated by Clara Zetkin and Rosa Luxembourg. These two women were only the most visible members of a large sisterhood that determinedly fought the nationalist chauvinism of the majority of their male colleagues in the socialist movement. They fought, and lost. Spiritual and socialist visions intertwined in the work of women like Elise van Calcar of the Netherlands, and Annie Besant and Olive Schreiner of England.

Groups of women sprang up all over Europe throughout the second half of the nineteenth century, women moving to a different rhythm from that of the military drumbeats to be heard everywhere. Among them were Concepcion Arenal in Spain, Frederika Bremer, Rosalie Olivecrone, and the controversial Ellen Key, all of Sweden, and Beatrice Webb and Octavia Hill in England. Frederika Bremer was the first to propose an international association of women for peace. Priscilla Peckover, an English Quaker, built up an international network of women with members in France, the Rhineland, Hanover, Rome, Warsaw, Constantinople, Russia, Japan, Polynesia, Portugal, and the United States (Stanton, 1970; Posthumus-van der Goot, 1961).

Austrian Bertha Sutner, author of one of the century's major works on disarmament, *Die Waffen Nieder* (Down with Arms) (1894), persuaded Alfred Nobel to found a peace prize. Jane Addams[2] of the United States helped convene a group of women at the Hague during World War I, a group which could continue and would provide both the moral conscience and the scholarly know-how to create alternative institutions to war as an instrument of national diplomacy. Frances Willard,[3] also of the United States, was an eloquent spokesperson for the new world view of women:

> We are a world republic of women—without distinction of race or color—who recognize no sectarianism in politics, no sex in citizenship. Each of us is as much a part of the world's union as is any other woman; it is our great, growing, beautiful home [Gordon, 1924: 69].

These women were responding to an intricate complex of issues; war, slavery, economic injustice, and the misery of the urban poor were all on their agendas. The women's rights movement developed almost incidentally, as women found civic problem-solving roles closed to them because of their sex. The new internationalism for women was not simply an extension of the older roles of creating public structures of nurturance. Something else was going on, a reconceptualization of social structures and social roles. Women were beginning to recognize their complicity in war and social injustice. They

Table 7.1: Occupations of Professional Women in the 1915 International Peace Movement

Occupation	Number
Doctor	2
Judge	1
Trade Union Movement	3
Lawyer	3
Social Work	1
Economists	4
International Relations	1
Government Officials	2
Members of Parliament	8
Physical Science	2
Education	6
Social Scientist	1
Suffragette, Public Figure	5
Total	39

SOURCE: Bussey and Tims (1965).

saw that their acceptance of traditional underside nurturance roles made the war business easier for men. Even the Florence Nightingales became politicized, and men fought against the new civic roles for women because they feared the changes that would follow.

By the early 1900s, we are struck with the high degree of professionalization and commitment to public life of the women in these international movements. Table 7.1 is a listing of occupations of professional women in one part of the 1915 international peace movement, the group that founded the Women's International League for Peace and Freedom. Between 1900 and 1915 the first three women's organizations focused primarily on international relations were born, as were five new international religious associations for women. By 1930 three more international relations groups and ten organizations for professionally specialized women had been born. All of these groups, and also the international educational associations for women founded before and after 1900, had international peace as one of their primary concerns. The international relations associations are distinct from the other groups, however, in that they focused primarily on the political institutions and processes of peace and war. Table 7.2 shows the founding dates of the ten international relations associations, and the number of national branches associated with each.

CONTEMPORARY PEACE ROLES

There is something of a hiatus between the women's peace movement as it took shape in the early part of this century and the movements involving

Table 7.2: Founding Dates for Women's NGOs Specifically Concerned with International Relations

Founding Dates and Organization	No. of Sections	Founding Dates and Organization	No. of Sections	Founding Dates and Organization	No. of Sections	Founding Dates and Organization	No. of Sections
1900-1915		1916-1930		1931-1945		1946-1970	
International Alliance of Women*	45	Associated Country Women of the World	67	Women's International Democratic Federation	97	All Africa Women's Conference	35
International Council of Social Democratic Women*	34	Pan Pacific and Southeast Asia Women's Association	14			European Union of Women	12
Women's International Alliance of Women	21	Women's International Zionist Organization	51			Federation of Asian Women's Association	11

SOURCE: **Yearbook of International Organizations, 1973** and **Yearbook of International Organizations, 1974** (Brussels: Union of International Associations, 1973 and 1974).

*The original name for IAW was International Women Suffrage Alliance, and the original name for ICSDW was International Socialist Women's Secretariat.

women activists today. The professional tradition of that earlier generation of women was buried in the back-to-the-home movement of the thirties and forties, so well described by Betty Friedan in *The Feminine Mystique* (1963). The six international relations organizations active before the thirties, and the four born since then, are all very much alive, but their organizational role is not as clear as in the earlier period. There has always been a Lysistrata component in their activities—protest and noncompliance. The public structures-of-nurturance component has also continued, for no women's organization has been willing to ignore the social suffering of the deprived. But the work of reconceptualization of society as a global system begun by women in the last century has slowed down somewhat. We will see from the figures to be presented in the following pages on women as scholars, activists, national and international public officials, and military personnel that few women have a significant opportunity to affect world peace potentials in any of these roles.

Women as Peace Researchers

Women are now moving back into the professional arena they occupied earlier. Women have been part of the post-World War II peace research movement from the beginning. This has been a social science movement to develop a body of peace-related knowledge that can substitute for military technology in handling international conflict. Table 7.3 reflects the participation of women in North America (and for one organization, the world participation of women) in this new research enterprise. The Consortium on Peace Research, Education, and Development (COPRED), and the Sociology of World

Table 7.3: Percentage Women in Professional North American Peace Research and World Order Associations, 1974

Organization	% Women
IPRA	
North American members	8
ISA	
General membership	12.4
Executive Committee, 1975	10.0
COPRED	
Council members	14
Individual members	24
Executive Committee, 1975	28
Sociology of World Conflict*	
(Section of American Sociological Associations)	

*The total membership of the American Sociological Association includes 15 percent women, and the total membership of the American Economic Association includes 6 percent women.

Conflicts groups have noticeably better participation of women, with figures ranging from 14 to 28 percent, than the International Peace Research Association (IPRA) and the International Studies Association (ISA), with figures ranging from 8 to 12 percent. The participation of women in the social sciences is generally not high. In the United States, the American Sociological Association does the best, with 15 percent women in general membership, and the American Economics Association is among the poorest, with 6 percent women in general membership. Some peace research settings, then, have been unusually open to the participation of women. Historically, the reasons for this are not unconnected with the fact that members of the Women's International League for Peace and Freedom in Scandinavia, England, Japan, India, and North America were instrumental in promoting the concept of peace research in the earliest stages of the idea. They not only promoted the concept, but they also assisted in the formation of the International Peace Research Association, of the Japanese Peace Research Society, and of the North American COPRED.

Peace research represents an important subset of peace roles for women. Societal reconstruction has to take place on the basis of knowledge, and we have far too little knowledge of planetary social systems. The scholarly world also has its limitations, however. After twenty years the findings of peace research remain modest and unattended to. Policy makers are not beating a path to the peace researcher's door. In one sense the peace research movement represents a scientific revolution, a revolution in paradigms, as Kuhn (1970) puts it. That type of shift in science takes a long time to translate into value changes in the general population, and into new policy perspectives for decision makers. (In policy terms, the scientific revolution set in motion by Copernicus in the 1500s could be said finally to have borne fruit in the creation by the United Nations in 1967-1968 of International Geophysical Year.)

Furthermore, the researcher is continually being pushed and pulled about by the pressure of the competitive academic achievement system, and by the "hard-nosed" view of what is "realistic" research on problems of peace and war. Is the woman peace researcher just engaging in a more sophisticated version of the old behavior of creating nurturant backgrounds (via "scientific" rationalizations) for public aggression? Or is she reconceptualizing the social order? A significant number of these women scholars are, in my opinion, seriously at work on the reconceptualization process. Documentation of that belongs to another study.

Women's Nongovernmental Organizations

Many women are turning back to that other set of instruments for peacemaking, the international nongovernmental organizations (NGOs), first created at the end of the last century. The potentialities and limitations of these organizations will be fully discussed in Chapters 8 and 9; thus they will be only briefly examined here.

The new women's peace organizations among the NGOs, born in the sixties, include the Voix des Femmes, Women Strike for Peace, and Another Mother for Peace. They are somewhat different in character than the older organizations discussed earlier. Responding initially to the threat to the lives of the babies of that decade through the strontium 90 fallout from nuclear testing, they began with a focus on the mother role as the basis for an international antiwar movement. Determined to remain grass-roots organizations, their international networks have stayed small and informal. They have avoided the development of an official NGO communication structure. However, they have not been able to break out of the Euro-North American mold, and their activity is only intermittently visible. They have certainly played an important part in the U.S. antiwar movement, and most of them have regular contact with Indochina. With the end of the Vietnam war and increasing international involvement in the conflicts of the Middle East and Africa, more third world women are becoming internationally active, and we may witness a decline in Eurocentrism by the end of this century.

Since international paid staffs are small or nonexistent and resources are very limited for most of these groups, both the old and the new women's NGOs are not able to serve as an effective and informed "people's presence" at international conferences on crucial topics like disarmament, the seabed, outer space, population, food, and the environment. Every one of the forty-seven organizations probably has a number of women among its members with a combination of expertise and social imagination that could bring a significant new perspective to the problems UN agencies are struggling with. The organizations have the right to make that kind of contribution; it is in fact one of the major legitimations of their existence. Yet any one organization sends its own experts to very few international meetings. Time and money to free up their experts for participation are usually lacking. So the UN and the nation-states that comprise it stay locked in their old patterns, and the women who could help them break out of those patterns stay outside. The reconceptualizing potential of women's NGOs on behalf of the international system is largely thrown away.

Women in the UN

For all its limitations, the UN itself is one of the major instruments for global change in the twentieth century. Yet the UN system itself is a very typical male stronghold, as Table 7.4 shows. There are no women in the top echelons (the new assistant secretary generalship created for International Women's Year changes this), and only 12.9 percent women overall, concentrated in lower staff levels. Women's NGOs will have to make a concerted and

Table 7.4: The Number of Women on the Professional Staff of the United Nations and Related Agencies

Organization	Number of Women at Each Professional Level*							Total of Women on Professional Staff	Total Professional Staff (Both Sexes)	% of Women on Total Professional Staff
	D-2	D-1	P-5	P-4	P-3	P-2	P-1			
United Nations	3	5	28	105	189	144	43	517	2,374	21.7
UNICEF	—	—	2	2	10	10	1	25	209	12.0
UNDP	—	2	3	4	13	17	8	47	493	9.5
ILO	—	2	2	10	63	4	40	121	640	18.9
FAO	—	—	3	41	48	60	35	189	4,073	4.6
UNESCO	—	1	20	99	50	66	23	267	1,795	14.8
WHO	—	2	9	64	189	90	33	387	1,794	21.5
IBRD	—	1	3	19	38	42	—	103	1,483	6.9
IMF	1	2	11	19	33	37	—	103	617	16.6
ICAO	—	—	—	1	7	11	1	20	222	9.0
UPU	—	—	—	—	1	—	1	2	68	2.9
ITU	—	—	—	1	8	5	3	17	143	11.8
WMO	—	—	—	1	3	2	3	9	114	7.8
IMCO	—	—	—	—	1	2	3	6	42	14.2
GATT	—	—	2	1	7	9	5	24	88	27.2
IAEA	—	—	1	3	12	12	12	40	344	11.6

SOURCE: Szalai (1973).
*Two top levels of appointment are missing from table: there is no woman Deputy Director General, and there is now one Assistant Secretary-General, Helvi Sipila.

long-enduring effort if this is to be changed. A one-year campaign focused on International Women's Year won't do the job.

But what will be the basis of their efforts? The more highly educated women become, the more effectively they are trained to operate within existing economic-political and social institutions. When women for so long have had so few rewards in the public sphere, can we expect them to toss those rewards lightly aside, in order to demonstrate the value incongruities and institutional deficiencies of the system that would reward them? Yet there is substantial scope for reconceptualization within the UN. The new secretariat established for IWY demonstrates this. In spite of the fact that International Women's Year is by far the most underfunded "major" year ever established as a program of the UN, the first woman Assistant Secretary General of the UN and her co-administrators in a reorganized program on the status of women are already making an impact beyond what was intended or anticipated when the year was approved.

WOMEN AS SOLDIERS, PROFESSIONALS, AND TOP-RANKING ADMINISTRATORS

Women in the Military

At the national level, many women are responding, understandably, to opportunities for employment and advancement within war-oriented systems. In the United States, for example, women have eagerly flocked to the new place opened up for them in the Reserve Officers Training Corps (ROTC). I know of no major anti-military service movement among women in any of the three countries in the world that conscript women: Israel, Guinea, and Mali.[4] To my knowledge, wherever military training is offered to women, it is eagerly accepted.

Some of the most remarkable liberation struggle sagas of the twentieth century are tales of women guerrilla fighters. When the accounts of the participation of women in the independence struggles of the countries of Africa and Asia (Boulding, 1969b; 1972) are combined with the accounts of participation of women in the liberation struggles currently under way, we will have a picture of the more violent aspect of women's nurturant roles—the struggle aspect—which is going to destroy a great many myths about the meekness of women. While women are usually a small minority in permanent national armies, in guerrilla and other types of underground warfare, they may reach as high as 40 percent participation levels, as in the PLAF (People's Liberation Armed Forces) in Vietnam.

The social meanings of women's roles in liberation armies are very complex. In part their presence is the age-old response of being where needed. This involves taking on exhausting workloads in field and factory as well

Table 7.5: NGOs, Military Expenditures and the Status of Women in Eleven Countries Reporting the Percentage of Women

Country	Number Women's NGOs[a]	Rank Order Women's NGOs	Number NGOs[b]	Rank Order All NGOs	% Women in Military[a]	Rank Order % Military Expenditures of GNP[c]	Rank Order GNP Per Capita[a]	% Women in Administrative Posts[a]	% Women Professionals[a]	% Women Single Widowed Divorced[a]
United Kingdom	39	1	1,238	6	4	6	18	7	38	36
France	36	2.5	1,609	1	3	8	8	21	43	41
United States	36	2.5	1,019	8	2	2	1	17	39	—
Australia	35	4	669	17	4	12	14	12	42	37
Canada	33	5	804	14	3	16	3	14	42	35
Netherlands	32	6	1,440	4	1	10	12	4	39	—
New Zealand	30	7.5	456	31	6	27	15	12	44	34
Denmark	30	7.5	946	11	1	17	7	14	51	39
Spain	20	9	871	12	2	33	34	4	33	—
Uruguay	17	10	403	36	1	50	44	5	57	41
Malaysia	13	11	241	57	0.3	49	62	2	28	—

a. Boulding Global Data Bank, Institute of Behavioral Science, University of Colorado.
b. Data from Chadwick Alger, Mershon Center, Ohio State University.
c. Data from **World Military Expenditures, 1968** (1969).

as on the battlefield. It also involves commando raids. Le Thi Rieng, who led the women's commando group that occupied the U.S. Embassy during the Tet offensive, killed two hundred U.S. personnel, and left the National Liberation Front (NLF) flag flying over the building, is a military heroine in every sence of the word. As a role model, Le Thi Rieng conveys many conflicting messages. So does Madame (General) Binh, Deputy Commander of the PLAF after her leadership in the 1960 Ben Tre uprising. So do the many heroines described in Bergman (1974). There is one underlying theme, however, that of *participation*. These women are shaping the new society of Vietnam side by side with men.

It is too early to tell whether these women will be able to maintain this equality of participation in the peacetime society to come. It is a further question (for both the women and the men) how their wartime experience will affect the quality of their peace-building skills. In Algeria women are back in the kitchen, their role in the liberation struggle forgotten. We do not know what their peace-building skills might have accomplished. World War II saw the enrolling of many women in the armed forces of the western world, and we see the faint shadow of that wartime participation of women in the far more modest contemporary figures on women in the armies of the British Commonwealth. Women are 4 percent of the armed forces in Britain and Australia, 6 percent in New Zealand. The figures are 1 to 3 percent for other European and North American armies (see Table 7.5, fifth column).

In general, participation in the military does not seem to open up other kinds of public participation for women unless other forces are also operating on behalf of their participation.

Women as High Governmental Officials

We have already seen how few positions are open to women in the UN— 12.9 percent overall—and how few of these are at the higher levels. No figures are available on the proportion of women in high governmental posts involving national and international responsibility, by country, but Table 7.5 indicates presence or absence of women in such high posts, including diplomatic posts, for ten countries that also report percentage of women in the armed forces. The countries are listed in rank order by number of women's NGOs, and the total "score" for women in high posts does bear some relationship to the number of women's NGOs. It is not a strong relationship, but it may be that the level of NGO participation of women in a country does establish a background level of international participation that makes it more probable that women will be given high public responsibility. However, it should be noted that no country reaches the maximum score of twelve, which would signify that there are women in each category of high government post. The size of the women's army bears no relationship either to women's NGOs or to the number of women in high office—a finding which will be reassuring to the women's peace movement.

The general conclusion to be drawn from an inspection of Tables 7.4 and 7.5 must be that not many women are "in the system" in responsible positions where they might affect peace potentials, either from the civil or the military side.

There is no way to judge to what extent the UN and national administrative positions filled by women offer opportunities for reconceiving and restructuring social processes. Generally women have lesser status, even in their administrative roles, and do not have the entrepreneurial freedom that women have in NGOs or in individual professions. To the extent that they humanize the settings they work in, much of their activity would come under the heading of public nurturance.

WOMEN'S RESOURCES FOR SYSTEM CHANGE AND PEACE WORK

International Rosters of Qualified Women

Systems change in contrast to systems support is difficult for isolated individuals. One of women's greatest problems is the fact that they are not only invisible to the systems in which they work, but they are also invisible to each other. This means that they cannot support each other in social change roles. In the past five years systematic efforts have been made to develop rosters of qualified women in all kinds of fields from education to medicine to development and world order. The number of able and experienced women who are being uncovered in every field is surprising everyone. Women's greatest resources lie in their own "socially hidden" skills, now being made visible. They have been working all along in the lower echelons of every type of institution. These daily-lengthening lists of trained and ready women give the lie to any attempts to say that "we cannot find qualified women."[5]

During the International Women's Year these rosters became internationalized for the first time. Women will have far more courage to work for innovations both at home and in the international system if they know they are part of an international community of women who support that kind of innovation. The contacts organized around specific problem-solving may be more durable than those organized around protest alone.

Network Skills

While women's NGOs are weak now, they will become stronger in the future as more attention is paid to network skills. A much closer collaboration between women scholars and activists is needed to develop the new networks. A hundred years ago that collaboration was much closer than it is today. Certain subnetworks now exist, as for example between socialist and nonsocialist women in Euro-North America, and between North American and Indochinese women. Perhaps nowhere is the network as effective as in Africa, where the All-African Women's Conferences has brought together seventeen women's NGOs that might not have been in touch with each other otherwise. African women's network skills go back a long way and might well be studied by Europeans. Now that contacts with all of Asia are easier in the West, there are many network skills to be learned from Asia, too. Each part of Asia from west to east has its own traditions and its own skills of social organization. They are all very different from patterns in the Americas. On all continents there will be a conflict between the more centralized and cosmopolitan "establishment" women's networks and the traditional village-level networks. It will take good listening to find the latter.

Women as New Role Models in Public Life

Another source of strength for women is in the styles they have already developed on the invisible fifth continent. They are freer, more varied, more interesting styles than the styles of the international establishment. One hears so often, from conference goers, what fun it is to have women participating in professional and public occasions—how fresh their perspectives are, how free, varied, and enjoyable their presentations and modes of interaction. Along with the variety goes the creativity, the free drawing on intuitive perceptions. This can be "professionalized" out of women. They must consciously avoid downplaying their own special styles.

Women as Futurists

The greatest strength of all for women is the strength of their commitment to a different future, and a lack of attachment to the existing international system. This strength needs to be developed; it cannot be taken for granted. As a matter of fact most women have thought, studied, and prepared themselves less for alternative futures than have many men. There are good reasons for this—there has been no support in their domestic environments for alternative futures thinking. The UNESCO time budget studies carried out in the sixties (Szalai, 1972) clearly showed that women in every one of the twelve countries studied spent less time on reading, study, and organizational work than men, in spite of the fact that there is a strong image, particularly in North America, of women doing the reading and the civic work in our communities. We are thinking of a select group, not the average woman. Women's triple role of breeder-feeder-producer insures that she has less leisure than men in every society, so it is no wonder that she has less time to read, think, and organize.

What women have is the potential for alternative thinking, but it has to be encouraged and trained, like any talent. Most futurists are men, and the narrow range of imagination shown in futures thinking reflects this. Every profession, every NGO, every community needs women futurists. In the world order field, women futurists are needed most of all, since it is here that the most radical departures from existing ways of doing things need to be visualized. The Institute for World Order, which has had a world order models program since 1967, has finally—in 1975—added women futurists, albeit at first only as commentators, to its team. There is no world order model prepared by a woman in the book series that has resulted from that program (Mendlovitz, 1975; Kothari, 1975; Falk, 1975). The lack shows, in both the style and content of the models. However, the senior author of the Club of Rome's study, *Limits to Growth,* is a remarkable woman scholar, Donella Meadows. Many, many more such women futurists are needed.

Alternative futures are the business of everyone of every age, sex, occupation, and social status, and most especially of householders, female and male. The household is one of the best places to begin experimentation with alternative ways of organizing life in terms of work, play, and consumption patterns. It is also a good place to begin freeing up the rest of the institutions of society, and the male role patterns with which they are encumbered.

The spontaneous capacity for sisterhood, the knowledge of the inner workings of neighborhoods and community life, the skills of the scientist, the scholar, the humanist, and the politician—all these belong to women. If ever there was a time to reconceive what society is about, and to create new working models of public roles to make possible behaviors that will recreate the body social, it is now. The old roles will not disappear. Nurturers will always be needed, but women are increasingly teaching men to share these roles. In the long run, the old hearth-battlefield dichotomies are better solved by teaching men to be nurturers than by teaching women to be soldiers. The public structures of nurturance, the welfare institutions of society, are no longer women's exclusive province. Nonetheless, the historic role of protest, the Lysistrata role, cannot and must not disappear. Public demonstrations can harness anguish to new social directions, but the emphasis now needs to be on the new direction, not only on the anguish.

The bold emigration of women from the invisible continent to the arenas of public life that began 150 years ago continues today. These immigrants are the teachers for a new set of social learnings about the nature of society. They are role models for new ways of working. The old continents have needed new colonists, and the new colonists are coming. They are women.

NOTES

1. Fuller descriptions of the phenomena and events referred to in this section are to be found in (Boulding (1976).
2. Jane Addams was a founder of the Women's International League for Peace and Freedom. See Addams et al. (1972).
3. Frances Willard was a founder of the Women's Christian Temperance Union. See Gordon (1924).
4. Israel does permit conscientious objection of women to military service.
5. Some examples of international rosters: the roster of women experts on development started in 1974 by Irene Tinker, Director of International Programs for the American Association for the Advancement of Science; the roster of women sociologists started by the Research Committee on Sex Roles of the International Sociological Association; the Women's International League of Peace and Freedom network; the ISIS network; the Ad Hoc Committee for the Participation of Women in the UN University; and others. National rosters are being developed by committees on the status of women in almost every American professional association at this time.

Chapter 8

NGOs AND WORLD PROBLEM-SOLVING:
A Comparison of Religious and Secular Women's NGOs

The interest in transnational actors as an additional set of participants on the world scene along with nation states, intergovernmental units, and others grows as we see the inter-nation system becoming increasingly rigid and inflexible in the face of increasing numbers of problems that can only be handled at the world level. Researchers in the field of transnationalism are dealing with emergent phenomena, with recent and fragile developments that can be regarded either as indicators of future directions in societal evolution or as pipedreams. Nongovernmental associations enabling private individuals to engage in collaborative action on behalf of world concerns across national boundaries have grown from a couple of hundred at the beginning of this century to close to three thousand in 1976. While pitifully small and poor compared to nation states, each organization is a repository for the knowledge and skills of its members, and for some modest physical resources. Optimists see them as increasingly important contributors to world problem-solving. Pessimists dismiss them as insignificant. While many studies have been made of the distribution of NGOs around the world, few have been done of their programs and organizational capacities.

This study will examine organizational subsets within the larger NGO universe, organizations that may have special properties useful for world problem-solving: (1) the religious transnational associations and (2) the forty-seven women's transnational associations. Religious transnationals have the

Author's Note: Paper prepared for the International Studies Association Comparative Interdisciplinary Studies Section INTERNET on Religion, February 1975; this article originally appeared as the lead Research Note in Volume 3, Issue 1, Spring 1976 (incorrectly identified on its cover as Volume 2, Issue 3, Spring 1976) of the *International Studies Notes.* ©1975 by the International Studies Association.

special character of being, in theory at least, ultimately rooted in local churches and parish communities, and therefore have the best potential grass-roots bases of any transnational actors. Every town and village everywhere has a church, chapel, or shrine of some kind. Most transnationals are urban-based and far removed from the needs and interests of ordinary individuals (Boulding, 1973, and Chapter 7 of this book). Religious transnationals also have a double commitment to global universalism on one hand, and to immediate personal and community responsibility on the other. Women's transnationals have the special character of being organized by the politically powerless half of the human community, those who live on society's "underside" by virtue of their culturally defined gender roles. Historically, women have had responsibility for the day-to-day immediacies of life, for human nurturance.

Religious and secular NGOs have very different histories, since the religious transnational associations have roots going back several thousand years, in the journeying made by wandering clerics, monks, and nuns from village to village and kingdom to kingdom, a phenomenon in Asia that antedates Christianity by at least 700 years. Special-purpose transnationals for persons of similar occupational, social, or cultural concerns, while they can be linked to ancient craft guilds, did not acquire global characteristics until the nineteenth century. They are an urban phenomenon, and have few grass-roots linkages.

To the extent that women participated in the nineteenth century growth of the new secular transnationals, they also participated in an urban-based set of enterprises. The women who were free to enter this sphere were frequently upper class women free of domestic responsibility and with few grass-roots contacts. Were the religious NGOs started by women any different, because of the ancient village base of religious life, and because of the kind of day-to-day responsibilities that most women have? Were these transnationals better grounded, less insulated from ordinary folk? In this chapter we will explore these questions by looking at the characteristics of secular and religious women's transnational associations in terms of their purposes and functioning on the world scene.

Transnationals are ordinarily referred to as nongovernmental organizations, or NGOs. For an organization to qualify as an NGO it must have members or sectors in at least three countries, and an international headquarters that operates autonomously for that organization and is not subsidized by any national government.

What do we look for in nongovernmental organizations in general, and in women's NGOs, whether religious or secular? Since NGOs by definition are identified with interests that transcend national boundaries, we expect all NGOs to define problems in global terms, to take account of human interests and needs as they are found in all parts of the planet. Because they have neither armies nor large bureaucracies at their command, we assume that they will utilize the power of shared values and concerns, rather than the power of political dominance to carry out aims. Their small budgets dictate use of communications technology to compensate for tiny infrastructures, with a minimum of hierarchical structures, in assembling and disseminating information relevant to organizational goals, and in arriving at policy decisions among widely separated groups. We expect NGOs to use the same communications technology to compensate for regional differences in wealth and capabilities, in aid of planetary redistribution of resources. Since they are emergent structures, we may also assume that they will reflect new perceptions of planetary society, and of appropriate social roles for individuals and groups. In short, we might look to them for new definitions of problems based on global frames of reference, and new ways of thinking and working. Since we also know that emergent social phenomena are constrained in their development by the social technologies available at the historical moment of development (Stinchcombe, 1965), we are aware that NGOs will, to a considerable extent, reflect familiar organizational patterns in their era of emergence. We must also take note of a peculiar public-but-private attitude on the part of NGO organizations. There is no ethic of accountability to the world community, and they can do as they please.

The forty-seven women's NGOs[1] provide a special set of cases for viewing the innovative potentials in NGOs as emergent structures. Of these forty-seven, nine are religious in orientation, ten are in the international relations arena, eighteen are for professional and working women, seven are educational/cultural, and three are for sportswomen. How do the religious organizations compare with the secular ones in terms of type of work and creativity in meeting problems? Do they add a spiritual-intuitive dimension to the social vision of planetary needs? What are the performance capacities of the religious as compared with the secular organizations in relation to local human needs, and how are the national branches distributed in relation to regional need? We will begin by examining the history of women's participation in modern world networks, and then examine capabilities and distribution of organizations by region. In the analyses that follow the historical background we will not only look at the performance of NGOs, but we will also use the concept of region, already used in earlier chapters as a shorthand device for reporting the status of women in various parts of the world, to provide an exercise in conceptualizing various kinds of geographic entities and identities.

THE HISTORICAL BACKGROUND: WOMEN ENTER THE WORLD SCENE

The rapid development of transport and communication facilities in the nineteenth century was paralleled by increasing attention to the education of women and the plight of the exploited lower middle class and lower class working woman. Women of the upper and middle classes acquired new public spheres of action simultaneously in the national and the international community, as we saw in the previous chapter. Traditional community nurturance roles took on new dimensions as women participated in the series of international fairs that helped to build the infrastructure of the new world community between 1851 and 1893. The first international exposition was held in London in 1851, and it was followed by expositions in Paris in the next decades. By 1893 at the Chicago Exposition, a great congress of women was formally organized for the first time. The papers presented at the congress give an overview of the process of translation of the older "lady of the manor house" style of service into modern approaches to social needs (Burdett-Coutts, 1893).[2] Many of the innovations in education and welfare services and home services for working women and children, for prisoners and for migrants, which were developed at that time, have yet to be generally adopted by any society.

Between 1880 and 1900 five international women's organizations were born. Two of them were religious in orientation, the World Young Women's Christian Association (WYWCA) and the World Women's Christian Temperance Union (WWCTU); one was professional, the International Council of Nurses (ICN); and two were cultural, the General Federation of Women's Clubs (GFWC) and the International Council of Women (ICW). In each case they began as local women's organizations in one country, but quickly spread elsewhere because there existed a high level of readiness among women to enter into transnational community.

Women were also entering other international organizations and working with men during this same period, but since there was a persistent problem with men accepting women as full collaborators in the mixed organizations, all-women's organizations continued to grow and multiply. The contributions of women in the mixed organizations were substantial but often invisible. In the all-women's organizations, however, they were (and are) highly visible. It is because of the relative invisibility of women in mixed organizations that we confine this analysis to all-women's organizations.[3]

While socialist women were active during this early period, holding separate international councils, they stayed within the international socialist movement and did not regroup separately until 1909. By far the most activist separate women's groups in this early period were the YWCA and WCTU.

Urban-based, with a strong commitment to the problems of the young working woman and the deserted, widowed, and single woman, they combined an instinct for practical community problem-solving with a powerful aspiration toward a kind of moral purity and spiritual welfare that does not translate easily into late twentieth century vocabulary. The nearest analogies today would be those of the whole person, the autonomous person, the liberated person. The effect of both organizations was to liberate women into the public sphere and to bring a new set of standards about community welfare and social justice into the public arena. Both organizations included a commitment to international peace along with domestic welfare goals—an unusual conception in organizational terms, though the language of "peace and justice" fitted the utopian euphoria of the end of the nineteenth century. These women's organizations tried to translate rhetoric into service for underprivileged women.

The next era of growth of women's international organizations came in the period 1900 to 1915. Five more religious organizations were born in this period, and the first three international relations associations. (See Table 8.1 for the founding dates of all forty-seven organizations analyzed in this study, and Table 8.2 for the full name of each organization.) Women's peace groups with international contacts date back to 1852 (Anglo-American Olive Leaf Circles), but viable permanent international organization for such groups did not occur until 1900. Both the religious and the international relations groups were informed by strong ethical and social service ideals. As was one of the international relations groups, the Women's International League for Peace and Freedom, which until recent decades often opened its meetings with prayer.[4] Since 1916, the main growth in women's organizations has been in the professional arena. Peace, justice, and social service themes have been strong in the professional organizations, but religious themes have received less emphasis.

The apparent decline of religious orientation in the transnational organizational life of women as they have mobilized around their economic roles in society is only part of the picture, however. The nineteenth century also witnessed an explosion of new teaching and service sisterhoods within the Catholic Church, groups that are not registered as NGOs. New Protestant religious service organizations also came into being. Although I have not been able to obtain a complete count of Catholic sisterhoods for the purposes of this chapter, records show that five hundred were founded between 1800 and 1899, counting only those with branches in the United States. Cita-Malard (1964) estimated over a decade ago that there were about one million women in Catholic orders at that time. A study of a sample of 116 sisterhoods with branches in the United States gives the picture of dates of founding as shown in Table 8.3.

Table 8.1: Founding Dates for Women's NGOs and Number of Section Memberships*

Organization Category	1880-1901	1900-1915	1916-1930	1931-1945	1946-1970
Religious	WYWCA (81) WWCTU (59)	GB (40) ICJW (21) IULCW (9) SJIA (12) WUCWO (82)		WFMW (20)	IFMW (27)
International Relations		IAW** (45) ICSDW** (34) WILPF (21)	ACWW (67) PPSAWA (14) WIZO (51)	WIDF (97)	AAWC (35) EUW (12) FAWA (11)
Professional	ICN (74)	IFHE (63)	ICM (42) IFBPW (52) IFUW (56) IFWLC (39) MWIA (37) NNF (5) ODI (12) SIA (48) ZI (44)	IFWL (68) WAWE (11)	IAWHPJ (22) ICWES (11) IUWA (32) PAMWA (13) WEGN (12)
Educational	GFWC (50) ICW (64)	IALC (13)	AI (12) IIW (42) WAGGGS (101)		WMM (46)
Sports			IFWHA (34)		IAPESGW (58) IWCC (8)

*From **Yearbook of International Organizations, 1973** and **1974.**
**The original name for IAW was International Women Suffrage Alliance, and the original name for ICSDW was International Socialist Women's Secretariat.

Table 8.2: Key to Initials of Women's NGOs*

Initials	Organization Name
AAWC	All African Women's Conference
ACWW	Associated Country Women of the World
AI	Altrusa International
EUW	European Union of Women
FAWA	Federation of Asian Women's Associations
GB	Girls' Brigade
GFWC	General Federation of Women's Clubs
IA	International Association of Lyceum Clubs
IAPESGW	International Association of Physical Education and Sports for Girls and Women
IAW	International Alliance of Women
IAWHPJ	International Association of Women and Home Page Journalists
ICJW	International Council of Jewish Women
ICM	International Confederation of Midwives
ICN	International Council of Nurses
ICSDW	International Council of Social Democratic Women
ICW	International Council of Women
ICWES	International Conference of Women Engineers and Scientists
IFBPW	International Federation of Business and Professional Women
IFHE	International Federation for Home Economics
IFMW	International Federation of Mazdaznan Women
IFWHA	International Federation of Women Hockey Associations
IFWL	International Federation of Women Lawyers
IFWLC	International Federation of Women in Legal Careers
IFUW	International Federation of University Women
IIW	International Inner Wheel
IULCW	International Union of Liberal Christian Women
IUWA	International Union of Women Architects
IWCA	International Women's Cricket Association
MWIA	Medical Women's International Association
NNF	Northern Nurses Federation
ODI	Open Door International
PAMWA	Pan-American Medical Women's Alliance
PPSAWA	Pan Pacific and Southeast Asia Women's Association
SIA	Soroptimist International Association
SJIA	St. Joan's International Alliance
WAGGGS	World Association of Girl Guides and Girl Scouts
WAWE	World Association of Women Executives
WEGN	West European Group of Nurses
WFMW	World Federation of Methodist Women
WIDF	Women's International Democratic Federation
WILPF	Women's International League for Peace and Freedom
WIZO	Women's International Zionist Organization
WMM	World Movement of Mothers
WUCWO	World Union of Catholic Women's Organizations
WWCTU	World's Women's Christian Temperance Union
WYWCA	World Young Women's Christian Association
ZI	Zonta International

*From **Yearbook of International Organizations, 1973** and **1974**.

Table 8.3: Date of Founding of 116 Women's Religious Orders

pre-1200	2
1200-1399	5
1400-1799	13
1800-1849	28
1850-1899	47
1900+	20
Not ascertainable	1
Total	116

NOTE: The countries of origin of these orders are Algeria, Belgium, Brazil, Canada, England, France, Germany, Italy, Mexico, Netherlands, Spain, Switzerland, South Africa, and the United States.

SOURCE: This information is taken from **Guide to the Catholic Sisterhoods in the U.S.** (McCarthy, 1955).

Some of these orders were founded for women by men. A reading of the histories, however, makes it clear that a substantial majority were founded primarily through the initiative of women. Because of the structures of the Church, they are all under male ecclesiastical authority. While the orientation of the sisterhoods is very profoundly religious, particularly in the founding decades, the organizations have administered a great variety of institutions and services that fall squarely within the main tradition of the women's international organizations begun at the turn of the century, in terms of human welfare.

The shift seen in Table 8.1 from the type of organization founded up to 1916 to the type founded afterwards, from religious to international political to professional, reflects the change in the kinds of public spaces allowed to women. With their increasingly large-scale entry into the skilled labor force, they organized around new perceptions of the types of contributions they could make, and of the types of social needs they wished to address.

CURRENT CHARACTER AND DISTRIBUTION OF WOMEN'S NGOs

Tables 8.4 and 8.5 give a summary picture of the characteristics and current distribution of women's organizations around the world. While some of the aims and activities of organizations in different categories overlap, the classification of organizations into the major categories of (1) religious, (2) international relations (including political), (3) professional and working women, (4) educational and cultural, and (5) sports, is fairly clear-cut in terms of the self-characterization of each organization and its own statement of major emphases. Organizations are characterized as religious only when the promotion of religious ideals is explicitly articulated in the goals.[5]

All of the organizations have certain common characteristics. They all promote international cooperation and understanding, as well as some concept of justice and social welfare, both for people in general and for women in particular. They all have a high ethical and altruistic tone. To some degree, therefore, they are all addressing themselves to some of the major problems of the twentieth century. They are all to an extent concerned with the gathering of data that will enable them to act more effectively in solving the problems they address, and for each of them the very existence of the organization itself provides a new set of social roles for acting on the world scene.

Utimately each organization is itself identity-creating and identity-affirming for its members. For religious organizations, the religious component of human identity becomes a significant enabler for social action. International political organizations invoke the civic component of human identity and rely on political analysis and skill for world problem-solving. Professional organizations perceive occupational training as a particular resource which can be applied to world problem-solving in ways different from normal occupational routines. Professional training is not necessarily specifically drawn on in the pattern of work, however; it may simply be a basis of widespread recruitment for social betterment work which deals with problems to which that profession is particularly sensitized. Educational/cultural organizations address themselves less to particular social problems and more to the realization of the wholeness of the person through education and culture. The early women's clubs that preceded the general federation fought hard for the right to be general enrichment associations, not bound to serve specific welfare needs. Nevertheless, the concern for the right to wholeness quickly became a transnational concern. Sports organizations are really a special category of professional associations, drawing on a particular set of skills as a basis both for recruitment and for creation of experiential settings that further a sense of world identity.

It will be seen from the first two columns of Table 8.4 that professional organizations represent by far the largest category of women's groups. If we add sports to them, they make up almost half of all women's groups. Since each profession also has a mixed NGO for both women and men, the existence of these women's NGOs is a significant statement about women's lack of opportunity to give expression to their public concerns within their "mainstream" professional associations. In fact, of course, each category of organization represents a special development by women within a field that contains similar mainstream organizations. In a future study it would be interesting to ascertain to what extent women hold double memberships in mixed and in all-women's organizations. Whether women's organizations facilitate isolation or participation in relation to the larger society depends in part on the extent to which there are cross-links between them and mixed

Table 8.4: Organizational Characteristics*

Organization Category	N	%	Mean Program Score	Mean Size of Organizational Network**
Religious	9	20	3.8	39.0
International Relations	10	21	4.5	38.7
Professional	18	38	3.8	35.6
Educational	7	15	3.7	46.8
Sports	3	6	2.0	33.3
All	47	100	3.8	38.4

*From **Yearbook of International Organizations, 1973** and **1974**. Additional information for Africa from African Bibliographic Center (1969).
**Mean number of national sectors per organization in that category.

Table 8.5: Distribution of Women's NGOs by Region*

	Percentage Branches in Regions				
Organization Category	Africa	Americas	Asia	Australasia	Europe
Religious	18.1	25.2	15.0	30.3	16.6
International Relations	27.8	17.8	22.4	21.3	19.9
Professional	27.2	34.1	37.7	27.0	41.6
Educational	22.3	17.4	19.2	15.7	16.0
Sports	4.6	5.6	5.7	5.6	5.9
All	100.0	100.1**	100.0	99.9**	100.0

*Data are from the **Yearbook of International Organizations, 1973** and **1974**. Additional information on Africa is from the African Bibliographic Center (1969).
**Error due to rounding.

organizations. It also depends in part on the extent to which women's groups work with each other across organizational boundaries. Chapter 9 analyzes the phenomenon of cross-connectedness of women's groups with each other and with mixed groups.

The mean program rating score for each category found in the next column of Table 8.4 will be further discussed in connection with Table 8.5. The score is based on an eight-point checklist (*not* a scale) and the highest rating that any individual organization has is seven. It will be seen that in terms of program capabilities, international political groups, not religious or professional organizations, have the highest average score. The average size of networks within each category is found in the next column, and here it will be seen that the educational groups have achieved the widest coverage of the world community with an average number of nearly forty-seven branches. After a noticeable drop in average size, religious, international political, and professional groups cluster fairly closely around means from thirty-nine to thirty-six. The maximum possible number of branches for an NGO is 216—the number of countries and territories in the world. It will be seen that even the larger NGOs only cover a small part of possible total membership (Table 8.7).

Regional Distribution of NGOs

Table 8.5 gives the picture by regions of the relative "strength of presence" of different types of NGOs. It will be noted that regional aggregations are created here that do not correspond to aggregations used elsewhere in this book. This grouping has been determined by the fact that the *Yearbook of International Organizations* reports national section memberships in NGOs in this way, for Africa, the Americas, Asia, Australia (sometimes called Oceania), and Europe. Elsewhere in this book North America is combined with Europe, South America is separate, West Asia (the "Middle East") is combined with North Africa, and East Asia is kept separate. The regrouping of countries for this chapter to match the NGO reporting provides an illustrative exercise regarding the major psychological task that lies before NGOs in particular and the world in general—thinking in a variety of ways about regional wholes in order to make global wholes meaningful. The "country mixes" represented in the groupings will be discussed later.

As we look across the regions in Table 8.5 we can compare the representation of each organizational category in the regions (percentage of branches in region) with the representation of the same category in the total set of women's NGOs (the percentage in column 2 of Table 8.4). Reading down the columns, we can see what the total organizational mix is for each region. In terms of local regional presence, religious organizations compared to other organizations are substantially underrepresented in Asia and Europe, underrepresented in Africa, and overrepresented in the Americas and Australasia. Australasia in particular appears to bear the imprint of the missionary movements of the late 1800s and early 1900s.

International relations groups have done better in Africa, are given less attention to the Americas, and on the whole are represented more evenly throughout all regions. Professional organizations are most intensively represented in Europe, where practically all of them were born, next best represented in Asia, somewhat underrepresented in the Americas, and very underrepresented in Africa. Education, like international relations, is best represented in Africa, and fairly well distributed elsewhere. Sports, with only three available networks, is perhaps not surprisingly evenly distributed across regions. This category will not be given further separate discussion.

In other analyses of the distribution of NGO networks, much has been made of the fact that they represent a Euro-North American elite and that their presence elsewhere is essentially colonial. One bit of evidence frequently cited for the colonial character of the networks is the fact that the international headquarters tend to be located in Europe and North America. There is no gainsaying the truth of this; NGOs were born in Euro-North America, and nothing can change that historical fact. Because of their global commitments, however, they represent a potential network for beginning the monumental task of redistributing power and resources in order to even out the world standard of living. NGOs can do this largely by providing information, training, and grants to members in poorer countries, and by helping them to become incorporated into decision networks. They also represent an international source of legitimation for the setting of new standards for domestic civil rights and social welfare, and they provide international collaborators for domestic projects in countries with few trained leaders.

While it is undoubtedly true that NGOs can and do serve imperial interests, consciously and unconsciously, it is also true that many of the kinds of people who become active in NGOs stand outside conventional power structures. They are, particularly in women's NGOs, an elite of the powerless. To the extent that these organizations become aware of the contradictions inherent in the very existence of NGOs, dependent as they have been on Euro-North American wealth and the leisure of middle and upper class women, the conditions will emerge for them to become instruments for other kinds of changes in the world system than those they now visualize. In the meantime, our task is to assess their contributions to world betterment as they presently conceive it.

Assessing NGO Program Capabilities

It is extraordinarily difficult to arrive at any kind of assessment of program capabilities of organizations for global social change based on the kind of statements that NGOs send in to the *Yearbook of International Organizations*. Since this is the only source of information across the board for all women's organizations, however, an effort has been made to rate each organization in terms of its stated goals and structural capabilities. Certain general statements can be made about the goals of all women's NGOs, beyond the overall one of increasing international understanding and cooperation among peoples of the world. They all have as their task an *improvement of the life conditions of women*, which includes attention to one or more of the following areas:

(1) redistribution of resources toward third world women;
(2) basic education;
(3) improvement of health, welfare, and living conditions;
(4) special skills training;

(5) improvement of economic, social, and legal status;
(6) cultural enrichment; and
(7) spiritual enrichment.

In addition, they all have an implied concern for *promoting the participation of women in society,* which may include attention to one or more of the following areas:

(1) training for community service roles for women;
(2) leadership training for participation in civic affairs;
(3) training for participation in policy-making;
(4) promotion of international collaboration of women on common concerns through establishment of cross-national task forces and committees;
(5) promotion of political activity on behalf of peace and justice;
(6) promotion of international understanding, friendship, and peace through experience-centered projects and development of educational materials; and
(7) promotion of awareness of religious dimensions in human life through experience-centered projects and the development of educational materials that foster spiritual awareness.

The rating system used here is distilled from the above listings of areas of concern. Each organization is rated according to the emphasis given to each of the following areas: (1) legislation; (2) training and/or specialized information-gathering; (3) community service; (4) grants; (5) cultural enrichment or specialized information dissemination; and (6) spiritual enrichment. An additional area considered for each organization is extent of program diversity and size of staff, and finally there is an "other" category, which makes possible an extra point for an organization with a special feature not covered by the above.

It is not always clear whether an organization is actually working on legislation (at national or UN levels), but when such activity is implied, the group is given the benefit of the doubt. Training and specialized information-gathering are lumped together because organizations tend to do one or the other, not both; they tend to be either activist in a very special sense, or information-centered. Community service is only checked when it appears that the organization supports specific community service projects. Grants refer to specific scholarship and funding projects. Cultural enrichment or information dissemination covers both general humanistic educational materials and task-oriented reports, newsletters, and bulletins. (Not all organizations that gather materials place emphasis on disseminating them. One has the impression that international headquarters of many organizations are vast treasure-houses of undisseminated information.) Program diversity and staff size are related, but not all organizations with high program diversity have large paid staffs. Some are particularly good at utilizing high-quality volunteer work. "Other" usually refers to playing consultative and linking roles not covered by the other categories.

Table 8.6 gives a detailed assessment of program capabilities of the religious, international relations, and educational NGOs. This rating process was done with considerable hesitation, in full awareness that more complete information might change ratings substantially. The absence of a check in a given category for a given organization does not mean that the emphasis is absent, but only that it is minimally present. Given the minuscule resources available to most of these organizations, the wonder is that they exist at all, not that they do not do more. However, given the extent of world need at present, performing the older symbolic function of affirming certain sets of values by simply existing, which was indeed a legitimate function of a number of NGOs, might now need rethinking. The tabulation is intended to raise questions, not to mislead or obfuscate. Additional analysis based on a questionnaire asking each of these organizations for further details is a necessary next step.

The religious, international relations, and educational NGOs are chosen for comparison because they all have generalized human welfare goals. Most of the professional organizations do also, but their particular emphasis on improving the status of the professional woman, and the quality of the profession itself, make them somewhat different from the other organizations.

Specific emphasis on legislative activity, not surprisingly, is found most generally in the international relations organizations, but also in four of the nine religious organizations. Training and/or information-gathering is found in every category of organizations, indicating a unanimous emphasis on relevant skills and/or knowledge stock, given the issues the organization deals with. Specific community service projects are not supported more by one category than another—about half of each set of organizations does this type of work. There may be local groups within an NGO that do community service, but according to their own statement such service is not specifically promoted at the international level of the organization. Religious NGOs do not do better with grass-roots linkages than secular organizations, it appears. The religious organizations do least well on grants, an area in which the professional organizations, not included here, do best. This may be poor reporting, or it may be that funding of educational and community service projects has not been seen as a priority. Some grants may be "hidden" in training programs which are not called scholarships. In terms of emphasis, the religious organizations apparently do least with preparation of materials which will increase the information level of members. Since every organization has a newsletter, this has more to do with preparation of special additional materials. Again, this *may* be poor reporting. Interestingly, not all of the religious organizations mention spiritual enrichment, though all are explicit about the religious context of their work or they would not be listed here. Two of the international relations organizations do mention spiritual enrichment. Both are regional federations which apparently see as one of their major purposes the infusion of a Christian element into political affairs. However, according to their own statements, they are not religious organizations.

To find program diversity and larger staff size, we must look to the larger religious organizations—the World Union of Catholic Women, the World YWCA, the World WCTU—and to two smaller ones with very active programs, the Girls Brigade and St. Joan's Alliance. Network size (see last column in Table 8.6) obviously has something to do with diversity and staff. The reasons why some organizations have spread widely and attracted many workers, while others have remained small, cannot be dealt with here; only the figures are recorded. While just one of the international relations groups, the Women's International Democratic Federation, has as large a network as the larger religious organizations, seven out of the ten international relations organizations have notable program diversity. It is possible that the kinds of questions that politically oriented international relations groups ask lead to more kinds of activities than the kinds of questions religious groups ask.

If we look at the mean program scores and the mean network size score, we find that the religious and educational organizations have about the same program capabilities (3.8 is the mean score), both less than the international relations groups (mean of 4.5). In terms of size, the educational organizations have considerably more spread than either of the other two, a mean size of 46.8 compared with 39 and 38.7 for the other two. The mean program score for the professional organizations is the same as the religious and educational, 3.8, and mean size is somewhat smaller, 35.6. If it seems surprising that the women's organizations with a primarily educational and cultural focus should have the largest global reach, rather than the religious ones, it might be remembered that the missionary activity in the religious spheres of the past one hundred years was not primarily a women's movement; it was initiated largely under male auspices. Indeed, many women were to be found working under male auspices. The "women's club movement," as indicated earlier, was one of the first autonomous outreaches of women, and the energy unleashed by that sense of autonomy is reflected in the spread of the women's clubs networks. Autonomous roles for women in religious and political settings have been slower in coming, although the religious organizations are among the very earliest to have been founded. The first of them, the YWCA and the WCTU, share the vitality and many of the characteristics of the women's club movement, and their network size reflects this fact.

Table 8.6: Program Capabilities of Women's NGOs*

	Legislation	Trading and/or Information Gathering	Community Service	Grants	Cultural Enrichment/Information Dissemination	Spiritual Enrichment	Program Diversity and Staff Size	Other Features	Program Score	Network Size
Religious										
GB			X		X	X	X		5	40
ICJW	X	X	X						3	2
IFMW	X	X							2	27
IULCW		X					X		1	9
SJIA	X	X						Consult.	3	12
WFMW		X						Consult.	2	6
WUCWO		X	X	X	X	X	X		6	82
WYWCA	X	X	X		X	X	X		7	81
WWCTU		X	X		X	X	X		5	59
Means				Mean Program Score 3.8				Mean Network Size 39		
International Relations										
ACWW			X	X	X		X	X	6	67
AAWC	X	X			X		X	X	5	35
EUW	X	X			X	X			4	12
FAWA	X	X			X	X			3	11
IAW	X				X		X		4	45
ICSDW	X	X		X	X		X		5	34
PPSAWA			X		X			X	2	14
WIDF	X	X	X		X		X		6	97
WILPF	X	X	X		X		X		5	21
WIZO	X	X	X	X	X		X		6	51
Means				Mean Program Score 4.5				Mean Network Size 38.7		

Table 8.6: (Continued)

	Legis-lation	Trading and/or Information Gathering	Com-munity Service	Grants	Cultural Enrichment/ Information Dissemination	Spiritual Enrich-ment	Program Diversity and Staff Size	Other Features	Program Score	Network Size
Educational										
AI		X	X	X					4	12
GFWC		X		X			X		4	50
IALC					X		X		1	13
ICW	X	X	X		X		X	X	6	64
IIW			X		X				2	42
WAGG		X	X	X	X		X	X	6	101
WMM		X			X		X		3	46
Means		Mean Program Score 3.7			Mean Network Size 46.8					

*Data are from the **Yearbook of International Organizations, 1973** and **1974**; additional information on Africa from African Bibliographic Center (1969).

Participation Opportunities for Women

Table 8.7 gives a summary picture of the availability of NGO participation opportunities for women by region, in terms of the presence of national branches. Africa, with 26 percent of the world's countries and territories, has 19 percent of the world's women's NGO branches. The Americas, with 23 percent of the world's countries, have 25.5 percent of the NGO branches. Asia, with 21 percent of the world's countries, has 18.5 percent, and Australasia, with 12.5 percent of the world's countries and territories, has 2 percent of the NGO branches. Europe, with 17 percent of the world's countries, has 31.8 percent of the NGO branches; the "mother of NGOs," Europe has served itself best. While in every region there are countries and territories that have no NGOs at all—always the poorest and less often the smallest units—it is interesting to think in terms of mean number of branches per country in a region. While the NGO networks are transnational, people *live* in countries, and enter NGOs through countries. If there is no local branch, the network does not represent an opportunity for transnational participation for the women of that country. The women of Asia and Africa (see column 3 in Table 8.7) continue to be substantially deprived of opportunities to enter NGO networks. In the Americas, had we separated the rich and poor countries, it would be found that the rich have the most NGOs, and Europe has most of all. That Australasia has only 1.9 branches per country is a reminder that the women of Oceania have little opportunity to enter the world community through NGO activity.

In terms of how each category of NGO distributes itself among the regions, international relations and education do best in Africa; international relations, professional organizations, and education do best in Asia; and religion does best in the Americas. All divert substantial amounts of their total resources toward Europe. The distribution of branches of religious NGOs to favor the

Table 8.7: Distribution of Organizational Strength of Women's NGOs by Number of Branches Located in Each Region*

Region	Countries and Territories		All NGO Branches		Mean No. Branches Per Country	% Branches in Each NGO Category				
	N	%	N	%		Religions	Int'l. Rel.	Professional	Educational	Sport
Africa	56	26	349	19.3	7.4	18.0	25.1	14.8	23.8	16.0
Americas	50	23	461	25.5	9.8	33.1	21.1	24.5	24.4	26.0
Asia	46	21	334	18.5	7.1	14.2	19.4	19.7	19.5	19.0
Australasia	27	12.5	89	5.0	1.9	7.7	4.9	3.7	4.3	5.0
Europe	37	17	574	31.8	12.2	25.4	29.4	37.3	28.1	34.0
WORLD	216	99.5**	1807	100.1**	8.4	98.4**	99.9**	100.0	100.1**	100.0

*Data are from the **Yearbook of International Organizations, 1973** and **1974**; additional information on Africa is from the African Bibliographic Center (1969).
**Error due to rounding.

Americas and Europe runs counter to the image we have of how such organizations might seek to be distributed. That professional organizations are weak in Africa and somewhat less so in Asia is perhaps in part a reflection of the recency of formation of many of these associations. They have not had time to spread out of Europe.

TRANSLATING STATISTICAL AGGREGATES INTO HUMAN IMAGERY

Table 8.8 represents an effort to depict basic social problems in the regional and world terms appropriate for NGO thinking. It is a statement of the world needs NGOs must address and a challenge to the human imagination. Here is where we get the full impact of the meaning of the regrouping of countries so that "the Americas" become one region. Normally we mentally divide the Americas into two parts: North America, which includes Canada and the United States, and represents a certain way of life and standard of living, and Latin America, which represents another way of life and other standards of living. No effort has to be made, and no challenges are presented. It is very hard to think of the United States and Haiti as part of one aggregate, sharing a common hemispheric standard of living. It is not just a verbal trick to say that no citizen of the United States is any richer than the poorest citizen of Haiti. Rather, it is an effort to reconceptualize human identity by region in terms of the mandate to share and redistribute resources.

The concept of region is both arbitrary and without substantive meaning, and should in the long run be discarded in favor of multiple special-purpose groupings of human beings. All its contradictions show up in the figures presented in Table 8.8. Ultimately we need to feel that we are an earth family sitting at an earth table being fed from the earth family farm. But for now this formulation is only rhetorical. In the meantime, getting a handle on the diversity encompassed within the term "regional" is a particular challenge to NGOs as they work at creating new kinds of identities across national borders. I ask the reader, in continuing the perusal of this chapter, to try to stretch her/his imagination to the concept of regional standards of living, with all the contradictions that such a concept implies. When the contradictions become intolerable, we will do something about them. Keeping countries and territories with less than one million population in the analysis is important for the same reason—to develop a more comprehensive understanding of wholes. Furthermore, each of those tiny units—there are sixty in all—is a potential member of innumerable NGO networks. We will build up our mental image of these regions by using the conventional economists' categories of gross national product[6] and percentage annual growth rate of gross national product, calories consumed per capita per day, and protein con-

Table 8.8: World Economic and Nutritional Profile, by Region and with World Means (1968 Figures)

Region	GNP Per Capita			% Annual Growth Rate			Calories Consumed Per Capita Per Day			Protein Consumed, Grams Per Capita Per Day		
	Low	High	Mean	Low	High	Mean	Low	High	Mean	Low	High	Mean
Africa	50 (Brunei)	1020 (Libya)	191	−3.5 (Algeria)	19.4 (Libya)	1.92	1760 (Tanzania)	2835 (Egypt)	2190	32.7 (Zaire)	32.4 (Egypt)	57.7
Americas	70 (Haiti)	3980 (U.S.)	737	−3.3 (Haiti)	11.6[a] (French Guinea)	2.13	1760 (Bolivia)	3210 (U.S.)	2404	45.8 (Bolivia)	101.7 (Argentina)	63.2
Asia	60 (Bhutan)	3540 (Kuwait)	495.5	−4.9 (South Yemen)	9.9[b] (Japan)	3.91	1780 (Indonesia)	2930 (Israel)	2232	40.1 (Indonesia)	92.9 (Mongolia)	60.7
Australasia	130 (Western Samoa)	2070 (Australia)	801	−3.4 (Tonga)	10.7 (French Polynesia)	2.59	—[d]	3380 (New Zealand)	—	—[d]	108.4 (New Zealand)	—
Europe	400 (Albania)	2620 (Sweden)	1339	0.8 (Italy)	7.8 (Rumania)	4.0	2370 (Albania)	3450 (Ireland)	3045	71.3 (Albania)	103.0 (France)	87.8
World	50 (Brunei) (also Upper Volta and Malawi)	3980 (U.S.)	631	−4.9 (South Yemen)	19.4 (Libya)	2.85[c]	1760 (Bolivia and Tanzania)	3450 (Ireland)	2443	32.7 (Zaire)	108.4 (New Zealand)	66.6

SOURCE: Boulding Global Data Bank.

a. Highest growth rates are in: French Guiana, American Virgin Islands, Bahamas, Puerto Rico and Bermuda.
b. Two small oil-rich territories rank higher: United Arab Emirates, 37.3, and Oman, 15.4.
c. Means are distorted upwards through high growth rates of very small units.
d. Information not available for 13 of 15 units in Australasia.

sumed in grams per capita per day. Table 8.8 shows us the lowest, the highest, and the mean, or average, figure for each of these categories for each region, and the world figure. Here we see clearly the basic discrepancies in world standard of living. Africa and the Americas contain the poorest, most economically stagnant, and least well fed populations of the world. They also contain the richest and fastest growing: the United States is the richest, and Libya has the highest annual growth rate. Asia runs a close second in containing both the richest and the poorest, the most stagnant and the most rapidly growing. The disparities in Australasia are somewhat less pronounced, and Europe is the most comfortably cushioned from extremes of riches and poverty. Had we used the country groupings followed in earlier chapters we would have discovered similar disparities in wealth in those regions also. Reality resists the intellectually attractive idea of finding similar countries to be placed in homogeneous regional groupings.

We can see from the juxtaposition of rich and poor in the Americas and in Asia, as well as in Africa, that the third world is everywhere. Extremes of poverty and riches are everywhere. The fourth world, the oil-rich "backward countries," accentuate this phenomenon. We could draw North-South lines, but the extremes would still remain within each region. The "we" of the world mean with an annual income of $631, with a daily intake of 2,443 calories and 66.6 grams of protein includes you and me. To put it more strongly, the "we" with an income of under $50 a year, slipping backward economically at −4.9 percent a year, living on 1,760 calories and 32.7 grams of protein a day, the "we" made up of the citizens of Brunei, Upper Volta, Malawi, the Republic of Yemen, Tanzania, Bolivia, and Zaire also includes you and me. This is the constituency of the NGOs.

Within the "fourth world" is a fifth world, the world of women. In every region, in every country, where there are poor people, the women are poorer —simply because in every society there are substantial numbers of women who raise children alone without the help of a second breadwinner.

CREATING NEW PARTNERSHIPS

Women's NGOs, by their own statements of purpose, have taken on a double set of constituencies—the first four worlds, commonly referred to as *the* world, and the fifth world. It is a large task for the women's NGOs to deal with the needs of their fifth world constituencies. The NGOs that touch the greatest numbers of that constituency are the World Association of Girl Guides and Girl Scouts (educational) with 101 sections, the Women's International Democratic Federation (international relations) with 97 sections, the World Union of Catholic Women (religious) with 82 sections, the World

YWCA (religious) with 81 sections, the International Council of Nurses (professional) with 74 sections, and the Associated Countrywomen of the World (international relations) with 67 sections. It might be said that six out of forty-seven women's NGOs carry the main burden of world network.

The problems are enormous. Even the most privileged women in the "mother-countries" of Europe have difficulties. The problems of the least privileged women are almost ungraspable in their magnitude. The old helping hand approach is rapidly becoming obsolete as we come to realize that excluded minorities of the world society generally have types of know-how that are crucial in the problem-solving process, particularly when their own problems are at issue. This means that NGOs have to become more like alliance structures, bringing into partnership excluded minorities who have inputs to make into the planning and decision-making processes in both the nongovernmental and the governmental arenas. Yet women's NGOs, as much as men's, were largely born during the helping hand era. While the hierarchical structure of NGOs is generally minimal, depending more on the size and elaboration of national sections than on the international machinery, which tends to the confederacy pattern, there is in fact a hierarchy of European-style competence, linked to European wealth and education. The world distribution of NGO branches, and the fact that most of their headquarters are in Europe, make that clear. The vast infrastructure of traditional women's organizations in Africa and Asia scarcely connects with twentieth century women's NGOs, but the All-African Women's Conference represents a beginning in linking some of these traditional organizations to the new NGOs. More developments like this may bring new strength to the fifth world, as well as new problem-solving capabilities.

It is difficult for western and westernized women to cross the cultural barriers set up by western-style industrialization, in order to develop easy working partnerships with their sisters in the third and fourth worlds, even when they share continents. Both ideologies and styles of work are very different. Also, now for the first time, grave questions are being raised about the development process itself, on both sides of the "development curtain." What does it mean to improve the quality of life on the planet?

PROBLEMS AND CHALLENGES FOR RELIGIOUS NETWORKS

The one set of organizations that might be able to cross the cultural barriers because of shared communication in another dimension, the religious organizations, often seem to be as culture-bound as the others. The women who work in them are probably as urban-based, and out of touch with village life, as women in any secular NGOs. Size has something to do with their lack of effectiveness. The larger the network, the fuller the partnership, as more third world women are brought into transnational activity. Religious networks are generally weak in Africa and Asia in relation to other types of networks, and only three of them have reached the critical size that makes it possible to bring third world women into significant partnerships.

Since it was the potential reach of religious networks that led to the initial focus on comparing religious transnationals with other types of transnational actors, this finding in regard to women's religious NGOs suggests that the NGO structure may not be the best organizational method for tapping grassroots religious activity in the world, particularly for women. Missionary and church networks exist largely outside the NGO structure. They do not need it, perhaps, since as pointed out they antedate the NGO pattern as world entities in their own right. The Methodist, Jewish, and Catholic women have organized themselves on the NGO pattern; however, there is little indication that they have direct communication links with local congregations. Other Protestant women, and Moslem, Buddhist, Hindu, and Animist women do not enter the women's NGO world organizationally. It is hard to discover what cross-national links may exist among women in the nonwestern religious communities. The significance of becoming an NGO as compared with remaining within a self-contained religious entity is that an NGO has direct access to all other types of transnational associations through several linking mechanisms, including the Union of International Associations and UN agencies, and that the NGO can make direct inputs to the work of the world community through other international bodies including the UN. Non-NGO women's religious groups sacrifice the possibility of such impact, though it must be acknowledged that no women's NGO groups use that possibility as they should or could.

The YWCA-WCTU vision of the new society and of new roles for women was by all accounts a very powerful shaper of the general secular vision of the good society and of women's roles in particular, earlier in this century. In this double process of envisioning and of creating interorganizational linkages to share visions and skills, these pioneer religious organizations themselves became secularized. We might say that the early religious associations "shot their bolt" in creating the conditions for other women's organizations to be formed. Once the main lines of communication were established, using the best social technology available early in this century, there has been little further innovation in communication patterns to facilitate information flow and decision-making among the religious NGOs (see the communication ratings, Table 8.6). International relations women have done better with this task. Redistribution of resources has also not been a major achievement of women's religious groups, though concepts of religious stewardship would suggest a stronger redistribution activity than is revealed. International relations, educational, and professional women's NGOs have done better at this too. Program statements give little emphasis to new ways of doing things. The majority of the religious organizations do not even aspire (officially, at least) to contribute to spiritual enrichment, a function that might compensate for many other weaknesses.

To get a fuller picture of the potentialities of the religious dimension in the transnational sphere, however, one probably has to step entirely outside the NGO structure. Religious and missionary orders are a major component of religious transnationalism, and rarely are they affiliated as NGOs. They stay inside church structures.

One of the strongest hints about the potentialities of women's organizations nested in church structures outside the NGO structure lies in the radicalization in recent decades of several sisterhoods within the Catholic Church. The sudden proliferation of sisterhoods with substantial female leadership in the nineteenth century, extending into the twentieth, has already been mentioned. Some of these sisterhoods are celebrating their centennials by expressing revolutionary intentions, as in the case of the Franciscan sisterhood which held a Chapter of Mats in 1974 in the style of their revolutionary founder, St. Francis himself (Boulding, 1974). If we look at the range of activities of these sisterhoods, and imagine that one after the other they might become radicalized, we see that there are exciting and unsettling intimations for the future.[7]

A radical network that acts as an action-information center for the American branches of sisterhoods is centered in Washington, D.C. Ex-sisters, who usually remain committed to poverty and service, have their own special network. How many other such radical networks there are, I do not know. Given the range of institutions they administer, and the sheer mass of health, education, and welfare services they provide, if the Catholic sisterhoods of the world want to start a revolution they have more of a resource base to start from than any other group of women on the planet.

Any comparison of religious and secular women's NGOs must take account of a very important late twentieth century development: the gradual emergence of women into the public sphere in the political and occupational sectors of their respective societies. When we add to this acceptance (however slow) of more public roles for women the general trend toward secularization in this century, we see that able women who in earlier times might have worked in religious NGOs now work in secular ones. Also, women who earlier worked in voluntary organizations now work in professional ones. This means an increase in certain kinds of problem-solving capabilities in women's NGOs as actors on the world scene. These are still substantially elite organizations consisting of women who have succeeded by a certain narrow set of criteria in a Western-style achievement, however. It remains a question to what extent we can expect from them new kinds of global humanism and innovative transnational approaches to social and political organization.

In one sense, the very concept of women's organizations is traditional, and twentieth century women's organizations are neotraditional versions of tribal women's councils, but with far less power. Will the new transnational networks developing outside the formal NGO structure include a significant component of women's networks such as WIN (Women's International Networks), or ISIS (Women's International Information and Communication Service), or will these networks tend to look beyond concepts of gender-based division of labor and social organization of any kind? The network concept itself is anti-organizational in the formalized sense: opposed to hierarchy and rigidly designated channels of communication and decision, official designations of membership, binding constitutions, detailed budgets. Is the concept of *potential association* described by Donald Schon and Anthony Judge (Judge, 1971), emphasizing the ad hoc quality of task groups, forming and reforming according to task perceptions and changing situational requirements, the transition concept that will bring the world community of transnational actors into the twenty-first century? Unfortunately there is nothing in the concept of "ad hoc" that guarantees better contact with the grass-roots or with daily problems at local village levels, than existing urban-based NGOs have achieved. The ad hoc concept too is a sophisticated, city concept. At its worst it can mean depersonalization and evasion of responsibility through failure to make long-term commitments.

Networks cannot work without some kind of continuity. Neither can they function without skills and knowledge. Only a major effort at skills-sharing between the old NGOs and the new networks, between the old religious transnationals and the new ones, between the religious and the secular, between the elite-oriented and the grass-roots-oriented, and between women and men, will make world sharing a more realistic prospect in the twenty-first century than it has been in the twentieth.

NOTES

1. There are many transnational organizations that have women's branches within them, but such auxiliary-status organizations, while they may be very significant in their own right, are not treated in this study. For one thing, they are almost impossible to identify with any degree of completeness. For another, it would be hard to judge the extent of their autonomy within the parent organization. Women's NGOs are autonomous by definition.

2. They also give a glimpse of American-style approaches to the same problem (Eagle, 1893).

3. It has been pointed out that representation at UN headquarters for mixed NGOs is often handled by women, who are freer than men for such essentially volunteer jobs. This gives them a lot of responsibility, but little status (Beverly Woodward, 1976).

4. This was more true in the United States than in Europe.

5. This is a departure from the practice of an earlier study of religious networks, when religious contexts were sometimes imputed if the name of the organization included a religious identification. Since a follow-up study indicated that some of the imputations were incorrect, this is no longer being done (see Boulding, 1973, 1974).

6. The formulae for arriving at the figure for gross national product are absurdly inadequate for depicting the total productivity of any society, but because GNP is reported and used so widely, and does measure a certain industrially oriented sector of national productivity, it continues to be used.

7. Activities of 116 service sisterhoods in contemporary Catholic religious orders are: *administering schools and teaching:* elementary, secondary, college, university, nursing school; *administering other health and welfare institutions:* orphanages, institutions for the handicapped, homes for the elderly, homes for unwed mothers, residence houses for working girls, urban settlement houses, schools and community centers for Indians, blacks, Mexican-Americans, centers for juvenile delinquents, hospitals, nursing homes; *community ministry:* home and community service to categories of people listed above, outside institutional settings (derived from a sampling of sisterhoods in McCarthy, 1955).

Chapter 9

FEMALE ALTERNATIVES TO HIERARCHICAL SYSTEMS, PAST AND PRESENT: A Critique of Women's NGOs in the Light of History

Because it is generally believed that women historically have operated outside hierarchical systems, there is understandable interest in assessing the innovative potential of large-scale participation by women in the public arena, particularly with regard to a possible bypassing or dismantling of the kinds of hierarchical systems that have patterned urban-based organizational life in all human societies for the past 9,000 years or so. The underlying thought is that women must have developed other organizational techniques that work outside power structures and do not require the exercise of dominance. Women are the nurturers, and nurturance is nonhierarchical.

There is a mixture of wish, fantasy, and truth in this line of reasoning. If women are to contribute to decentralist innovation in contemporary society it must be on the basis of a realistic assessment of their historical experience and capabilities, including their handicaps. This chapter continues the analysis of women's nongovernmental organizations begun in the preceding chapter by attempting that assessment, concluding with a brief analysis of extent of decentralism, and the use of linkage practices among women's NGOs.

First, it must be clear that class structures have always included women, and that women have had differential power in each society based on class position just as men have. The fact that at each level in the class system they have less power than the males at the same level should not obscure the basic fact that women of the elite in all historical eras have wielded substantial amounts of public power. While the immediate political and cultural settings

Author's Note: Reprinted from *International Associations,* Issue 6-7, June-July 1975, pp. 340-346, by permission of the Union des Associations Internationales.

are different, Indira Gandhi, Mrs. Bandaraika, and Golda Meir all came to power out of ancient traditions of women rulers in Eastern cultures, including the Judaic tradition of women judges and an Indian tradition of ruling queens. Industrialization generally acted to limit the power of women, partly because of the associated dismantling of the large landed estates that had been the source of much of women's power from Sumerian times on. It happened that western historians interpreted the position of women in industrial societies as the human norm. Their anti-woman bias has produced a rewriting of world history that substantially obliterates the contributions of upper class women (see Beard [1946] and Boulding [1977] on this subject).

Second, hierarchical systems emerge as solutions to problems of scale. Until the industrial era, most human beings lived in household enclaves of an essentially craft-based society. The hierarchical structures that emerged with the first kingdoms and became elaborated into empires were a kind of minimum hierarchy that left most families intact as producing units. With increasing human densities, new technologies, and greater productivity, members of producer households were increasingly siphoned off into administration, beginning with the elite and continuing down into the middle class. Women as well as men were administrators of temple bureaucracies, warehouse complexes, cities, and provinces in Egypt, Sumeria, and elsewhere in the Mediterranean right through Roman times. As more and more public offices developed in a society, however, women filled proportionately fewer and fewer of them. Only as long as there were plenty of women from the lower classes to care for the children of the women of the elite were women free to enter the public spaces. Differential responsibility for the care of children anchored nonelite women to the home and nearby work places as new work opportunities developing further from home took away the fathers who had earlier shared in househole-based tasks.

The anchoring effect of children meant that women remained inside the mini-society of the home and neighborhood while men entered the public arenas. While in some societies women had more authority inside the home than men, and in other societies it was the other way around, in general the small scale of the household meant a minimum of hierarchy. There were dominance patterns, but they were situational and shifted from setting to setting.

This anchoring effect not only left women closer to, and therefore more aware of, nurturance needs of their own family, but also sensitized them to their neighbors. Community redistribution systems, whether in terms of sharing food, nursing the sick, or caring for children, became the business of the women anchored to the households. For one thing, they were the only ones who knew about neighborhood needs. Men were not there, could not see, did not know. The female role in redistribution operated at every level of society from the poorest to the richest. The elite counterpart of the poor woman who shared a pot of food with an even hungrier neighbor[1] was the princess who founded hospitals and orphanages. The historical role of the women of every royal family was to develop the health, education, and welfare infrastructure of their societies. This role died out only when independently wealthy land-based royalty died out, during the industrial revolution. The queen's distribution system was, however, hierarchical; the sharing among the urban poor was not.

Did women ever actively try to contravene dominance systems? To an extent they did, through their diplomatic roles in the marriage alliance systems that developed side by side with the institutions of chiefdom, kingship, and empire. Women of the aristocracy were usually married to potential enemies, after careful education and training. They had to survive in an often hostile court through sheer skill in mediation and nonviolent conflict resolution. Calling in the armies from back home to rescue a beleaguered queen was rarely a possibility. Women had few threat systems at their command.[2]

Historically, women have been the mediators in every society, largely through the marriage alliance systems. Every woman, not just royalty, is such a mediator. When a couple is married, it is usually the woman who leaves her home village, not the man.[3] A woman's skill in developing networks for communication and cooperation in an alien setting, not only in terms of making friends with hostile relatives of her new husband in her new home, but also in terms of linking them in positive ways with her own family back in her old home, is one of the major unstudied sets of social organization skills to be found in the human record. The record can be found in the correspondence of women around the Mediterranean during the Middle Kingdom in Egypt; it can sometimes be picked up in the observations of anthropologists. It lies everywhere, in bits and pieces.

The women of the West who lost their power with industrialization reentered the public spaces of society toward the end of the last century. Middle and upper class women developed new kinds of alliances as they finally came to understand the stripping process they had been through. By 1880 they were prepared to bypass the nationalistic struggles of Europe and forge alternative structures for the solution of what they already perceived to be global, not national problems, of social justice and human welfare. Although they had begun nationally, in associations for peace, in anti-slavery organizations and groups that dealt with the many faces of urban misery from alcoholism to bad housing to destitution to the inability of poor working mothers to care for their children, by the 1880s they were prepared to act internationally.

In the international socialist movement as elsewhere they stood for decentralism, nonviolence, and grass-roots activity on behalf of human welfare.

The phenomenon of the women's NGOs stemmed in part from the inability of women to get men to give priority to decentralism and nonviolence, and in part from the fact that men could not perceive women as individual human beings in their own right, let alone as partners in major public enterprises.

Each of the forty-seven women's NGOs active today is in its own way highly task-oriented. However, even though these organizations were born out of a perception of the need for decentralism and worldwide problem-solving, the international women's movement has not stayed clear in those perceptions. Deflected in substantial measure by the persistent failure of men to recognize their existence and their seriousness of purpose, many NGOs became caught up in a kind of identity struggle which has isolated each of the organizations from the others. Instead of using their network skills to work together whenever possible, these groups have tended to emphasize separate programs and separate identities. Instead of thinking in terms of the overall magnitude of the global problems they try to address and their responsibility for the world society, they function like private clubs free to decide when and where to "develop a program." This privatistic approach to public problems is a function of their privatized roles in their home societies. On the whole they do not like to come together to discuss how work and resources might be distributed among the women's organizations, and they do not even do well on networking with the UN agencies. While no one can blame the women's NGOs for having been largely born in Europe—that was where the conditions were first ready for this new set of roles—they do not seem to study the map very carefully. The distribution of their sections, and particularly of their headquarters, in relation to the needs they set out to deal with, is very poor, as we noted in Chapter 8. Table 9.1 shows the headquarters distribution for each category of women's NGOs, and Table 9.2 shows the linkage relations and staff picture for each category. Europe continues to serve itself best.

Given the number of possible links, the paucity of connections with UN agencies is distressing, particularly when one hears from UN agency people the plea for more expert contributions from the nongovernmental sectors to free them from excessive dependence on overcautious governmental inputs. The forty-seven women's NGOs represent a substantial knowledge resource for the world community, but one that is not well used. Staff size and small budgets are the usual limitations. In one way every women's NGO is a miracle even in its existence, given the fact that the women in it have command over few of the resources in their own societies. It seems unkind to chide small, courageous NGOs for not being large and rich. However, their very low-power position ought to lead them to examine the age-old skills that women have exercised in operating from positions of lesser power, in terms of organizing resources differently. Table 9.3 shows the number of interwomen organiza-

Table 9.1: Headquarters Distribution of Women's NGOs*

NGO Category	Location of Headquarters	No. Headquarters
A. By NGO Category		
Religious	United Kingdom	3
	United States	2
	Israel	1
	France	1
	Switzerland	1
	Germany (FDR)	1
International Relations	United Kingdom	3
	Switzerland	1
	Germany (GDR)	1
	Germany (FDR)	1
	Algeria	1
	Philippines	1
	Korea (S.)	1
	Israel	1
Education	United States	2
	France	2
	United Kingdom	2
	Switzerland	1
Professional	United Kingdom	6
	France	5
	Austria	2
	Belgium	2
	Switzerland	2
	United States	2
	Iran	1
	Sweden	1

B. Summary of Headquarters Distribution

United Kingdom	14	Germany (FDR)	2
France	8	Germany (GDR)	1
United States	6	Algeria	1
Switzerland	5	Philippines	1
Israel	2	Korea (S.)	1
Belgium	2	Iran	1
Austria	2	Sweden	1

*Date developed from **Yearbook of International Organizations, 1973; 1974.**

tional links, by NGO category, one for the Liaison Committee of Women's International Organizations, the other for the All-African Women's Conference. Interorganizational cooperation through the Liaison Committee is rather minimal. The African linkage system is impressive by comparison, and one wonders whether the traditional African women's organizational skills have not functioned here, in contrast to the European suspicion of cooperative activity. Learning to work with third world partners, whether in the ghettos and rural slums of the West or in Africa and Asia, is a skill that women's NGOs are just beginning to discover (or rediscover). International

Table 9.2: Linkage Relationships and Staff of Forty-seven Women's NGOs

	UN Consultative Relationships*		NGO Consultative Relationships**		
	Number Organizations Having Consultative Relationships	Number Relationships	Number Organizations Having Consultative Relationships	Number Relationships	Staff Range
A. By NGO Category					
Religious	3	0	1	0	30
	1	1	4	1	paid
	3	2-3	3	2-3	to
	1	4-6	1	4-6	all
	1	7	——	7	volunteer
International Relations	——	0	4	0	17
	2	1	2	1	paid
	4	2-3	4	2-3	to
	4	4-6	——	4-6	all
	——	7	——	7	volunteer
Educational	2	0	5	0	30
	2	1	——	1	paid
	——	2-3	2	2-3	to all
	3	4-6	——	4-6	volunteer
Professional	9	0	13	0	2
	1	1	5	1	paid
	6	2-3	2	2-3	to all
	5	4-6	1	4-6	volunteer
B. Summary of Linkage Relationships					
	14	0	2	0	
	6	1	11	1	
	13	2-3	11	2-3	
	13	4-6	2	4-6	
	1	7	0	7	
Total	47		47		

SOURCE: Data developed from **Yearbook of International Organizations, 1973; 1974.**
*ECOSOC, UNESCO, UNICEF, FAO, ILO, WHO, Council of Europe, OAS.
**Special consultative relationship with any other NGO.

Women's Year has been very salutary for European and North American women, in helping them realize more about the condition of women around the world and the structural features that universally operate to reinforce that condition. As we can see, the needs are greatest where the NGO structure is weakest.

Not only are NGOs not well distributed, and effectively linked with each other, but also they are not as innovative as they might be in the use of communications to overcome time and space barriers on behalf of their own stated goals. In the previous chapter we looked at program capabilities of

Table 9.3: Linkage Relationships of Women's NGOs: Linkage Among Women's Organizations Only*

Organizational Category	N	LCWIO**	AAWC**
Religious	9	3	3
International Relations	10	4	4
Professional	21	1	7
Educational	7	1	3

*Data developed from **Yearbook of International Organizations, 1973; 1974.**
**LCWIO = Liaison Committee of Women's International Organizations;
AAWC = All African Women's Conference.

each of the forty-seven women's NGOs, and found that most of the organizations received relatively low scores.

While these low scores may in part be due to inadequate reporting, in part I suspect that they are due to women having abandoned their traditional networking skills and accepted male organizational patterns. Since the networking skills developed to a considerable extent in small-scale settings like the family and the village, the ability to translate the network approach to large-scale activities must by no means be taken for granted. In fanciful language, women are all embattled princesses married off to foreign kings; they must establish every conceivable kind of "unorthodox" relationship across class and national lines that bypass (and undermine) the power structure if their goals for the whole human society are to be realized.

In part women need to uncover older preindustrial network skills; in part they need to unlearn socialization into male dominance systems; in part they need to be freshly inventive about new nonhierarchical patterns for working in large-scale entities. None of this can happen as long as women are attached to old status systems, and yet the old status systems give them what recognition they do get from the "male world." In the United States, it has been very interesting to see the experiments in women's centers and alternative society groups with several people sharing one job slot and salary, and transforming the job description into a network description. This dismantling and reassembling along different lines of existing jobs in traditional sectors such as universities, church service groups, and community welfare organizations may have great possibilities for the future.[4] It involves commitment to a lower standard of living, ignoring some institutional status rewards, and building of small cooperative working groups around jobs that were formerly done by individuals. It also enhances, rather than reduces, individuality, since each member of such a network has more time to spend on other activities besides the network job, precisely because a group is sharing the responsibility.

Such network job performance requires communication skills that many people do not have. Women's centers particularly work at developing them.

In fact, nonhierarchical organizations in general require greatly enhanced communication skills and technologies. Hierarchies can shortcut communications—that is why they appear efficient and desirable. The price of that shortcut is the flattened-out, one-dimensional quality of the resulting society.

The greatest danger for the larger society is that these communication-oriented nonhierarchical approaches that experimental women's communes and centers are developing—and that mixed groups (including the new men's liberation groups) are also working with—will be perceived as traditional low-profile nurturant behavior useful only for "low-level" social maintenance activities. These innovative approaches may not be dealt with seriously in their own terms as task-oriented problem-solving behaviors carried out in a nurturant manner. It takes a great deal of persistence and a certain kind of assertiveness to win acceptance for this style of working as a legitimate task-oriented method. While the tree will be judged by its fruits, it may take a long time for this particular harvest to ripen. The difficulties of the new styles must not be underestimated. They will fit better into that future world where women and men alike have learned to operate in nonauthoritarian styles within fluid localist social structures connected to the world web but not dominated by it than in the present dominance-oriented world. At present women must concentrate on transition roles and try to translate the new communication styles to the macro-level. Only by such an effort of transition will women be able to hasten the coming of planetary commensalism.

NOTES

1. Accounts of such food sharing among the poor are found in the writings of antiquity, and also in contemporary studies of slum neighborhoods.

2. The exception to this was the royal women who ruled in their own right and led their own armies. The long succession of successful warrior queens (as, for example, from Ancient Arabia, Macedonia, and tribal Europe, in the classical empires of India and Byzantium, and in post-medieval Europe; see Boulding, 1977) demonstrates that women could effectively operate threat systems when these were available to them.

3. In matrilocal societies it is the men who must do this adapting, and in those situations the men develop traits that we usually associate with women.

4. Some examples include: The American Friends Service Committee, an American religious service organization, currently has several jobs formerly filled by one individual now being filled by a collective of from two to four people. In Norway, the Peace Research Institute at Oslo (PRIO) is experimenting with rotating all but clerical positions in the Institute, and equalizing salaries in a kind of reconstituted research collective. Communal living groups belonging to the transnational network known as the Movement for a New Society generally share out wage-earning opportunities in the communities where they live by having several members of a local group share the same job.

PART IV

THE FUTURE

Chapter 10

THE COMING OF THE GENTLE SOCIETY

We have seen that there is an enormous gap between reality and ideal with regard to the participation of women in shaping human society during this last quarter of the twentieth century. Yet there is a new consciousness abroad, and the convening of the World Conference of International Women's Year in Mexico City in June of 1975 was a significant expression of the new consciousness. It seems appropriate to begin this last chapter, which looks to the future, by considering some exercepts from the "World Plan of Action" issued from that Conference, the most significant and far-reaching document about the human role of women ever to be conceived and written. It could not have been written any earlier than 1975 because the knowledge base[1] for the understanding of the relationship between the situation of women in each of the world's societies and the global problems of war and poverty did not exist before this decade.

The document spells out that relationship and focuses on the need to place the situation of women squarely in the center of the United Nations commitment to social progress for the human community. If women remain peripheral in the eyes of the decision makers who are to implement that commitment, the human race cannot progress.

> (1) In subscribing to the Charter, the peoples of the United Nations undertook specific commitments: "to save succeeding generations from the scourge of war ... to reaffirm faith in fundamental human rights, in the dignity and worth of the human person, in the equal rights of men and women and of nations large and small, and ... to promote social progress and better standards of life in larger freedom."
>
> (2) Many conventions, declarations, formal recommendations and other instruments have been adopted since then, reinforcing and elaborating these fundamental principles and objectives.

(3) In these various instruments the international community has proclaimed that the full and complete development of a country, the welfare of the world and the cause of peace require the maximum participation of women as well as men in all fields.

(4) Despite these solemn pronouncements and notwithstanding the work accomplished in particular by the United Nations Commission on the Status of Women and the specialized agencies concerned, progress in translating these principles into practical reality is proving slow and uneven.

(5) There are significant differences in the status of women in different countries and regions of the world which are rooted in the political, economic and social structure, the cultural framework and the level of development of each country. However, basic similarities unite women of all countries, the most notable being the persisting *de facto* gap between the economic and social status of women and that of men.

(6) As a result of the uneven development which prevails in international economic relations, three quarters of humanity is faced with urgent and pressing social and economic problems. The women among them are even more affected by such problems and improvements in their situation must be an integral part of the global project for the establishment of a new economic order.

(11) The achievement of equality between men and women implies that they should have equal rights, opportunities and responsibilities to enable them to develop their talents and capabilities for their own personal fulfillment and the benefit of society. To that end, a reassessment of the functions and roles traditionally allotted to each sex within the family and the community at large is essential. The necessity of a change in the traditional role of men as well as of women must be recognized. In order to allow for women's equal participation in all societal activities, men must accept shared responsibility for home and children. The objective is not to give women a preferential role, but to ensure the complete assimilation of men and women in the social order.

(15) International co-operation and peace requires national independence and liberation, the elimination of colonialism and neo-colonialism, foreign occupation and apartheid, and racial discrimination in all its forms as well as recognition of the dignity of the individual and appreciation of the human person and his or her self-determination. To this end, the Plan calls for the full participation of women in all efforts to promote and maintain peace.

(16) It is the aim of the plan to ensure that the original and multi-dimensional contribution—both actual and potential—of women is not overlooked in existing concepts for development and an improved

world economic equilibrium [From the Introduction to the "World Plan of Action of the World Conference of the International Women's Year," UN (1975: 3-6, E./Conf. 66/5).]

The Introduction to the Plan is followed by a series of guidelines for national action for the decade 1975 to 1985 which include highly specific recommendations for: (1) the involvement of women in the strengthening of international security and peace through participation at all relevant levels in national, intergovernmental, and UN bodies; (2) furthering the political participation of women in national societies at every level; (3) strengthening educational and training programs for women; (4) integrating women workers into the labor force of every country at every level, according to accepted international standards; (5) more equitably distributing health care and nutrition services to take account of the responsibilities of women everywhere for the maintenance of health and provision of food for their families; (6) reordering priorities with regard to social support systems for the family unit; (7) directly involving women, as the primary producers of population, in the development of population programs and other programs affecting the quality of life of individuals of all ages, in family groups and outside them, including housing and social services of every kind.

The Plan recommends that each government establish a timetable for achieving specific objectives in each of these areas for the next five years. The statements on the world situation of women in the World Plan of Action are strong, and the guidelines sufficiently specific so that no government can complain that it does not know where to begin. Yet we all recognize that the instruments for implementation are weak, and the motivation to implement the Plan on the part of most government officials will be weaker still.

The reasons for the weakness of motivation and of implementation instruments have very deep roots in human history and cannot be laid to ill will on the part of officials and administrators. Many responsibile officials see attention to "women's problems" as a distraction from the serious business of attending to the world crises of war, hunger, and resource depletion. Thus we have a paradox: at the very moment in history when the conceptual framework and the appropriate data base have been joined for an approach to the problems of war, hunger, and resource depletion involving the integration of the excluded half of the world's population into the problem-solving process, the tremendous anxieties engendered by the gravity of these crises render most decision makers unable to open their minds to the new perspective offered. A situation of intense threat is the worst possible condition under which to engage in new learnings. Fear rigidifies people, narrows their available behavioral repertoire, and drives them back to old, "tried and true" ways of doing things.

The general paradigm shift[2] required to change thinking and behavior in a male-dominated world, the shift anticipated by the World Plan of Action, will not come about quickly. Most people will continue to operate for some time as if old models of the social reality were still applicable. Nevertheless, forces are at work which go beyond the capacity of any group of powerholders to stem. The old paradigms can no longer offer control of ongoing social processes. The very powerlessness of the powerful in the face of today's crises is what will in time open the way for the people with the new paradigm well in mind, particularly including women, to play new roles in the world scene. The rest of this chapter will be devoted to exploring the dimensions and meaning of this paradigm shift, and the place of women in facilitating the transition to a new social order.

First it must be made clear that we must not, dare not, underestimate the threats the world faces today. It is true that there appears to be a great gulf between the world's needs and the resources and potentials that women have to offer. Consider the suicidal priorities of nations, as reflected in Figure 10.1 (from the newly issued *World Military and Social Expenditures,* Sivard, 1976). Is there any effective role that can be created now for women in a world that has established such a priority system? We can see that the $300 billion now being spent on arms in 1976 represents a worldwide militarization, not just an East-West temperate-zone phenomenon. The United States and Western and Eastern Europe simply have the largest *share* in the militarization, being the richest countries. The insane preferences established during this great era of progress in technological know-how are shared by rich and poor alike. Figure 10.2 makes those priorities, as reflected in world public expenditures on the military, human welfare, and peacekeeping, starkly clear. Public expenditures for education barely outstrip military expenditures, health drops halfway down the chart, and international benevolence and aspirations for peace as measured by expenditures for aid and UN peacekeeping are miniscule indeed. Figure 10.2 also portrays the resulting tragedy for the third world in the widening gap between the rich nations, who can afford both guns and butter, and the poor, who cannot.

The deflection of all our skills, energy, know-how, and social idealism into systematic militarization of the planet is the ultimate pathology of the twentieth century and could be the final pathology of the human race. But it need not be so! What we must remember is that the future is not just something that happens to us. It is something that women and men help create. Human beings, however, can only create what they can envision. Who can construct magnetic images for us of a twenty-first century world community that will reorient our behavior, provide a guide for reordering our values, criteria for reordering our social technologies, and a touchstone for redefining expectations and aspirations? Make no mistake about it: It

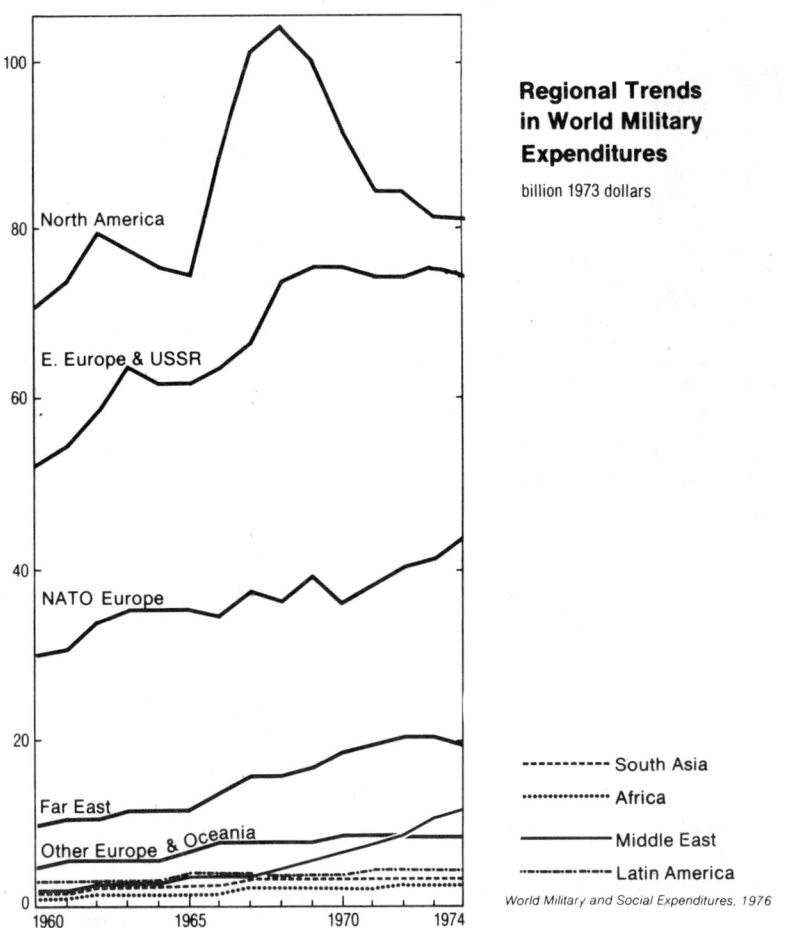

Figure 10.1

was the utopian images of the seventeenth and eighteenth centuries that moved us to where we are today, as Fred Polak (1973) has shown in his study of images of "scientifically" planned societies that harnessed technology to human welfare. While women wrote few if any of these utopias, they participated actively in creating the social technology of welfare planning, as briefly touched on in Chapters 7 and 8 (and further expounded in Chapter 11 of Boulding, 1977). With so much dynamism unleashed in the nineteenth century, what went wrong?

There is no space here to expound on so large a subject. The concepts and technology of centralized planning developed in this century to implement

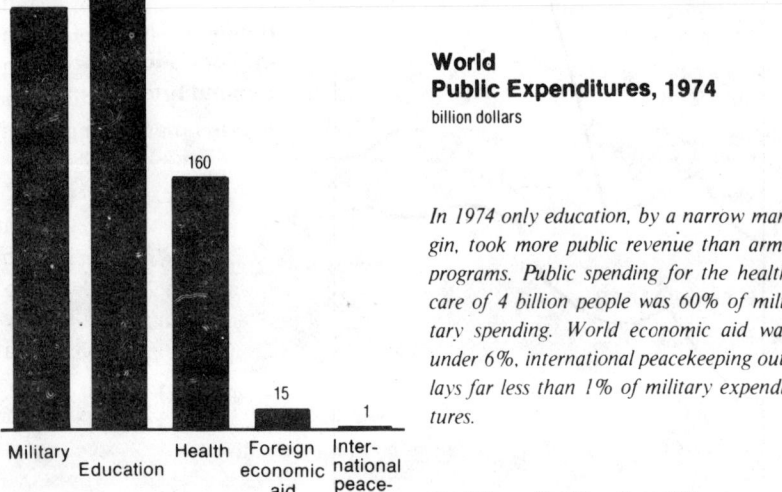

Figure 10.2

the utopias envisioned in the two previous centuries were not invented from scratch, but elaborated from more ancient know-how developed in Assyria, Egypt, India, China, and Rome, when the world was already from 1 to 2 percent urban. Centralized bureaucratic structures were adapted to the complex systems that evolved with increasing population densities. These adaptations worked sufficiently for centuries for both rulers and ruled, so that the costs in militarization and violence were simply accepted as part of the bargain humans made with history. Since women, except for the aristocracy, were never full participants in this urban infrastructure, rather deriving their economic strength from and finding their productive sphere in the landed estates and peasant farms of the rural areas, their role, as pointed out in Chapter 7, tended to be ameliorative rather than creative during the long centuries of urban-based empires.

Now we face a world society so complex that centralized planning can no longer work, yet even supposedly free enterprise, nonplanned societies like the United States are in fact highly planned. Furthermore, all the people who are trained in policy-making and administration, whether of political, economic, or social structures, are trained to plan and administer centrally coordinated systems. The militarization of the world can in one way be seen as a side effect of the centralization of national economies, and of the increasingly tight organization of regional alliances with the associated world arms trade. No one *intends* to blow the world up. National planners, doing the things they are trained to do, simply happen to increase military defense levels year after year in country after country.[3] The establishment of negotiation machinery such as the SALT talks to control militarization, only controls the *rate* of increase of armaments, but does not stop the basic escalation. United Nations disarmament machinery is helpless in this situation; the world's wealth of physical and human resources is increasingly being drawn into the maws of the world military machine.

What is needed now? I would answer, a new set of images of possible futures that involve a decentralist yet still interconnected and interdependent world, which will stimulate the development of a variety of new social techniques to enable that world to come about. Ultimately such a new set of images can only come out of a deeply spiritual faith that humankind is something more, and human society meant to become something other than what we have realized so far in the human experience.

Who will create the new images? It will be those who are marginal to the present society, who are excluded from the centers of power, who stand at the world's peripheries and see society with different eyes. All utopists, all visionaries have been marginal to the society they have lived in. Yet we need more than visions; we need marginal people with practical everyday skills who can begin translating the images of the future into new behaviors at the micro level, as well as helping with the development of intermediate social technology to replace centralist methods and structures.

It happens that the category of human beings I have been writing about in this book fulfills the requirements of marginality, of exclusion from the centers of power, and of possession of practical everyday skills at the micro and intermediate levels of human activity—the family, the neighborhood, the town. Since they also represent approximately half the human race, their aggregate potential is incalculable. I am referring, of course, to women.

The power of the marginals lies precisely in their lack of at-homeness in the world in which they live. Because they do not "belong" in the sense that they are never invited into society's back rooms where decisions that shape their lives are made, because they are usually treated as objects, never subjects, of the social process, they are driven to affirm belonging at another level.[4] The use of the metaphor of the human family to indicate a larger belonging comes easily to the marginals. It is also used by those in power, of course. When used by the powerful, the family metaphor emphasizes dependency, the helplessness of children who need a powerful father to guide them. When used by the powerless, the family metaphor emphasizes mutuality and sharing. Even within the Christian tradition, as the liberation movement among women theologians and ministers is now making clear, the metaphor of the world family has had very different meanings for women and for men.

The fatherhood of God and the priesthood of men has stood against the motherhood of the holy spirit and the sisterhood of believers.

A study of the writings of women over the centuries—saints, scholars, scientists, and poets—will I think reveal a different use of the metaphors of humanity and of the social order by women[5] than by men, though in every age there are also men who have already joined the "new society" based on the gentler metaphors. Women do not often, however, sit down and think systematically about the world social order. When women enter positions of power their metaphors tend to become coopted, and to take on a patriarchal cast. Most women rulers in history, for example, tend to behave like the father of their people rather than the mother or the sister. (Queen Elizabeth I was *called* the mother of her people, but she acted like a father.)

Another interesting phenomenon is the distortion of women's metaphors by men. Berit Aas (1975: 18) has compared the metaphors of personhood used by men about women and by men about men; the point I am making comes out clearly, from a slightly different perspective, in this study:

synonyms for woman

Dame, donna, Eve, Eve's daughter, women-folk, lady, matron, mother, nymph, sex-kitten, mam, madam, girl.
(collectively) The weak sex, the second sex, the distaff side.
(angry woman) Xantippe, Amazon, fury.
(dumb woman) Goose, hen.
(sexy woman) Coquette, prostitute.
(intellectual woman) Blue-stocking.

synonyms for man

Man, Adam.
(collectively) The strong sex, gentleman, a he, a master, men-folk, a male person, person, personality.
"The master of creation," the side of the sword, spouse, worker, crew, and
"to be a man for," which is translated from Norwegian as "being able" or "to master"[6] [Aas, 1975: 150].

Aas notes that "mother is offered as a synonym for woman while father is not given as a synonym for man" (1975: 151).

What will be the outcome of the movement for the participation of women in all sectors of society? Will the male distortion of the woman's metaphor stop? Or will women themselves lose their own metaphors and help the human race become an even more aggressive, dominance-oriented species than it now is? This could happen. As Margaret Mead showed us a few years ago (1950) individual societies can foster wholly aggressive characteristics in both females and males; they can also foster nurturant characteristics in both, or they can reverse what we think of as customary sex roles.[7] If we visualize 50 percent of the U.S. National Security Council as being composed of women (there have never been women on it, of course), it is hard to imagine that they would not quickly take on the mental habits and behavior patterns of the men they work with.

Yet matters are not that simple either. For example, the Research and Training Program of the U.S. Navy is recruiting increasing numbers of women to its service with both the awareness and the intention of changing ("improving," "raising the level of") the character of that service. Some of the senior administrators of this program feel that we are moving toward a substantially new type of society and that the navy will have a different kind of mission in the world of the future, a mission much less combat-oriented than the present one. They do not explicitly state that naval women will help reorient the naval mission, but the implication is there.[8]

There are two aspects of the woman's metaphor that bear on the question of the nature of the impact on society of increased participation by women in its public spaces. One has to do with *style* of role performance. Kanter (1975: 34-74) and (1976: 282-291) points to ways in which women can change interaction and decision-making styles of previously male dominant groups in business and industry, and notes very specifically that there is a necessary and critical sex ratio that has to be achieved in any group in order for women's more nurturant interactive styles to alter the behavior of a predominantly male group. (Militant feminists argue that women's liberation means liberation from nurturant roles and would measure progress for women by the extent to which they are free to use the more assertive masculine behavioral styles. This position must be taken into account because if it should come to prevail among women, their potential for effecting the kind of changes I am discussing might possibly be lost.)

The second aspect of the woman's metaphor has to do with the stance toward bureaucratic hierarchical structures. Is the decentralist nonbureaucratic model of social organization which is implicit in the woman's metaphor a viable alternative for modern society? If women "bring it with them," can it be used? Most literature on decentralized nonbureaucratic social organization, often referred to as "segmentary organization," deals either with nomadic or small-scale acephalous tribal societies (Barkun, 1968; Nelson, 1973: 43-60), or with social movements in industrial society. Gerlach and Hine (1970: 77) see the polycephalous, decentralized segmentary structure as an effective organizational format for social innovation, but not as an alternative model for the social order. Jo Freeman (1975: 222), applying the Gerlach and Hine approach to the feminist movement, also treats these techniques as movement strategies rather than as possible models of the social order.

Freeman sees them not only as techniques, but as ineffective techniques at that, vulnerable to the very development of elitism and goal subversion[9] that this approach is supposed to circumvent. I am taking the position that while we do not now have viable nonbureaucratic decentralist models of the social order that can be used at macro levels, they can, and I believe they will, be developed in the transition quarter-century that lies ahead. One particular set of women's techniques within the contemporary women's movement should not be taken to represent the totality of the contribution of the woman's metaphor to the political life of society. When that contribution does begin to take shape, it will very certainly draw heavily on the work of Mary Follett (1920), who early in this century was already laying the groundwork in political theory for the new social order along decentralist, participatory lines.

Since temperament, socialization, and past experience all to some extent affect both sex-role behavior and philosophic preferences in regard to the patterning of the social order, it does not seem fruitful to set up an either/or argument over whether "freedom" for women involves the general acceptance of more nurturant behavior by both sexes, and of a more localist social order, or whether that freedom involves the general acceptance of more assertive behavior by women and the incorporation of women into hierarchical authority positions. In the transition, at least, it certainly involves both.

There is an important underlying issue at stake here, however. Is there an ideal model for human performance of social roles that both women and men may be able to develop more fully in a future society not so fixated on gender differentiation as a determinant of role assignment and performance? Those who believe that we are moving toward an androgynous[10] society will answer yes. Once again, Margaret Mead has led the way in pointing out this possibility (Mead, 1967: 873), although she does not use the world androgynous. What would the androgynous—or what may alternatively be called the *gentle*-society look like? Would it be some horribly dull sexless society from which all human variety had disappeared, with all masculinity and feminity absorbed into a Caspar Milquetoast model of humanity, or would it be an excitingly diverse society in which each human being reached a degree of individuation and creativity such as only a few achieve in our present society? I am inclined to believe the latter. Science fiction has developed some interesting scenarios for androgynous societies. Most of these scenarios continue to assign the biologic function of child-bearing to women, but this function does not lead to stereotyped women's roles as we know them in contemporary societies. Rather there is a tremendous variety of social design around the themes of child-bearing, household composition, and economic productivity even though existing differentiation in procreative functions is postulated. Some conceptions of the androgynous society, however, involve the appearance of mutations enabling every individual to alternate the procreative functions of insemination and of carrying the fetus. Others visualize womb implantation for males who desire it, and still others picture test tube babies and the abandonment of the use of the human womb entirely.[11]

The issue is not whether women become like men or men become like women. The issue is whether by institutionalizing opportunities for the education, training, and participation of women in every sector of society at every level of decision-making in every dimension of human activity, and extending to men the procreation-oriented education we now direct exclusively to women, we will now set in motion a dialogic teaching-learning process between women and men that will enhance the human potentials of both. There have been great poets, artists, scholars, and saints as well as ordinary women and men in every age who have in fact been androgynous. Jesus is the prototypical androgynous human being in the history of western civilization. Buddha and Shiva are similarly androgynous figures in the history of eastern civilization. We recognize these persons when we meet them, in history or in the present, because they combine qualities of gentleness and assertiveness in ways that fit neither the typical male nor the typical female roles. Jonas Salk (1973) builds his model of social change around them, and describes them as "Epoch B people," surviving as best they can in Epoch A times. They will be the creators of the gentle society.

It is hard to envision a demilitarized, decentralist world of the future that is not also an androgynous world. The behavioral characteristics and mental orientations that human beings will need to develop in order to utilize non-military approaches to international problem-solving and to create more self-help devices to meet human needs at the community level are the behavioral characteristics of the nurturant, self-reliant androgyne.

On the other hand, the androgynous society seems like a far-out science fiction fantasy; on the other hand, unrecognized, partial androgyneity is already the fact in large areas of human experience. The world profile in Chapter 1, the historical review of women in the labor force in Chapter 3, and Chapters 4, 5, and 6 all describe the social reality of women toiling as men do, frequently carrying a heavier burden of physical labor than men, on top of the breeder-feeder function. In many ways men are the protected half of the species, not women. Equality for that vast majority of the world's women who carry such heavy dual burdens involves men sharing more of the parenting and feeding roles with women. Part III has emphasized the ambivalence involved for women in these perforce androgynous roles, as they attempt to create alternative world structures while operating from niches in role sets largely shaped for them by men—the work of nurturance they have performed through the centuries. The nineteenth century, as I have pointed out, created a new situation because of the possibility for the first time for women of having access to a level of education, global transport, and communication facilities that enabled them to think and act in global terms. The ensuing efforts of women over the past hundred years to reconstruct the world social order along more humane, peaceful, and equalitarian lines have been continuously distorted however by the center/periphery-patterned dominance structures in which they operate. Breaking out of these dominance structures and creating direct links with the world mass of peasant and village women at the grass-roots level has been very difficult.

Given the persistence of centralist dominance structures and the theme of conquering armies sent forth by weeping women in human history over the past eight thousand years or so, what indications are there that a shift toward a more androgynous society might take place? It seems implausible at this time, at the very zenith of world militarism, even to hint that a mutual transformation of gender-based roles toward a more shared nurturance might be possible.

Social change is glacially slow. Wars, revolutions, scientific discoveries, and technological inventions make it appear that the world, in the industrial nations at least, is changing very fast. The very attentive reception given in Europe and North America to such writers as Robert Jungk (1966) and Alvin Toffler (1970) suggests that most people feel battered by the changes they experience. Yet the changes are all variations on a small range of themes and hardly touch the lives of masses of third world peoples. As I tried to make clear earlier, industrial people are required to make relatively few adaptations to their environment compared to nomadic and peasant peoples. Technology insulates us from a great deal of our environment, even as it provides us with a kaleidoscope of images of what is happening "out there." In our homes, in our places of work, in our schools and gathering places, and even in our transportation media, as we move from one location to another, we are protected from having to respond to changes in the macro-environment except when wars or economic or natural catastrophes shatter our technological screening devices. Our range of behavioral repertoires—including the most intimate, involving the relationships of lovers, spouses, parents, children, and friends—have become so limited in this new technological shelter we live in that we have developed a whole series of specialized group therapy techniques to deal with the re-establishment of human contact in each set of relationships. One of the major obstacles to creating a demilitarized, peaceful, interdependent, and locally self-reliant society either nationally or internationally lies in the decline in interpersonal competence, and the lack of wholistic behavioral, as opposed to purely verbal, problem-solving skills.

In the long run, the factors that will contribute most to a shift toward a competent, peaceful, and androgynous society lie in the fragility of the technological shell, and in the hidden reservoirs of adaptability and human caring that remain concealed in all humans. There are profound disagreements among the best-trained scientists about the future energy utilization possibilities. The evidence seems to be counter to continuing the kind of technological innovation we have experienced in the past 150 years in hopes it will insulate us from the need to change our lifeways. While catastrophe scenarios are possible, triggered by nuclear war, individual acts of nuclear terrorism, widespread nuclear plant failures, or a variety of other types of dramatic breaks in our technological support systems, what is much more likely is a gradual attrition in resource availability and in the capacity of central planning systems to allocate dwindling resources effectively and to maintain health, education, and welfare services at anything like the levels we have now.

In the past decade we have had ample experience of the declining effectiveness of centrally administered service systems. Every socialist country—as well as European Common Market countries—has had to struggle with this. In the U.S. newspaper accounts, case study after case study can be read detailing how the application of centrally set standards and criteria for performance, and for the allocation of centrally budgeted funds, has weakened the effectiveness of local services to the poor, the elderly, children, and all populations with special needs. One day the story is about the collapse of nursing home care in a region under the impact of the application of new federal standards; another day we read about havoc in school lunch programs created by central computer programming for all local schools in an area. The newest developments in automated systems have become a nightmare for airports, causing a warning to be sent recently to all flight control officers about the increased likelihood of air traffic accidents as a result of system modifications requiring less frequent exercise of human judgment. The decline in national and world postal capabilities is one of the more visible and dramatic evidences of organizational disarray. The most recent automation disaster in the United States, as of this writing, is an expensive nationwide system of processing parcels developed by the post office. This process automatically destroys a certain percentage of the packages entrusted to it.

Technological developments in medicine make incredible life support systems possible for the elderly and the critically ill, but they leave diminished medical services available to middle and low income people. Educational technology makes books, audio-visual equipment, and computers available to children as part of a wide array of learning aids, but these are administered in schools with dwindling numbers of pupils interested in using them as the pupil dropout rate rises yearly for elementary as well as high school students.

Yet we do not have an uncaring society. There are teachers who agonize over children they cannot help; there are doctors and nurses who are deeply frustrated over their inability to give adequate medical care; there are welfare workers who lie awake nights worrying about their clients. Air traffic controllers get ulcers, and postal workers feel harassed by the unwielding bureaucracies that hamper the delivery of mail.

Fortunately, the technological shell does not insulate us completely from reality. We know that things are wrong. Can they be any different? Any better?

I pointed out in the chapter on women and peace work that women do not think of themselves as futurists, though every woman householder is daily a practicing futurist. Because their responsibilities and experiences tend to be local, they do not think in terms of large-scale systems or world futures. Precisely because of their intimate knowledge of local social terrains, however, they will be increasingly important in the development of the self-help systems that must replace poorly functioning centralized systems. We see this already in health services, as local doctors and nurses develop radio and TV programs to give a community the kind of medical advice that used to be available from the family doctor. We see it in the care of the elderly, as elderly activists give leadership to self-help programs for their own age groups, pooling skills and resources to meet their needs. We see it in the schools, as community persons help to develop a variety of apprenticeship programs, often in relation to pressing community needs, that bring children out of the isolation of the classroom into contact with people of all ages and backgrounds.[12] In all the activities I have mentioned, women have played a major role.

The post 1950s trend away from volunteer roles for women and toward their involvement in the paid labor force, including the paid helping professions, is being followed by an interesting counter trend, particularly in the United States. The volunteer is re-emerging as an important factor in community programs. The counter trend is not entirely welcomed by the women's movement, since it threatens to place women once more in the position of being expected to render unlimited service without recompense or recognition, and could undercut the status gains won by insistence that women be paid for the work they do. However, the new volunteerism wears a different face.

Because the new volunteer is likely also to be employed, and is volunteering time after working hours, there is more respect for the constraints under which the volunteer works. Also, there are increasing numbers of male volunteers. Professionals often handle the frustrations of their job constraints by working after hours on community redesign. Evaluation research on community programs is increasingly focusing on regaining an earlier ad hoc status and fluidity of informal network contacts between community groups. The goal is now to regain the greater local effectiveness that has been lost by compartmentalization and specialization. (See, for example, *Integration of Human Services in HEW;* and Litwak, 1970.)

None of these developments is peculiarly in the women's sphere. They are accomplished by women and men working side by side, but they depend heavily for their effectiveness on the special local fifth world knowledge that women have.

LEVERAGE POINTS FOR MOVEMENT TOWARD THE GENTLE SOCIETY

What I am describing is happening already, but very slowly, only in scattered locations. More conscious attention by women to their own innovative potential will increase the rate. There are three major leverage points that will move us more rapidly toward the gentle society. These points can be very effective in affluent western societies, although they may have less leverage power in poverty societies, and for "third world" poverty groups in affluent societies, where women's heavy burdens leave the majority of women with little energy for social change. An adequate discussion of third world strategies for women, and of how first and third world women can work together within and between countries, lies beyond my competence. Identifying the need for such alliances is the most that can be done here. One of the outcomes of the women's decade should be activities and writings by third world women that will educate first world women about the different perspectives and different strategies for social change being developed and practiced in various parts of the world. This will lay the groundwork for a broader spectrum of international cooperative activities than the western-initiated ones described in this book.

The first leverage point is the family. Consciousness-raising is already taking place in a certain middle-class sector of Euroamerican culture about equal parenting and equal sharing of what sociologists call the expressive (formerly female) and the instrumental (formerly male) roles (see Grönseth's study of work-sharing families, 1975: 202-221). These experiments in "liberated familism" are being supplemented by male liberation groups that do voluntary parenting for the children of women-headed households, as well as general resocialization of men for more nurturant social roles. They are further supplemented by community programs, some church-related and some not, to create extended families that will give the elderly, the lonely young, and the folk in between opportunities for intergenerational sharing and mutual aid. All such programs involve some redefinition of gender-based social roles.

The second leverage point is the early-childhood school setting—nursery school and early elementary school—where the majority of teachers (in most countries) are women. The opportunities for innovation by these women are legion. By giving major attention to the further development of apprenticeship relationships between children and other sectors of the community, crossing not only age but economic, ethnic, and cultural boundaries, teachers can see to it that no set of skills becomes the exclusive domain of any one section of the community. By involving male volunteers more heavily in the educational experiences of children, teachers can promote the resocialization of both children and adults away from gender-based roles to social roles that express individual human capacities. Textbook reform and classroom-based experiences alone will not do this. Adults and children must experience each other in a variety of settings, both task-oriented and recreational, for this resocialization to take place. Women teachers do not have to perpetuate the system they were trained in for the next generation. Expension of apprenticeship learning will if anything have even more impact in third world countries than in the first world, since classrooms tend to be even more divorced from daily life in the poor countries than in the rich. More Euroamerican women teachers need to visit Russia and China, where important educational innovations have been going on for years. The Chinese pattern of alternating very traditional classroom teaching with highly practical apprenticeships to local agricultural communes and factories provides for the West a set of educational models that needs to be carefully studied. Russian and Chinese educational systems both give a great deal of emphasis to children helping each other learn, something most American schools lost when the one-room schoolhouse was abandoned.

The third leverage point is the community itself. As more community services deteriorate or are discontinued because of economic difficulties in the first world, and fewer foreign-aid-based community development programs are available to the third world for the same reason, local initiative in the reconstruction of neighborhood self-help networks to deal with the problems of illness, child care, home maintenance, basic farming, food, and shelter will be an increasing challenge. For the third world this frequently involves rediscovery of traditional mutual aid systems that have been ignored or allowed to atrophy by development planners.[13] This goes so counter to the post-World War II trend toward specialization in every kind of human service that it may be hard to imagine and may appear, particularly to feminists, as a plot to get women back into domestic servitude. I am suggesting that women's leadership will be crucial in the development of local self-help in two ways: (1) they are the most likely to know where the hidden resources of the community are; and (2) they are the ones who must unremittingly attend to helping both girls and boys get the training they need in order to share community tasks more equally. Intentions without training will do little good. The development of community-wide continuing educational programs that begin in elementary school and continue to be available throughout life, permitting a variety of special skills training for all women and men, will be indispensable for the creation of the gentle society.

As local shortages develop, of water and of the prevailing currently used fuel, more imaginative resource monitoring and resource-conserving systems will have to be developed for home, school, and industry. If more intermediate technologies will be required in this more resource-conserving society, the local community is where they will have to be developed. The lifelong continuing education centers will become the workshops producing people able to engage in more labor-intensive economic activity if and when this is needed. The new peace corps of the future may involve sending women and men from those third world countries most advanced in intermediate technology to the high technology countries to help the latter to relearn the ingenuity they once had in earlier stages of the industrial revolution. Great effort may be required to keep such a shift from sweeping industrial societies into an emotional "reversion to the womb" that will involve insistence on kitchen-based roles for women, which will represent the very opposite of the types of productive roles they have traditionally had in the preindustrial world. As I have said, fear is a bad teacher. Unless women are exercising active leadership every step of the way in the years ahead, reaction to resource shortages, environmental pollution, and escalating societal violence might produce regressive movements that would drive society even farther from its androgynous potential than it now is.

We have seen in the studies of women in developing countries how much difference it makes to the well-being of a society whether women become a heavily exploited source of physical labor under highly unequal conditions, or whether they are relatively equal partners sharing resources appropriate to their labor. Both models represent possible futures for the West if we run out of high technology solutions and creative imagination simultaneously. To an optimist, neither will seem likely. Each of the three leverage points just discussed exist in arenas where the average woman is already active and knowledgeable. Moving from these familiar arenas to discussing androgynous approaches in regional, national, and global thinking that will create an interconnected, interdependent world society seems like an enormous step. It is one that women can and will take, once they begin preparing themselves for it, but it must not be forgotten that both the precondition and the continuing condition for women's involvement in the larger society is the gradual erosion of traditional gender differentiation in social roles at the local level.

A fourth leverage point, one that is much harder to locate and utilize effectively, and also one that requires extra training to use, is the domain of declarations and covenants concerning human rights that have gradually been evolving since the time of the French Revolution, though from far older sources.[14] In this century, first the League of Nations and then the United Nations have helped to create the specific covenants that spell out the rights of women, minorities, and children. To the extent that national parliaments adopt these covenants as a declaration of the rights of their own citizens, women have some leverage to expand their participation in the public arenas of the world. The simple obligation of a society to consider qualified women for any job, for example, has far-reaching implications for raising the aspiration levels of women. It creates, both at the national and the international level, a new incentive for women to get the appropriate training for global tasks. The following memo issued in January 1976 by the UN Centre for Economic and Social Information provides an illustration of the interconnected problems of aspiration level, training, and availability of women for UN work:

> Qualified women are being actively sought by the United Nations to work in technical assistance programmes in developing countries.
>
> The jobs available, which are some of the most challenging and interesting open to men or women with technical skill and experience, play a vital role in United Nations efforts to assist countries improve economic and social conditions.
>
> The Technical Recruitment Service of the United Nations, which handles applications for some 70 categories of skills, ranging from administrative reform to welfare programmes, is hoping that far greater numbers of women will apply for positions. Each year, the Service appoints some 1,000 technical experts from throughout the world, to work in more than 100 countries, but only a tiny proportion of the jobs have gone to women.

The reason, according to Mr. Leslie Schenk, who is charged with increasing the proportion of women applicants, is that "only a very disappointing number of women have been applying. We think that they don't know the opportunities exist." In recent years, the Service has recruited:

- a woman from New York to be attached to the Ministry of Trade in Malaysia to assess export potentials, market requirements, import systems, commercial channels, designs and prices, to assist in launching a marketing and promotional campaign for batik;
- a Filipino woman who is now serving as an adviser in Sri Lanka, developing training programmes in the field of family and child welfare. She is also training trainers in the skills required for demonstrators in creches and day care centres;
- a Ugandan woman to be manager of a multidisciplinary social and economic development project for full integration of women in rural development, a pilot project to serve as a pattern for the Swaziland national development effort;
- another Filipino woman as leader of a team of five government members of the Association of South East Asian Nations preparing negotiations on multilateral trade;

- a Panamanian woman who has for seventeen years been the Director of the Latin American Demographic Centre in Santiago, Chile, which among other services has provided population and census training for more than 1,000 professional demographers; and
- a woman from the Middle East to serve for several years as a welfare adviser in Mali, one month as an expert in community development in Burundi, and three years as a project coordinator in the Central African Republic.

Table 10.1 lists the technical fields for which international personnel is sought, and there is no sex barrier, legally, to employment in any of them.[15] The vacancy list issued in February 1976 from the UN Technical Assistance Recruitment Service lists 237 positions for which personnel are being actively sought. One hundred forty of these are open to any qualifying woman or man from any country, and ninety-seven are open to women and men from a special group of nine countries in Europe and Asia. The development of skill rosters from which technical assistance programs can choose qualified women, and the encouragement of more women to get the kinds of training in demand in the world community, must be high priorities for women. As mentioned in Chapter 7, such rosters are in the process of development, but they are still very incomplete. The same approach is necessary nationally, to encourage enough women to become available for national governmental posts and for international diplomatic careers.

There is nothing inevitable about the development of the gentle society I have envisioned here. The dangers pointed out are real. The dangers of rigidity of thought and action among decision-makers, induced by a paralyzing fear of impending crises, could create gigantic setbacks for the human

Table 10.1: Technical Cooperation Fields of Activity

Administrative Reform	Management Development
City Planning	Marketing
Community Development	Organization and Methods
Computer Research	Personnel Administration
Demography	Public Administration
Development Planning	Regional Planning
Ecology	Social Welfare
Economic Planning and Development	Statistics
Economics	Tourism Development
Electronic Data Processing	Training of Civil Servants
Housing	Training of Social Workers
Local Government Administration	Urban Development
Low-Cost Housing	Water Resources
	Welfare Program

SOURCE: Letter to Elise Boulding from Leslie Schenk, Recruitment Officer, Office of Personnel Services, United Nations (1976).

enterprise on the planet. The danger that women will not undertake an active enough role in envisioning and social problem-solving in the face of new opportunities is also serious. We may not make the transition to the gentle society because women do not have the confidence to act on their own metaphors. We may lose out because women throw away their metaphors and adopt those of men, either permanently or as a transition strategy. This has been a calculated transition strategy on the part of women revolutionaries in the past, a gamble on the possibility of being able to create the gentler society later. It is a grave gamble indeed, since we have no historical examples, to my knowledge, of violent revolution leading to the gentle society.

The issue remains a very real one, however, of whether what I have called the woman's metaphor is of any use as the basis for a transition strategy away from the crisis-ridden present to a new social order. It is a subject requiring much further study on the part of those seeking social change strategies. A study of the metaphors of women activists is one useful way to approach the problem. What social models did they work with, and how effective were they? Some fine examples of women's metaphors are to be found in *Woman as Revolutionary* (1973). This book provides a series of excerpts from the writings of twenty-two women ranging from the medieval and Renaissance figures of Christine de Pisan and Joan of Arc to early turn-of-the-century figures such as terrorist Sofia Perovskaya, anarchist Emma Goldman, and the great humanitarian Helen Keller. While they all work with variants of the basic commensalist theme in their metaphors of the social order, some of them have allowed their metaphors to be coopted by men. Others have not. All the metaphors foreshadow in some way the androgynous society, the gentle society, that I suggest represents women's contribution to imaging the future. Two passages from *Woman as Revolutionary* demonstrate the alternatives. The first is a biographical account of the Russian terrorist Sofia Perovskaya, from the *Memoirs of Vera Figner*. Perovskaya deliberately set aside her own metaphor to adopt that of her male colleagues.

> Perhaps Perovskaya had inherited her mother's tender heart, and this may explain her womanly gentleness and overflowing goodness toward the toiling masses, during the period of her activity as a member of the Tchaikovsky's circle. Upon completing her studies for the position of assistant physician, she came in contact with these people in the village, in her capacity of propagandist from the Populist group. Those who witnessed her life there have stated in their reminiscences that there was something maternally tender in her treatment of the sick, as indeed there was in her entire attitude towards the peasants with whom she came in contact. How morally satisfying to her was this contact with village life, and how difficult it was for her to tear herself away from that obscure and wretched village existence, was indicated by her atti-

tude at the conference of Voronezh, and her hesitation in the face of the breaking up of the party, Land and Freedom, into The Will of the People and the Black Partition. At that time both she and I had just left the village behind us, and were still bound to it with all our hearts. We were asked to take part in the political struggle, we were called to the city, but we felt that the village needed us, that without us it would be still darker there. Reason told us that we must follow the course chosen by our comrades, the political terrorists, who were drunk with the spirit of strife and animated by success. But our hearts spoke otherwise, our mood was quite different. It drew us to the world of the dispossessed. This mood, which we did not at that time analyze, was afterwards defined as an aspiration towards a clean life, towards personal saintliness. But, as I have before mentioned, after some hesitation we overcame our feeling, our mood, and having renounced that moral satisfaction which life among the people gave to us, we stood firmly side by side with our comrades, whose political sagacity was greater than our own.

From that time on, Perovskaya was first in all the terroristic projects of the Executive Committee of The Will of the People. It was she who took the part of the simple, hospitable housewife in the poor hovel bought for seven or eight hundred rubles in the name of Sukhorukov, who as a petty railroad clerk figured as her husband. At the decisive moment, it was she who was left in that hovel with Stephan Shiryayev, to turn on the electric current at the approach of the Tsar's train. Always watchful, always ready, she gave the necessary signal at the right time, and she was not to blame for the fact that it was not the Tsar's train, but the train in which his servants were travelling that was wrecked.

Later, after the explosion in the Winter Palace on the fifth of February, 1880, she went to Odessa to superintend the laying of a mine on Italyanskaya Street.

And finally, when on the first of March, 1881, the seventh attempt of the Executive Committee was in preparation, Perovskaya, together with Zhelyabov, organised the group of persons who were to observe the Tsar's goings and comings in the capital, and who were to be the signalists at the climax of the drama. She also directed the bomb-throwers, not only during the preparatory period, but also on the first of March, when she gave orders for a new disposition of forces, thanks to which the Emperor perished from the explosion of two bombs, hurled by the terrorists [Giffen, 1973: 95-97].

The second metaphor comes from Helen Keller, in an article entitled "The Hand of the World." While the language may appear a bit flowery, there was nothing flowery about her life. She experienced the extreme social marginality of those who are born both blind and deaf, yet found a way to discover and affirm a new kind of social belonging. Her firm insistence on probing the depths of her own metaphor, and her understanding of the underlying social processes involved, make her use of the gentle metaphor of the hand a powerful instrument for social change.[16] It represents the kind of wholistic, behaviorally oriented approach to problem-solving that I suggested earlier must replace a purely verbal facility with problem manipulation, if viable transition strategies to the gentle society are to be found.

All our earthly well-being hangs upon the living hand of the world. Society is founded upon it. Its life-beats throb in our institutions. Every industry, every process, is wrought by a hand, or by a superhand—a machine whose mighty arm and cunning fingers the human hand invents and wields. The hand embodies its skill, projects and multiplies itself, in wondrous tools, and with them it spins and weaves, plows and reaps, converts clay into walls, and roofs our habitations with trees of the forest.

The hand of the world! Think how it sends forth the waters where it will to form canals between the seas, and binds the same seas with thoughts incorporated in arms of stone! What is the telegraph cable but the quick hand of the world extended between the nations, now menacing, now clasped in brotherhood? What are our ships and railways but *our* feet made swift and strong by *our* hands? The hand captures the winds, the sun, and the lightnings, and dispatches them upon errands of commerce. Before its irresistible blows, mountains are beaten small as dust. Huge derricks—prehensile power magnified in digits of steel—rear factories and palaces, lay stone upon stone in our stately monuments, and raise cathedral spires.

Step by step by investigation of blindness led me into the industrial world. And what a world it is! How different from the world of my beliefs! I must face unflinchingly a world of facts—a world of misery and degradation, of blindness, crookedness, and sin, a world struggling against the elements, against the unknown, against itself. How reconcile this world of fact with the bright world of my imagining?

Why is it willing hands are denied the prerogatives of labor, that the hand of *one* is against *the other.* At the bidding of a single hand thousands rush to produce, or hang idle. Amazing that hands which produce nothing should be exalted and jeweled with authority!

Driven by the very maladjustments that wound it, and enabled by its proved capacity for readjustment and harmony, society must move onward to a state in which every hand shall work and reap the fruits of its own endeavor, no less, no more. This is the third world which I have discovered. From a world of dreams I was plunged into a world of fact, and thence I have emerged into a society which is still a dream, but rooted in the actual. The commonwealth of the future is growing surely out of the state in which we now live. There will be strife, but no aimless, self-defeating strife. There will be competition, but no soul-destroying, hand-crippling competition. There will be only honest emulation in cooperative effort. There will be example to instruct, companionship to cheer, and to lighten burdens. Each hand will do its part in the provision of food, clothing, shelter, and the other great needs of *humanity,* so that if poverty comes all will bear it alike, and if prosperity shines all will rejoice in its warmth.

The hand of the world will then have achieved what it now obscurely symbolizes—the uplifting and regeneration of the race, all that is highest, all that is creative in *humankind* [Giffen, 1973: 125-132].

One last metaphor to consider, closely linked conceptually to the hand of the world metaphor, comes from the writings of Mao Tse-tung: "Women hold up half the sky." I will leave you with the image of Helen Keller and Mao Tse-tung standing side by side, holding up the world.

Now what is *your* metaphor?

NOTES

1. There has been no lack of writing about the relationship between women's roles and status, war, and poverty, stemming from intuitions about the nature of the social order. Jane Addams, Ellen Key, and other nineteenth century internationalist women wrote at length on this subject. Marx and Engels (1962) and August Bebel (1971) all suggested that the extent of liberation of women into the labor force was a measure of the progress of women from an earlier condition of domestic servitude (Boulding, 1977). Only recently, however, have social science data been available to document the relationship between the status and participation of women in society, and the social and economic conditions of that society.

2. "Paradigm shift" is employed here in the sense used by Kuhn (1970).

3. Military expenditures in the developed world went from $97 billion (U.S.) in 1960 to $222 billion in 1974. In the developing world, military expenditures went from $10 billion to $48 billion. The world totals were $107 billion in 1960, $270 billion in 1974 (Sivard, 1976: 20).

4. Norwegian sociologist Ingrid Eide Galtung's study of international civil servants (1966: 198-209) makes a similar point about the marginality of UN civil servants in their home countries, and relates that marginality to their sense of commitment to world community.

5. A striking example of the woman's metaphor is found in the writings of the fourteenth century English anchoress, Julian of Norwich: "And then I saw that God rejoiceth that he is our Father: and God rejoiceth that he is our Mother: and God rejoiceth that he is our true spouse, and our soul his beloved wife. And Christ rejoiceth that he is our Brother."

6. "The young psychologist who first quoted these synonyms wrote a book which he entitled: Language is power" (Aas, 1975: 150; see Blakar, 1973).

7. In her study of three societies of New Guinea, Mead found that "The Arapesh is the mild responsive man married to the mild responsive woman.... The Mundugumor

ideal is the violent aggressive man married to the violent aggressive woman." Among the Tchambuli there is a sex role reversal, "with the woman the dominant, impersonal, aging partner, the man the less responsible and the emotionally dependent person" (1950: 279).

8. These observations are my own personal interpretation of the proceedings of a conference (in which I participated in December 1975) called to consider what world scenarios may be in the future and how the research and training program of the Navy should adapt itself to the changing world.

9. Freeman's discussion is in terms of the Weber-Michels model of "oligarchization, conservation, and goal transformation," and her use of the model is based on their writings (Weber, 1946; Michels, 1949).

10. Androgynous: "both male and female in one; hermaphroditic" in Webster's 2nd *Collegiate Dictionary*. This word is to be carefully distinguished from androgenous, "producing male offspring."

11. Some examples of sex role conceptualizations in science fiction: Theodore Sturgeon, "If All Men Were Brothers Would You Let Your Sister Marry One?" *Dangerous Visions* No. 3; Kingsley Amis, *New Maps of Hell,* Chapter 5 on utopias; Ursula K. LeGuin, *The Left Hand of Darkness* and *The Dispossessed;* and many others. Shulamith Firestone's *Dialectics of Sex,* which is *not* science fiction, suggests that the test tube may replace the womb.

12. More than half the school systems in the United States now have available to them funding to develop such locally conceived and locally based community apprenticeship programs. Will federal funding agencies be able to resist the hitherto inevitable process of institutionalizing specifications as the programs proliferate, turning the apprenticeship system into another standardized variation of the classroom experience?

13. Gandhi's *swaraj,* or community *self-help* programs in India, were almost entirely built on traditional concepts and models of village organization (Gandhi, 1951).

14. For these older sources, see Jenks (1958).

15. Frequently the courts have to be used to establish these legal rights to employment, which is one reason why the human rights leverage point is such a difficult one to exercise.

16. To do justice to the spirit of these paragraphs, I have replaced the word "man" with alternative wordings wherever it occurs, and italicized the replaced word so the reader can know where I have made the changes.

BIBLIOGRAPHY

Aas, Berit (1975) "On female culture: An attempt to formulate a theory of women's solidarity and action." Acta Sociologica 18: 142-161.
Aberle, David F. (1962) "Matrilineal descent in a cross-cultural perspective." Pp. 655-730 in David M. Schneider and Kathleen Gough (eds.), Matrilineal Kinship. Berkeley: University of California Press.
Addams, Jane, Emily G. Balch, and Alice Hamilton (1972) Women at the Hague: The International Congress of Women and Its Results. New York: Garland Publishing Company. (First published 1915)
Adelman, Irma and Cynthia Taft Morris (1973) Economic Growth and Social Equity in Developing Countries. Stanford, Cal.: Stanford University Press.
--- (1967) Society, Politics and Economic Development: A Quantitative Approach. Baltimore: Johns Hopkins Press.
African Bibliographic Center (1960) "Contemporary African women." Vol. 6. Special Bibliographic Series. New York: Negro Universities Press.
AID [Agency for International Development] (1974) "A seven country survey on the roles of women in rural development." A report prepared for the Agency for International Development by Development Alternatives, Inc., Washington, D.C. (mimeo)
Alger, Chadwick (n.d.) Columbus: Mershon Center, Ohio State University.
Ali, Ameer (1899) "The influence of women in Islam." The Nineteenth Century Magazine (May): 755-774.
Awad, M. (1959) "Settlement of nomadic and semi-nomadic tribal groups in the Middle East." International Labor Review 79 (January): 25-56.

Barkun, Michael (1968) Law Without Sanctions: Order in Primitive Societies and the World Community. New Haven, Conn.: Yale University Press.
Beard, Mary (1946) Woman as a Force in History: A Study in Traditions and Realities. New York: Macmillan.
Bebel, August (1971) Women Under Socialism. Tr. Daniel de Leon. New York: Schocken Books. (First published 1904)
Bennet, William S. (1967) "Educational change and economic development." Sociology of Education 40 (Spring): 101-114.
Bergman, Arlene Eisen (1974) Women of Viet Nam. San Francisco: People's Press.
Bernard, Jessie (1975) Women, Wives, Mothers: Values and Options. Chicago: Aldine.
Blakar, Rolv (1973) Spraak er Makt. Oslo: Pax.
Borgstrom, Georg (1973) Focal Points. New York: Macmillan.
Boserup, Ester (1970) Woman's Role in Economic Development. New York: St. Martin's Press.
Boulding, Elise (1977) The Underside of History: A View of Women Through Time. Boulder, Colo.: Westview Press.
--- (1974) "Futures for Franciscans." An address given Chapter of Mats, School Sisters of St. Francis, Alverno College, Milwaukee, August 12. (mimeo)

Boulding, Elise (1973) "Societal complexity and religious potential." Paper presented to Discussion Group No. 7, Special World Conference on Futures Research, "Human Needs–New Societies–Supportive Technologies." Rome, September 25-30.

――― (1972) "Women as role models in industrializing societies: A macro-system model of socialization for civic competence." Pp. 11-34 in Marvin Sussman and Betty Cogswell (eds.), Cross-National Family Research. Leiden: E. J. Brill.

――― (1969a) "The family, the NGO and social mapping in a changing world." International Associations 11 (November): 549-554.

――― (1969b) "The Effects of Industrialization on the Participation of Women in Society." Ann Arbor: University of Michigan. Unpublished Ph.D. dissertation.

――― (1966) "The road to parliament for women." A paper presented to the International Seminar on the Participation of Women in Public Life, Rome, October.

Boulding, Elise, Shirley A. Nuss, Dorothy Carson, and Michael Greenstein (1976) Handbook of International Data on Women. New York: Halsted Press (A Sage Publications Book).

Boulding Global Data Bank (n.d.) Boulder: Institute of Behavioral Science, University of Colorado.

Brown, Lester R. (1970) Seeds of Change: The Green Revolution and Development in the 1970's. New York: Praeger.

Brown, Norman L. and E. R. Pariser (1975) "Food science in developing countries." Science 188 (9 May): 589-592.

Burdett-Coutts, The Baroness (1893) Woman's Mission. New York: Charles Scribner's Sons.

Bussey, Gertrude and Margaret Tims (1965) Women's International League for Peace and Freedom: 1915-1965: A Record of Fifty Year's Work. London: Allen and Unwin.

Buvinić, Mayra et al. [eds.] (1976) Women and World Development: An Annotated Bibliography. Washington, D.C.: Overseas Development Council.

Chadwick, Nora (1970) The Celts. London: Cox & Wyman.

Cita-Malard, Suzanne (1964) Religious Orders of Women. Tr. George J. Robinson. New York: Hawthorn.

Cleveland, Arthur Rackham (1896) Woman Under the English Law. London: Hurst.

De Tocqueville, Alexis (1945) Democracy in America. Tr. Philips Bradley. New York: Alfred A. Knopf.

Drinker, Sophie (1948) Music and Women: The Story of Women in Their Relation to Music. New York: Coward-McCann.

Duby, Georges (1968) Rural Economy and Country Life in the Medieval West. Tr. C. Pasten. London: E. Arnold.

Dupire, Marguerite (1963) "The position of women in a pastoral society." Pp. 47-92 in Denise Paulme (ed.), Women of Tropical Africa. Tr. H. M. Wright. London: Routledge and Kegan Paul.

Dwyer, Johanna T. and Jean Mayer (1975) "Beyond economics and nutrition: The complex basis of food policy." Science 188 (9 May): 566-570.

Eagle, Mary Kavanaugh Oldham [ed.] (1893) The Congress of Women (held in the Women's Building, World Columbian Exposition). Chicago: Arno Reprint, 1974.

Eberhard, Wolfram (1967) Settlement and Social Change in Asia. Collected Papers. Vol. I. Hong Kong: Hong Kong University Press.

Falk, Richard A. (1975) A Study of Future Worlds. New York: Free Press.
Farrell, Warren (1974) The Liberated Man: Beyond Masculinity, Freeing Men and Their Relationships with Women. New York: Random House.
Firth, Raymond and B. S. Yamey [eds.] (1964) Capital, Saving, and Credit in Peasant Societies: Studies from Asia, Oceania, the Caribbean, and Middle America. Chicago: Aldine.
Follett, Mary P. (1920) The New State. New York: Longmans, Green.
Ford Foundation (1973) "Women and national development in African countries: Some profound contradictions." A position paper presented by the Human Resources Development Division, Women's Programme Unit, United Nations Economic Commission for Africa, to the Task Force on Women, Ford Foundation, February.
Freeman, Jo (1975) "Political organization in the feminist movement." Acta Sociologica 18: 222-244.
Friedan, Betty (1963) The Feminine Mystique. New York: W. W. Norton.

Galtung, Ingrid Eide (1966) "Are international civil servants international? A case study of UN experts twentieth century in Latin America." Pp. 198-209 in Proceedings of the International Peace Research Association Inaugural Conference. Assen, the Netherlands: Van Gorcum.
Gandhi, Mohandas K. (1951) Sarvodoya. Delhi: Ahmedabad, Mavajivan.
Gerlach, Luther P. and Virginia H. Hine (1970) People, Power, Change: Movements of Social Transformation. New York: Bobbs-Merrill.
Giffen, Frederick C. [ed.] (1973) Woman as Revolutionary. New York: New American Library, Mentor Books.
Gordon, Elizabeth Putnam (1924) Women Torch-Bearers: The Story of the Woman's Christian Temperance Union. Evanston, Ill.: National WCTU Publishing House.
Graves, Nancy (1971) City, Country, and Child Rearing: A Tri-Cultural Study of Mother-Child Relationships in Varying Environments. Boulder: University of Colorado. Unpublished Ph.D. dissertation.
Grönseth, Erik (1975) "Worksharing families: Adaptations of pioneering families with husband and wife in part-time employment." Acta Sociologica 18: 202-221.
Grousset, René (1970) The Empire of the Steppes: A History of Central Asia. Tr. Naomi Walford. New Brunswick, N.J.: Rutgers University Press.

Halpern, Joel M. (1964) "Capital, saving, and credit among Lao peasants." Pp. 69-81 in Raymond Firth and B. S. Yamey (eds.), Capital, Saving, and Credit in Peasant Societies: Studies from Asia, Oceania, the Caribbean, and Middle America. Chicago: Aldine.
Hansen, Donald A. and Reuben Hill (1964) "Families under stress." Pp. 782-819 in Harold Christensen (ed.), Handbook of Marriage and the Family. Chicago: Rand-McNally.
Herlihy, David (1962) "Land, family and women in continental Europe, 701-1200." Traditio 18: 89-120.
Hill, Polly (1969) "Hidden trade in Hausaland." Man 4: 392-409.

Ihromi, T. O. et al. (1973) The Status of Women and Family Planning in Indonesia. A Preliminary Report of the Study Conducted by the Research Team on the Status of Women and Family Planning in Indonesia. Jakarta, Indonesia: National Training and Research Center.

Integration of Human Services in HEW (n.d.) Washington, D.C.: Government Printing Office.
International Labor Organization (1973) 1972 Yearbook of Labor Statistics. Geneva: International Labor Office.

Jenks, C. Willfred (1958) The Common Law of Mankind. London: Stevens.
Judge, Anthony J. N. (1971) "Matrix organization and organizational networks." International Associations 3: 154-170.
Julian of Norwich (1961) Revelations of Divine Love. Tr. James Walsh, S. J. Naperville, Ill.: Allenson.
Jungk, Robert (1966) Die Grosse Maschine: Auf dem Weg in eine andere Welt. Bern: Scherz.

Kanter, Rosabeth Moss (1976) "The policy issues: Presentation VI." Signs 1 (Spring): 282-291.
——— (1975) "Women and the structure of organizations: Explorations in theory and behavior." Pp. 34-74 in Marcia Millman and Rosabeth Moss Kanter (eds.), Another Voice: Feminist Perspectives on Social Life and Social Science. Garden City, N.Y.: Doubleday/Anchor.
Key, Ellen (1911) Love and Marriage. Tr. Arthur G. Chater. New York: Putnam.
Kothari, Rajni (1974) Footsteps into the Future: Diagnosis for the Present World and a Design for an Alternative. New York: Free Press.
Kramer, Samual Noah (1963) The Sumerians: Their History, Culture, and Character. Chicago: University of Chicago Press.
Kuhn, Thomas S. (1970) The Structure of Scientific Revolutions. Chicago: University of Chicago Press.

Lacey, W. K. (1968) The Family in Classical Greece. Ithaca, N.Y.: Cornell University Press.
Laslett, Peter [ed.] (1972) Household and Family in Past Time. Cambridge, England: Cambridge University Press.
Latham, Michael C. (1975) "Nutrition and infection in national development." Science 188 (9 May): 561-565.
Lee, Richard B. and Irven DeVore [eds.] (1968) Man the Hunter. Chicago: Aldine.
Lev, Daniel S. (1972) Islamic Courts and Indonesia: A Study in the Political Bases of Legal Institutions. Berkeley: University of California Press.
Litwak, Eugene with J. Ajemian, G. Hamilton, J. F. McDonough, and G. Rhodes (1970) Towards the Multi-Factor Theory and Practices of Linkages Between Formal Organizations. HEW, Social and Rehabilitative Services Department. Washington, D.C.: Government Printing Office.

McCarthy, Florence E. (1976) "Bengali women as mediators of social change." Human Organization.
McCarthy, Thomas P., C.S.V. (1955) Guide to the Catholic Sisterhoods in the United States. Washington, D.C.: Catholic University of America Press.
McDonnell, Ernest W. (1969) The Beguines and Beghards in Medieval Culture. New York: Octagon Books.
Maher, Vanessa (1974) Women and Property in Morocco: Their Changing Relations to the Process of Social Stratification in the Middle Atlas. London: Cambridge University Press.

Marx, Karl and Friedrich Engels (1962) Selected Works. Volume II. Moscow: Foreign Languages Publishing House.
Mayer, Jean (1975) "Management of famine relief." Science 188 (9 May): 571-577.
Mead, Margaret (1967) "The life cycle and its variation: The division of roles." Daedalus 96 (Summer): 871-875.
——— (1950) Sex and Temperament in Three Primitive Societies. New York: New American Library.
Meadows, D. L. and D. H. Meadows (1972) Limits to Growth. New York: Universe Books.
Mendlovitz, Saul [ed.] (1975) On the Creation of a Just World Order: Preferred Worlds for the 1990's. New York: Free Press.
Michels, Robert (1949) Political Parties. New York: Free Press.
Mitchnik, David (1972) The Role of Women in Rural Development in Zaire. Oxford: Oxfam.
Monteil, Vincent (1959) "The evolution and settling of the nomads of the Sahara." International Social Science Journal 11: 572-585.
Moock, Peter Russell (1973) Managerial Ability in Small-Farm Production: An Analysis of Maize Yields in the Vihiga Division of Kenya. New York: Columbia University. Unpublished Ph.D. dissertation.

Nair, Kusum (1973) Three Bowls of Rice: India and Japan: Century of Effort. East Lansing: Michigan State University Press.
——— (1969) The Lonely Furrow: Farming in the United States, Japan, and India. Ann Arbor: University of Michigan Press.
——— (1962) Blossoms in the Dust: The Human Factor in Indian Development. New York: Praeger.
Nelson, Cynthia (1973) "Women and power in nomadic societies in the Middle East." Pp. 43-60 in Cynthia Nelson (ed.), The Desert and the Sown: Nomads in the Wider Society. Berkeley: University of California Press.
"Nomads and Nomadism in the Arid Zone" (1959) Part I of the International Social Science Journal 11: 481-585.

O'Faolain, Julia and Laura Martines [eds.] (1973) Not in God's Image: A History of Women in Europe from the Greeks to the Nineteenth Century. New York: Harper & Row.
Official Associated Press Almanac, 1973 (1972) New York: Almanac Publishing Co.

Paddock, William and Paul Paddock (1967) Famine—1975! Boston: Little, Brown.
Papanek, Hanna (1975) "Women in South and Southeast Asia: Issues and research." Signs: Journal of Women in Culture and Society 1 (Autumn): 193-214.
Penzer, N. M. (1935) The Harem: An Account of the Institution. Philadelphia: J. B. Lippincott.
Piet, David L. and Lukas Hendrata (1974) "Karet KB and Jamu: An integrated approach to condom marketing." International Development Review 12: 2-7.
Planetary Citizens (1975) "Food and famine." Resource Sheet No. 1. New York: 777 UN Plaza.
Polak, Fred L. (1973) The Image of the Future. 2 volumes. Tr. Elise Boulding. New York: Oceana Press, 1961. (Edition abridged by Elise Bounding, San Francisco: Jossey Bass/Elsivier).

Poleman, Thomas T. (1975) "World food: A perspective." Science 188 (9 May): 510-518.
Posthumus-van der Goot, W. H. (1961) Vrouwen Vochten Voor de Vrede. Arnhem: Van Loghum Slaterus.
Power, Eileen and M. M. Postan (1933) Studies in English Trade in the Fifteenth Century. London: George Routledge & Sons.
Prawdin, Michael (1940) The Mongol Empire: Its Rise and Legacy. Tr. Eden and Cedar Paul. London: Allen and Unwin.

Renard, Georges (1968) Guilds in the Middle Ages. New York: Augustus M. Kelley.
Rudé, George (1974) The Crowd in History, 1730-1848. New York: Wiley.

Salk, Jonas (1973) The Survival of the Wisest. New York: Harper & Row.
Schenk, Leslie (1976) Recruitment Officer, Office of Personnel Services, United Nations.
Sherrard, Philip (1966) Byzantium. New York: Time.
Silberman, Leo (1959) "Somali nomads." International Social Science Journal 11: 559-569.
Simons, H. J. (1968) African Women: Their Legal Status in South Africa. Evanston, Ill.: Northwestern University Press.
Sivard, Ruth Leger (1976) World Military and Social Expenditures. Leesburg, Va.: WMSE Publications.
Smith, W. Robertson (1966) Kinship and Marriage in Early Arabia. Stanley A. Cook, (ed.), Oosterhout N. B., the Netherlands: Anthropological Publications.
Social Indicators (1973) Written and compiled by the Statistical Policy Division, Office of Management and Budget, and prepared for publication by the Social and Economic Statistics Administration, U.S. Dept. of Commerce. Washington, D.C.: Government Printing Office.
Stanton, Theodore [ed.] (1970) The Woman Question in Europe. New York: Source Book Press. (First published 1884)
Stinchcombe, Arthur (1965) "Social structure and organizations." In James G. March (ed.), Handbook of Organizations. Chicago: Rand McNally.
Strathern, Marilyn (1972) Women in Between: Female Roles in a Male World, Mount Hagen, New Guinea. New York: Seminar Press.
Sudarkasa, Niara (1973) Where Women Work: A Study of Yoruba Women in the Marketplace and in the Home. No. 53, Anthropological Papers, Museum of Anthropology. Ann Arbor: University of Michigan.
Sullerot, Evelyne (1968) Historie et Sociologie du Travail Féminin. Paris: Société Nouvelle des Editions Gonthier.
Swift, M. G. (1964) "Capital, saving, and credit in a Malay peasant economy." Pp. 133-156 in Raymond Firth and B. S. Yamey (eds.), Capital, Saving, and Credit in Peasant Societies: Studies from Asia, Oceania, the Caribbean, and Middle America. Chicago, Ill.: Aldine.
Szalai, Alexander (1973) The Situation of Women in the United Nations. New York: United Nations, UNITAR.
――― (1972) The Use of Time. The Hague: Mouton.

Taeuber, Irene B. and Conrad Taeuber (1971) People of the United States in the Twentieth Century. United States Bureau of Census Monograph. Washington, D.C.: United States Government Printing Office.

Bibliography

Taylor, Charles Lewis and Michael C. Hudson (1972) World Handbook of Political and Social Indicators. New Haven, Conn.: Yale University Press.

Thompson, Louis M. (1975) "Weather variability, climatic change, and grain production." Science 188 (9 May): 535-540.

Thrupp, Sylvia L. (1964) Change in Medieval Society: Europe North of the Alps, 1050-1500. New York: Appleton-Century-Crofts.

Tinker, Irene and Michèle Bo Bramsen [eds.] (1976) Women and World Development. Washington, D.C.: Overseas Development Council.

Toffler, Alvin (1970) Future Shock. New York: Random House.

Topley, Marjorie (1964) "Capital, saving, and credit among indigenous rice farmers and immigrant vegetable farmers in Hong Kong's new territories." Pp. 157-186 in Raymond Firth and B. S. Yamey (eds.), Capital, Saving, and Credit in Peasant Societies: Studies from Asia, Oceania, the Caribbean, and Middle America. Chicago: Aldine.

Toynbee, Arnold J. (1935) A Study of History. Vol. 3. New York: Oxford University Press.

Turnbull, Colin (1968a) The Forest People. New York: Simon and Schuster.

--- (1968b) "Hunting and gathering: Contemporary societies." International Encyclopedia of the Social Sciences. Vol. 7. New York: Macmillan.

United Nations (1976) Memorandum issued by the UN Centre for Economic and Social Information. January.

--- (1975a) 1974 Report of the World Social Situation. New York: United Nations.

--- (1975b) "World plan of action of the World Conference of the International Women's Year." Mexico City, June 19-July 2. New York: United Nations.

--- (1974a) "The data base for discussion on the interrelations between the integration of women in development, their situation, and population factors in Africa." Regional Seminar on the Integration of Women in Development with Special Reference to Population Factors, Economic Commission for Africa, United Nations Economic and Social Council, Addis Ababa, May. (mimeo)

--- (1974b) The Changing and Contemporary Role of Women in African Development. UNECA. New York: United Nations.

--- (1974c) "Study on the interrelationship of the status of women and family planning." Addendum, World Population Conference. Bucharest, Romania, August. (mimeo)

--- (1974d) "The role of women in population dynamics related to food and agriculture and rural development in Africa." ECA/FAO, Women's Program Unit. (mimeo)

--- (1974e) "Report of the world food conference." Conference held in Rome in November, 1974. New York: United Nations.

--- (1973) "Report of five workshops in home economics and other family-related fields. UNECA. New York: United Nations.

--- (1972-1974) "Country reports on vocational and technical training for girls and women." UNECA. New York: United Nations.

--- (1972a) United Nations Demographic Yearbook. New York: United Nations.

--- (1972b) UNESCO Statistical Yearbook, 1972. New York: United Nations.

--- (1972c) United Nations Statistical Yearbook, 1972. New York: United Nations.

--- (1971a) United Nations Demographic Yearbook. New York: United Nations.

--- (1971b) UNESCO Statistical Yearbook, 1971. New York: United Nations.

--- (1971c) United Nations Statistical Yearbook, 1971. New York: United Nations.

United Nations (1966) Progress in Land Reform. Dept. of Economic and Social Affairs. Fourth Report, prepared jointly by the Secretariats of the UN, FAO, and ILO. New York: United Nations.

--- (1953) The Determinants and Consequences of Population Trends: A Summary of the Findings of Studies on the Relationships Between Population Changes and Economic and Social Conditions. Population Studies No. 17. New York: United Nations.

Vreede-De Stuers, Cora (1968) Parda: A Study of Muslim Women's Life in Northern India. Atlantic Highlands, N.J.: Humanities Press.

Ward, Barbara [ed.] (1963a) Women in the New Asia: The Changing Social Roles of Men and Women in South and South-East Asia. Paris: UNESCO.

--- (1963b) "Men, women and change: An essay in understanding social roles in South and South-East Asia." Pp. 25-99 in Barbara E. Ward (ed.), Women of the New Asia: The Changing Social Roles of Men and Women in South and South-East Asia. Paris: UNESCO.

Weber, Max (1946) Max Weber: Essays in Sociology. H. J. Gerth and C. W. Mills (eds.). New York: Oxford University Press.

Wenig, Steffan (1970) Women in Egyptian Art. New York: McGraw Hill.

Westermann, William L. (1955) The Slave Systems of Greek and Roman Antiquity. Philadelphia: American Philosophical Society.

White, Gilbert F., David J. Bradley, and Anne U. White (1972) Drawers of Water: Domestic Water Use in East Africa. Chicago: University of Chicago Press.

Woodward, Beverly (1976) Personal Communication. Boston: International Fellowship of Reconciliation.

World Military Expenditures (1969) Washington, D.C.: United States Arms Control and Disarmament Agency.

Yearbook of International Organizations (1974) Brussels: Union of International Associations.

--- (1973) Brussels: Union of International Associations.

Ziegler, Philip (1970) The Black Death. Great Britain: Pelican Books.

APPENDIX

Table A.1: Figures on Participation in Agriculture of Women and Total Population Based on ILO Estimates and E. Boulding Estimates

Country	% of All Economically Active Women in Agriculture and Herding (from ILO data)[a]	% of Total Economically Active Population in Agriculture and Herding	% of All Economically Active Women in Agriculture and Herding (E. Boulding Estimates)
Countries with Substantial Numbers of Women-Headed Households			
Botswana	95	90	95
Central African Republic	No Data	90	95
Congo	No Data	60	60
Gambia	No Data	90	90
Ghana	65.1	56	65
Ivory Coast	No Data	86	80[b]
Kenya	No Data	88	85
Lesotho	No Data	98	90
Malawi	No Data	90	90
Mali	No Data	90	90
Nigeria	27.8	80	60[c]
Senegal	No Data	85	80
Sierra Leone	91.6	90	92
Uganda	No Data	90	90
Countries with Substantial Numbers of Women-Headed Urban Households			
Benin	No Data	84	80
Malagasy Republic	No Data	90	70[d]
Tanzania	97.7	95	98[e]
Other Countries with High Women's Participation in Agriculture			
Cameroon	No Data	90	90
Egypt	33.9	51	50[f]
Gabon	94	No Data	94
Guinea	No Data	85	85
Liberia	93.7	80	93
Swaziland	19.9	80	80
Zaire	99	70	95[g]
Zambia	36.7	80	70
Countries with Substantial Nomad Population[h]			
Algeria	23.4	60	60
Ethiopia	No Data	96	80
Libya	22	36	20
Morocco	56.5	No Data	41
Niger	No Data	95	96
Somalia	No Data	95	85
Sudan	No Data	80	80
Tunisia	12.7	47	45

a. Distribution index from Boulding, Nuss, Carson, and Greenstein (1976).

(Notes continued on next page)

NOTES TO TABLE A.1: (Continued)

b. In Ivory Coast, 47 percent of female population are reported to be economically active, and 19 percent of the population as urban. In a region where women are very active in trading, it seems reasonable to allow for more women in towns, and therefore, fewer women than men in agriculture.

c. Allowing for women in Moslem areas not working in the fields.

d. Allowing for substantial urban migration of women, and women's urban small industry projects.

e. The Ford Foundation report (1973) states that women spend twice as many hours farming in Tanzania as men.

f. Earlier official estimates of women in agriculture in Egypt: 1927—15 percent; 1947—51 percent; 1960—4 percent.

g. Zaire currently has a special new program for agricultural training for women.

h. I have less confidence in estimates in this category. Nomadic women participate equally in herding activities with men, but settled women participate substantially less in agriculture. Not knowing to what extent nomadic women enter into official figures for these countries, it is hard to make corrections.

Table A.2: Problems with UN Data on Women in Agriculture

Type of Problem	Number Countries Reporting Problem, by Region			
	Africa	Asia	Americas	Oceania Europe
Specific mention of non-reporting of women in agriculture	3	— —	1	1
Exclusion of nomads or tribals	3	4	8	1
Female agriculturalists and unpaid family workers lumped with "other" or included with employers and workers on own account; or female in religious orders; or lumped with livestock, hunting and fishing, mining and manufacturing; or, in socialist countries, female in producer's co-ops.	1	2	— —	10*
Numbers based on official "estimates" only	10	4	2	6
Numbers based on sample surveys	5	8	11	11
Warning of under-enumeration	3	1	2	— —
Number of countries reporting data limitations**	25	19	23	29
Total number countries and territories in region	56	46	50	64

SOURCE: Based on analysis of footnotes to statistics on economically active persons for the 1972 **ILO Yearbook of Labor Statistics.**

*High number of European countries due to different reporting systems of socialist countries.

**Some countries may be listed more than once.

Appendix

Table A.3.

AFRICA

- Angola
- Benin, formerly Dahomey
- Botswana
- Burundi
- Central African Republic (Ubangi-Shari)
- Chad
- Cameroon
- Congo, People's Rep. of the—Brazzaville
- Equatorial Guinea, formerly Rio Muni
- Gabon
- Gambia, The
- Guinea-Bissau, formerly Portuguese Guinea
- Ghana (Gold Coast and British Togoland)
- Guinea
- Ivory Coast
- Kenya
- Liberia
- Lesotho, formerly Basutoland
- Malagasy Republic (also Madagascar)
- Mauritius
- Mali
- Malawi, formerly Nyasaland
- Mozambique
- Namibia (also Southwest Africa)
- Nigeria
- Niger
- Rhodesia, formerly Southern Rhodesia
- Rwanda
- South Africa
- Senegal
- Sierra Leone
- Somalia
- Swaziland
- Togo, formerly French Togoland
- Uganda
- Upper Volta
- United Republic of Tanzania
- Zambia, formerly Northern Rhodesia
- Zaire Democratic Republic of the Congo—Kinshasa

ASIA

- Afghanistan
- Australia
- Bhutan
- Bangladesh, formerly East Pakistan
- Burma
- China, People's Republic of (including Tibet)
- Fiji
- Hong Kong
- India
- Indonesia (including West Irian)
- Iran (Persia, before 1935)
- Japan
- Khmer, formerly Cambodia
- Korea, Dem. People's Rep. of (North)
- Korea, Republic of (South)
- Laos
- Maldives (Maldive Islands)
- Malaysia (Sabah, Sarawak and West Malaysia)
- Mongolia
- Nauru
- Nepal
- New Guinea
- New Zealand
- Pakistan (including Bangladesh before 1971)
- Philippines
- Ryukyu Islands (returned to Japan, 1972)
- Singapore
- Sri Lanka, formerly Ceylon
- Taiwan (also, Republic of China)
- Thailand (officially Siam until 1939)
- Tonga
- Vietnam, Democratic Republic of (North)
- Vietnam, Republic of (South)
- Western Samoa

Table A.3 (Continued)

EUROPE/NORTH AMERICA

Albania
Andorra
Austria
Belgium (data frequently include Luxembourg)
Bulgaria
Canada
Czechoslovakia
Denmark
Finland
France
German Democratic Republic (East)
Germany, Federal Republic of (including West Berlin)
Greece
Hungary
Iceland
Ireland
Italy
Liechtenstein
Luxembourg
Malta
Monaco
Norway
Netherlands, Kingdom of the
Poland
Portugal
Romania
San Marino
Spain
Sweden
Switzerland
United Kingdom of Great Britain and Northern Ireland
United States of America
Union of Soviet Socialist Republics
Vatican City, the State of (Holy See)
Yugoslavia

LATIN AMERICA

Argentina
Barbados
Bahamas
Bolivia
Brazil
Chile (including Easter Islands and Juan Fern Arch.)
Colombia
Costa Rica
Dominican Republic
Ecuador
El Salvador
Grenada (in the Windward Islands)
Guatemala
Guyana
Haiti
Honduras
Jamaica
Mexico
Nicaragua
Panama (excluding the Canal Zone)
Paraguay
Peru
Puerto Rico
Surinam
Trinidad and Tobago
Uruguay
Venezuela

NORTH AFRICA AND THE MIDDLE EAST

Algeria
Bahrain
Cyprus
Egypt (officially, United Arab Republic)
Ethiopia
Iraq
Israel
Jordan
Kuwait
Lebanon
Libya
Mauritania
Morocco (including Ifini, excluding Spanish North Africa)
Oman, formerly Sultanate of Muscat and Oman
Qatar
Saudi Arabia
Sudan
Syria
Tunisia
Turkey (once center of the Ottoman Empire)
United Arab Emirates, formerly Trucial Oman
Yemen
Yemen, People's Democratic Republic of formerly Aden

SOURCE: Boulding, Nuss, Carson, and Greenstein (1976).

AUTHOR INDEX

Aas, Berit, 228, 243 n.6.
Aberle, David F., 58.
Addams, Jane, 182 n.2.
Adelman, Irma, 77, 79, 80, 81, 82, 88, 89, 90, 91, 94, 95.
Ajemian, J., 234.
Alger, Chadwick, 179.
Ali, Ameer, 41.
Awad, M., 53 n.8.

Balch, Emily, 182 n.2.
Barkun, Michael, 229.
Beard, Mary, 212.
Bebel, August, 243 n.1.
Bennet, William S., 93.
Bergman, Arlene Eisen, 177.
Bernard, Jessie, 73.
Blakar, Rolv, 243 n.6.
Borgstrom, Georg, 157, 164 n.11.
Boserup, Ester, 74 n.6, n.8, 78, 80, 81, 84, 85, 86, 92, 103, 112, 119, 122, 137.
Boulding, Elise, 19-30, 33, 43, 44, 46-50, 53 n.13, n.15, 57, 60, 80, 82, 88, 96, 97, 107, 109 n.3, n.5, 118, 137, 141, 143, 145, 146, 148, 150, 152, 153, 154, 177, 186, 207, 209 n.5, 212, 218 n.2, 225, 243 n.1, 253, 255, 256.
Bradley, David J., 145.
Bramsen, Michèle Bo, 182 n.5, 75 n.1.
Brown, Lester R., 161.
Brown, Norman L., 156.
Burdett-Coutts, The Baroness, 188.
Bussey, Gertrude, 171.
Buvinić, Mayra, 75 n.1.

Carson, Dorothy, 19-30, 80, 82, 97, 118, 137, 141, 143, 145, 146, 148, 150, 152, 153, 154, 253, 255, 256.
Chadwick, Nora, 37, 38.
Cita-Malard, Suzanne, 189.
Cleveland, Arthur Rackham, 63.

De Tocqueville, Alexis, 39-40.
DeVore, Irven, 53 n.5, 56.
Drinker, Sophie, 38.
Duby, Georges, 74 n.9.
Dupire, Marguerite, 37, 97.
Dwyer, Johanna T., 156.

Eagle, Mary Kavanaugh Oldham, 209 n.2.
Eberhard, Wolfram, 53 n.4.
Engels, Friedrich, 243 n.1.

Falk, Richard A., 181.
Farrell, Warren, 74 n.13.
Firth, Raymond, 80, 96.
Follett, Mary P., 229.
Freeman, Jo, 229.
Friedan, Betty, 53 n.10, 171.

Galtung, Ingrid Eide, 243 n.4.
Gandhi, Mohandas K., 244 n.13.
Gerlach, Luther P., 229.
Giffen, Frederick C., 239.
Gordon, Elizabeth Putnam, 170, 182 n.3.
Graves, Nancy, 43.
Greenstein, Michael, 19-30, 80, 82, 97, 118, 137, 141, 143, 145, 146, 148, 150, 152, 153, 154, 253, 255, 256.
Grönseth, Erik, 235.
Grousset, René, 37, 38, 39.

Halpern, Joel M., 99.
Hamilton, Alice, 182 n.2.
Hamilton, G., 234.
Hansen, Donald A., 39.
Hendrata, Lukas, 136 n.10.
Herlihy, David, 40, 59, 63.
Hill, Polly, 80, 101-102, 104.
Hill, Reuben, 39.
Hine, Virginia H., 229.

Ihromi, T. O., 101.

Jenks, C. Willfred, 244 n.14.
Judge, Anthony J.N., 208.
Julian of Norwich, 243 n.5.
Jungk, Robert, 232.

Kanter, Rosabeth Moss, 299.
Key, Ellen, 68.
Kothari, Rajni, 181.
Kramer, Samuel Noah, 59.
Kuhn, Thomas S., 174, 243 n.2.

Lacey, W. K., 53 n.7.
Laslett, Peter, 64, 65, 66, 147.
Latham, Michael C., 156.
Lee, Richard B., 53 n.5, 56.
Lev, Daniel S., 100.
Litwak, Eugene, 234.

McCarthy, Florence E., 104.
McCarthy, Thomas P., 192, 209 n.7.
McDonnell, Ernest W., 74 n.12.
McDonough, J. F., 234.
Maher, Vanessa, 80, 98, 99, 104.
Martines, Laura, 62, 74 n.11.
Marx, Karl, 243 n.1.
Mayer, Jean, 80, 147, 149, 156, 158.
Mead, Margaret, 228, 230, 243 n.7.
Meadows, D. H., 181.
Meadows, D. L., 181.
Mendlovitz, Saul, 181.
Michels, Robert, 244 n.9.
Monteil, Vincent, 45, 46, 53 n.5, n.8.
Moock, Peter Russell, 117.
Morris, Cynthia Taft, 77, 79, 80, 81, 82, 88, 89, 90, 91, 94, 95.

Nair, Kusum, 80, 103, 104, 106.
Nelson, Cynthia, 229.
Nuss, Shirley A., 19-30, 80, 82, 97, 118, 137, 141, 143, 145, 146, 148, 150, 152, 153, 154, 253, 255, 256.

O'Faolain, Julia, 62, 74 n.11.

Paddock, Paul, 164 n.10.
Paddock, William, 164 n.10.
Papanek, Hanna, 100.
Pariser, E. R., 156.
Penzer, N. M., 53 n.7.
Piet, David L., 136 n.10.

Polak, Fred L., 224.
Poleman, Thomas T., 156.
Postan, M. M., 64.
Posthumus-van der Goot, W. H., 170.
Power, Eileen, 64.
Prawdin, Michael, 37.

Renard, Georges, 40.
Rhodes, G., 234.
Rudé, George, 62.

Salk, Jonas, 231.
Schenk, Leslie, 237-238.
Sherrard, Philip, 64.
Silberman, Leo, 45.
Simons, H. J., 97.
Sivard, Ruth Leger, 224-226, 243- n.3.
Smith, W. Robertson, 37.
Stanton, Theodore, 170.
Stinchcombe, Arthur, 187.
Strathern, Marilyn, 97.
Sudarkasa, Niara, 101.
Sullerot, Evelyne, 60, 74 n.4.
Swift, M. G., 99.
Szalai, Alexander, 68, 69, 176, 181.

Taeuber, Conrad, 43.
Taeuber, Irene B., 43.
Thompson, Louis M., 159.
Thrupp, Sylvia L., 63.
Tims, Margaret, 171.
Tinker, Irene, 182 n.5, 75 n.1.
Toffler, Alvin, 232.
Topley, Marjorie, 100.
Toynbee, Arnold J., 53 n.2.
Turnbull, Colin, 53 n.2, n.5.

Vreede-De Stuers, Cora, 80, 104.

Ward, Barbara, 80, 100.
Weber, Max, 144 n.9.
Wenig, Steffan, 53 n.7, 59.
Westermann, William L., 74 n.5.
White, Anne U., 145.
White, Gilbert F., 145.
Woodward, Beverly, 209 n.3.

Yamey, B. S., 80, 96.

Ziegler, Philip, 63.

SUBJECT INDEX

Adaptation, 33, 35, 39, 87, 106, 232.
Ad hoc groups, 182 n.5, 208, 234.
Administration, 25-28, 40, 59, 83, 106-107, 151, 154, 212.
Agriculture: agribusiness, 77; aid, 24, 111-136; cash crops, 62, 112-113, 135, 136 n.2, 142, 155; herding, 34-38, 42, 45, 57; third world, 96-103, 157; settlement, 56-58; slash-and-burn cultivation, 57, 78; subsistence, 21, 77-78, 81-83, 112, 113, 118-119, 124, 130, 155.
Aid: agriculture, 24, 111-136; breeding, 109 n.3, 118; development, 106, 154-156; neighborhood, 213-214; NGO, 202, 205, 214, 215; self-help, 125, 135, 231-234, 236; traditional, 236, 244 n.13.
All-African Women's Conference, 180, 214.
All-African Women's Voluntary Task Force, 135.
Alternatives: economic, 78; food, 149-153; future, 181-182, 229-231; hierarchy, 211-218, 229-231; role, 35, 66-67; war, 170, 229-231.
American Economics Association, 173.
American Sociological Association, 173.
Androgynous society, 230-231, 236-239, 244 n.10.
Another Mother for Peace, 173.
Antiwar movement, 174-175.
Anti-woman bias, 212.
Apprenticeship, see Education.
Aristocracy: expatriate, 79; nomad, 52 n.4; nurturance, 169, 212-213; politics, 35-38, 169, 213; purdah, 41; trade, 58.
Aspiration, 25, 237, 240.
Assimilation, 46, 50, 136, 222, 223.
Autonomy, 35, 39-40, 43, 46, 49, 70-72, 102, 134, 186, 201, 209 n.1.
Awareness, 107, 111-118, 150, 155-158, 161-162, 170, 192, 208, 213.

Bargaining, 63.
Barriers, 35, 41, 77, 81, 82, 99, 101, 105, 107.
Barter, 21.

Baths, 41, 99.
Beating daughters, 65, 74 n.11.
Beguinages, 66-67.
Belief structures, 39.
Biology, 70-73, 149, 230.
Black Death, 63.
Bonding, 39.
Breast-feeding, 113, 139, 147-149.
Breeder-feeder-producer, 22, 55, 62-73, 79-80, 109 n.3, 111-113, 118-131, 181, 231.
Bureaucratic efficiency, 80-82, 101.
Byzantine empire, 41.

Camilla project, 104.
Capital: accumulation, 97, 104, 107; availability, 21; flow, 97; formation, 79-80.
Cash cropping, see Agriculture.
Celibacy, 61, 65-68.
Census, 18, 43; see also Counting.
Centralization, 58, 100, 107-108, 211, 213-214, 225-233.
Ceremony, 21, 38-39, 56, 160.
Change: assessment, 154-155; dynamics, 81-96; International Women's Year, 180; NGO, 196-201; potential, 211, 215-218, 234-235; production, 41, 111, 132, 156-157; resistance, 104, 111, 117, 154, 170; social, 229-235; systems, 179-182; U.S. Navy, 228-229.
Children: abuse, 65-66; anchoring effect, 212; autonomy, 43; care, 21-25, 41, 56, 61, 63-69, 101; education, 152-153; feeding, 113, 139, 147-149; labor, 61-62.
Child-woman ratio, 21-22, 147-149.
Choice, 34, 64, 65-67.
Civic skills, 51, 68.
Civilizing model, 41.
Clerical and sales labor, 25, 28, 82-87, 91-92, 100.
Code of Hammurabi, 59.
Collaboration, 180, 195, 196, 234-235.
Colleagueship, 68, 107, 134, 169, 188.
Colonialism, 79, 93, 100, 195.
Commensalism, 218, 239.

[259]

Communes, 66-68, 70-72, 160.
Communication: networks, 35, 51, 112, 121, 206-208, 211, 213-217; NGO, 175, 180, 187, 194, 206; public space, 41, 105; technology, 46.
Competition, 58, 60, 61, 67, 74 n.5, 102, 151, 174.
Compliance, 168, 173.
Consortium on Peace Research, Education and Development, 173, 174.
Constraint, 55-74, 83.
Counting problems, 17-21, 25-30, 82, 93, 98, 118, 125-130, 140-145, 154-155.
Credit, 80, 97, 100, 102, 104, 107, 113, 132-135.
Crusades, 40, 63.

Data: access, 38, 80, 82, 114; analysis, 117, 136; base, 81, 221, 223; collection, 96-97, 192-200, 214; cross-national, 44, 46; food, 151, 155; limitation, 17-18, 21, 28, 30, 33, 80, 140-141.
Decentralization, see Centralization.
Decision-making: aspiration, 20, 24, 25, 237, 240; crisis, 223-224; dualism, 78-80, 104, 108; economic, 93-96; education, 93; food, 140, 149-156; marginality, 227; memory, 157-159; NGO, 174, 205; resource, 43, 93-96; tribal, 56; women, 44-45, 79, 97, 104, 107, 112-117, 121, 133-136, 140, 149, 154, 221, 239.
Development: aid, 106, 154-156; cooperative, 113, 114, 120, 122, 133, 134; education, 25, 157-159; industrial, 77-79, 82; International Women's Year, 18, 31, 222, 223, 236; migration, 42; participation, 29, 117, 157-159, 165, 206, 222, 223, 236; technology, 111-112, 117, 157-159, 236; urban-based, 44, 46.
Disarmament, 170, 175, 226.
Division of labor, 38, 62-64, 78, 106, 208.
Divorce, 21, 37, 61.
Dominance, 62, 72, 212, 213, 217, 218.
Drawing rights, 73.
Dualism: decision-making, 78-80, 104, 108; definition, 81-82; economic, 77-109; education, 100, 103-104, 108; extent, 82-85; gender-based, 78, 80, 98; production, 77-78, 100-106; third world, 78-80; triple, 78-79.

Economic Commission for Africa, 113, 118, 135.

Economy: analysis, 44-49, 57-58, 79-80, 101, 204, 209 n.6; capital-intensive, 77; cash, 80; deprivation, 22, 56, 59, 78-79, 100-103; dualism, 77-109; education, 23-25, 91, 93, 106; exchange, 20-21, 35, 80; growth, 88-91, 98, 99, 103, 105-107, 120, 124-130; integration, 82; international, 79; labor-intensive, 78, 236; market, 77-78; non-market, 98-99; polygamy, 37; subsistence, 20-21, 55, 57, 60, 99, 103.
Education: access, 113-114, 119, 125, 133, 231; apprenticeship, 64, 88, 234-235, 244 n.12; dualism, 100, 103-104, 108; employment, 23-25; fertility, 131; food, 150-153; investment, 25, 91, 93, 106; modernization, 48-49, 105, 235; organization, 193-201; vocational, 93, 119, 121-124, 130, 136 n.5.; women, 23-25, 50, 91, 93, 99, 106, 150, 153, 187-188, 223.
Egalitarianism, 18, 29, 31, 34-43, 56, 58, 78, 222, 231.
Elite, see Aristocracy.
Empire, 168-169, 195-196.
Employment, 23-25, 28, 46, 67, 113, 177.
Enclaves, 77, 96, 212.
Enclosure: upward mobility, 99, 105; urbanism, 33, 40-43, 45, 52, 59, 63-64, 104, 107; work, 83, 101-102.
Enfranchisement, 44.
Exchange economy, 20-21, 35, 80.
Exclusion, 29, 67.
Exploitation, 63, 78-79, 106, 160, 187-188, 237.

Family: constraint, 55-74; crisis, 39, 98; extended, 66, 99; labor, 17, 20, 62-64, 88, 140, 154, 160; law, 59; metaphor, 227; migration, 34, 39-40, 51; militarism, 167-168; planning, 131-133; workshops, 18, 21, 25, 87-88, 93, 106.
Famine, 149, 155.
Femaleness of labor, see Labor.
Fifth world, 17, 111-112, 140, 157, 167, 181, 205, 206, 234.
Fluidity: data, 77, 79, 207, 234; nomads, 33-39; power, 33-39, 185, 239; resources, 79, 97, 99, 107-108; social, 40, 59, 218.
Food: banks, 147, 159-160, 163 n.8; distribution, 112, 139, 144-145; eating out, 101; knowledge, 149-153; planning, 113, 149-151; preservation, 133-134; production, 31, 55-57, 121, 124,

142-144, 146-149; shortage, 149, 155-160; starvation, 62, 63.
Foreign Assistance Act of 1973, 116.
Fourth world, 162.
Fulani women, 97.
Futurism, 52, 181-182, 221-242.

Gap bridging, 135, 155-157, 169-170, 221.
General Federation of Women's Clubs, 188.
Global systems, 169-174, 186, 195-201, 214, 231.
Golden Age of Women, 36.
Grants, 21, 78, 159, 200.
Gray, Lady Jane, 65.
Guilds, 40, 63-67, 186.
Gynaeceum, 33, 40-41.
Gypsies, 34, 36, 38, 39, 42.

Habit, 161, 228.
Hakka women, 100.
Harems, 33, 37, 40, 53 n.7.
Hausa women, 101-102.
Health, 45-46, 113, 131, 132, 156, 223.
Helplessness, 43, 46.
Herding, see Agriculture.
Hierarchy, 187, 205, 211-218, 229-230.
Home industry, 18, 21, 25, 87-88, 93, 106.
Homemakers, 17, 20-21, 142-144, 163 n.2.
Horses, 35, 52 n.4.
Households, 59-68, 71, 97, 103; size, 22, 56, 66, 70-72, 99, 147.
Housework, 68-72, 101.
Hunters and gatherers, 34-36, 56-57.

Identity, 192-193, 202-205, 214.
Imaging, 23, 111, 159-161, 167-168, 177, 181, 197, 202-205, 224-227.
Imbalance, 78-79, 124-130.
Income: counting, 21; inequality, 59-62, 63-74, 77-78, 80, 88-92, 100, 111; maintenance, 73; separate, 97, 101; source, 21; supplemental, 60, 61, 67, 133.
Independence, 97, 102, 177-178.
India, 103-105.
Indicators: economic, 81-82, 88-91, 105-107, 118-130; participation, 33, 44, 46-51, 55, 81-82, 140; significance of, 18-19, 40.
Individuation, 46-49, 160, 230.
Indonesia, 99-100, 107.
Industrialization, 28, 33, 77-79, 87, 169-171, 206, 213, 232.

Infant mortality, 56, 65, 109 n.3, 113, 131, 133, 147.
Infanticide, 37, 56.
Inheritance rights, 97.
Innovation, see Change.
Institute for World Order, 181.
Insulation, 114, 136 n.3, 157-159, 186.
Intermediaries, 101-102.
International Council of Nurses, 188, 205.
International Council of Women, 188.
International labor movement, 169.
International meetings, 174-175.
International Peace Research Association, 173, 174.
International relations associations, 171, 189, 195, 200, 205, 207.
International rosters, see Rosters.
International Studies Association, 173.
International Women's Year, 18, 31, 112, 175-177, 180, 214, 221-224, 236.
Internationalism, 169-171, 174-178, 192-196.
Investment, 25, 45, 97-100, 106.
Invisibility, 17-18, 56-59, 78-79, 93-96, 99, 154, 161-162, 180, 181.
Isolation, 31, 41, 65-67, 180, 193-194, 214, 234.

Japan, 105-107.

Keller, Helen, 241-242.
Key, Ellen, 68.
Kinship, 98, 159, 208.
Kitchen gardens, 130, 139, 142, 144, 155.
Knowledge: recognition, 77, 112, 136; women's, 163, 173-175, 205; see also Data.

Labor: auxiliary, 18; femaleness of, 18-21, 26-30, 44, 79, 82-87, 91, 92, 99, 103, 107, 108, 140-155, 190-192; inequality, 62, 231; non-market, 98-99; see also Family, Workload, Household.
Labor-intensive economy, 78, 236.
Land, see Property.
Latin America, 83.
Law, 24, 59-60, 97, 135, 197-201.
Leadership, 35, 79, 82, 101, 236.
Leisure, 56, 70, 181.
Le Thi Rieng, 177.
Liaison Committee of Women's International Organizations, 214-215.
Life-cycle, 97-98.
Love, 72-73.
Lysistrata, 168, 173.

Managerial ability, 25, 117, 119, 131.
Manufacturing, 141, 142.
Mapping, 17-19.
Margaret, Queen of Navarre, 65.
Marginality, 21, 34, 58, 99, 227, 241, 243 n.4.
Markets, 77-78, 98-99, 102, 103, 114, 117, 119, 124, 134, 155.
Marriage, 21-22, 37, 56, 63-73, 120, 124, 130, 136 n.4, 213.
Matriliny, 36-38, 58, 74 n.3.
Measurement, see Census, Counting, Indicators.
Mechanization, 62, 77, 112.
Media use, 69-70.
Medicine, 60, 156.
Metaphor, 227-229, 239, 241, 242, 243 n.5.
Migration, 22-23, 33-34, 39-45, 51, 62-68, 106, 119, 121.
Militarism: change, 228-229, 231; nurturance, 167-170, 174, 177-178, 182; participation, 25-26, 28, 31 n.2, 35-38; poverty, 224; spending, 224-226, 243 n.3.
Missionary movements, 193, 206.
Mobility, 34-35, 42-45, 51, 63-68, 105.
Modernization: cushion for, 93; economy, 78-87, 93, 112-113, 120; education, 23-25, 48, 49; euphoria, 157-159; model of, 39-40; participation, 46-51, 100-107, 114; third world, 78-80.
Monetary value, 17-18, 80.
Morocco, 98-99, 107.
Moscosa, Flora Tristan, 169.

Networks, see Communication, NGOs, Trade.
New Guinian women, 97.
NGOs, 51, 120, 125, 174-177, 178, 180, 181, 185-208, 211-218.
Niches, 35, 66-67, 231.
Nigeria, 100-103.
Nomads: definition, 34; general, 33-52.
Not economically active, 17, 20-21, 28-29.
Nuclear threat, 174-175, 232.
Nurturance: awareness, 212, 228-231; hierarchy, 211, 212, 217; militarism, 167-170, 174, 177-178, 182; roles, 64, 186, 188, 235; scale, 72-73.
Nutrition, 113, 122, 133, 149, 155-157, 161.

Observation, 116-117, 142, 157, 164 n.9, 241.

Occupations: involvement, 28; profiles, 25-29, 60, 83-87; ratios, 50; recognizing, 18.
Opportunity: economic, 25, 43, 93-101; education, 24-25; migration, 40; NGO, 201-202.
Own account workers, 17-18, 21, 82-87, 91-93, 100, 101, 118, 133.
Ownership, 37, 97, 135.

Paradigm shift, 223-224.
Paris Commune, 169.
Partnership, 21-23, 37, 63-64, 72-73, 108, 167-168.
Paston, Agnes, 65.
Patriarchy, 36-37.
Patron-client system, 98-99, 107.
Peace: adaptability, 232; exclusion, 29; groups, 167-181, 188-189, 213; International Women's Year, 18, 31, 221-224; nomads, 35, 46; roles, 165, 167-181.
Perception, 35, 51, 108.
Percy Amendment, 116.
Performance, 44, 230.
Perovskaya, Sofia, 240-241.
Policy-making, see Decision-making.
Politics, 37-38, 41, 45, 65, 79.
Polygamy, 37, 61, 68, 101, 119, 121.
Population: control, 37, 56, 223, 225-226; growth, 37, 88-91, 96, 120, 130; resources, 37, 112; scale, 33; shifts, 43.
Populism, 79, 175, 208, 213-214.
Potential association, 208.
Poverty: Black Death, 63; census taking, 18; militarism, 224-226; prostitution, 21, 61; trap, 43, 77-80, 88, 96, 98, 100, 103; urban, 43, 60-61, 77, 102, 124, 157.
Power: base, 186; differentials, 33, 59; enclosure, 40-42; hierarchy, 211-214, 217; marginal, 224, 227; religion, 186; tribal, 38-39.
Problem-solving: colonialism, 93; education, 93; hierarchy, 212, 214, 217-218; International Women's Year, 223-227, 231; organizational, 193, 205, 208, 214; scale, 33, 35; women, 93, 170, 212, 217-218, 223-227, 231.
Procreation, 25, 230.
Production: capital deprivation, 100, 102, 103; craft, 36, 38; decline, 111-113, 114, 132; differentiation, 25, 55-59; dualism, 77-78, 100-106; enclosure, 41, 83, 101-102; increasing, 156-157;

Subject Index

mass, 41; technology, 77, 106; see also Agriculture, Family, Home industry.
Professionals, 24-28, 83-87, 91-92, 150-154, 171-178, 193-194, 208.
Property, 37, 40, 59, 63, 100.
Prostitution, 21, 61.
Protected space, 39, 66-67, 103.
Protests, 168-171, 173.
Public space, 36, 41, 63, 99, 168-169, 173, 175, 208, 213.
Purdah, 41, 99, 101-102, 104, 107.

Reform movements, 68-69.
Regionalism, 187, 194-196, 202-205.
Regression analysis, 117.
Religion: generalized response, 38-39; NGOs, 185-187, 189, 200-201, 206, 207; participation, 82-91, 121; service orders, 61, 65-67.
Resources: access, 40, 41, 78, 131; allocation, 17, 40, 99, 105, 112, 114, 119, 136, 160, 163 n.6, 165, 168-170, 195, 196, 202, 207, 212-214, depletion, 78-79; deprivation, 56, 59, 78-79; education, 91-95; limitations, 61, 91, 117, 149-151, 175, 224, 236; population, 37; regionalism, 187, 194-196, 202-205; utilization, 35, 36, 39, 42, 53 n.8.
Responsibility, 21-22, 25, 41.
Rewards, 56, 134, 175, 217.
Ritual, see Ceremony.
Role: clusters, 33; differentiation, 25, 33, 38, 55, 72, 101; government, 178; reshuffling, 34; reversal, 72, 99-100, 228, 243 n.7; status, 47-49, 53 n.15.
Roster development, 180, 182 n.5, 239.
Ruling women, 37, 38, 58, 211-212, 218 n.2, 228.

Savings, 80, 97.
Scale, 33, 35.
Scavenging, 21.
Science fiction, 230, 231, 233 n.11.
Seclusion, see Enclosure.
Sectoral cleavage, 81, 82, 99, 101, 105, 107.
Segmentary organization, 229.
Service work, 25, 36, 98-99, 188, 189, 200, 207-208, 209 n.7, 232-233, 236.
Settlement, 33-34, 40, 42-46, 53 n.8, 56-58.
Shamanism, 39.
Sharing: child care, 72-73; communication, 206; food, 159; housework, 212; jobs, 217, 218 n.4; responsibility, 217, 222, 231, 232; wages, 62; work, 133.

Sin, 62.
Single women, 21-23, 63-64, 72-73, 167-168.
Sisterhoods, 181, 189, 207-208, 209 n.7, 227.
Skill, 25, 39, 42, 43, 51, 68, 217-218.
Slavery, 35, 42, 45, 60, 61, 74 n.5.
Social interaction, 35, 41, 70, 211, 213.
Social service, 62-68.
Socialism, 68-71, 169-170, 213-214.
Sociology of World Conflicts, 173, (ASA).
Somalia, 44-46.
Soup kitchens, 67.
Space, 38, 39, 41, 52, 65, 111, see also Public space.
Specialization, 38, 58, 101, 134.
Spiritual enrichment, 196, 197, 200, 207, 227.
Standard of living, 79, 195, 204, 217.
Status: agriculture, 103-107; dualism, 78, 93, 103-107; industrialization, 25-28, 93; International Women's Year, 222; nomad, 34-42, 45, 47-49, 53 n.15; planning, 24-25, 157; social research, 175-178, 217.
Statute of Laborers, 62-63.
Stratification, 34-35, 52 n.4, 58-59.
Style, 181, 229.
Submarginal land, 36, 42, 53 n.8.
Subsistence, see Agriculture, Economy.
Support systems, 61, 70-73, 131-133, 223.
Survival, 155-156, 160.
Systems analysis, 153-163, 204.

Technology: adaptation, 106, 232; communication, 46, 79; competing, 151; equality, 34; imaging, 232; insulation, 77, 232-233; intermediate, 93, 111-112, 131-134, 156, 227, 236; military, 173; organizational, 79.
Third level training, 24, 25, 31 n.1.
Third world: census, 18; change, 232, 234; definition, 162; dualism, 78-80; exports, 164 n.11; food, 155-157; infant mortality, 147; internationalism, 175, 204, 214-215; militarism, 224; wages, 18, 62.
Threat systems, 213, 223.
Time budgets, 68-70, 96, 181.
Trade, 36, 38, 41, 55-63, 96-103, 146.
Tradition, 38, 78-87, 121, 135, 236, 244 n.13.
Transnational organizations, see NGOs.
Triage, 160.

Unit of participation, 82, 113.
United Nations, 175-176, 178, 237-239.
United States Navy, 228-229.
Unpartnered women, 21-23, 63-64, 72-73, 167-168.
Upward mobility, 41, 99, 105.
Urbanism: centralization, 58, 100, 107, 108, 211-214, 225-233; dualism, 77-78; enclosure, 33, 40-43, 45, 59, 63-64; fertility, 130-131; food, 111-113, 124; participation, 46-51; poverty, 43, 60-61, 77-78, 102, 124, 157; stratification, 58-59; trade, 101, 119.
Utopianism, 68-69, 189, 224-227.

Vietnam, 177-178.
Vision, 46, 79, 93.
Visiting husbands, 36, 119, 121.
Vocational education, see Education.
Voix des Femmes, 169, 174.
Volunteerism, 234-235.

Wage labor, 20-25, 62-63, 83-87, 91, 92, 99, 102, 103; see also Income.
Wastage, 161-162.
Weeding and irrigation, 57, 112, 130.
Wholeness, 188, 193, 195, 241.
Widowhood, 21, 61, 62, 65.
Women and Food Resolution, 162, 201.
Women Strike for Peace, 174.
Women's courts, 37, 40-41.
Women's International Democratic Federation, 200, 205.
Women's International Information and Communication Service (ISIS), 182 n.5, 208.
Women's International League for Peace and Freedom, 171, 174, 189.
Women's International Networks, 208.
Women's movement, 168, 174, 189, 201, 208, 229-230.
Women's quarters, 44, 103-104, 116.
Workload: biological endurance, 149; conservatism, 157; home, 154-155, 160; inequality, 231; length of day, 55-63, 106, 112-113; liberation struggles, 177; organizational, 125, 130, 205; unpaid, 45, 58-60.
World Plan of Action, 221-224.
World Union of Catholic Women, 200, 205.
World we, 19, 28, 204-205.
World Women's Christian Temperance Union, 188, 189, 200, 201, 207.
World Young Women's Christian Association, 188, 189, 200, 201, 205, 207.

Yoruba women, 101.

Zenana modernization, 104-105.
Zero population growth, 37, 56.

MICHIGAN STATE UNIVERSITY
LIBRARY

AUG 14 2025

WITHDRAWN

PLACE IN RETURN BOX to remove this checkout from your record.
TO AVOID FINES return on or before date due.

DATE DUE	DATE DUE	DATE DUE
MAY 1 9 1996	AUG 2 5 200	
	08 1 3 04	
DEC 08 1997		
JAN 2 9 2000		
JAN 1 1 2000		

MSU Is An Affirmative Action/Equal Opportunity Institution

c:\circ\datedue.pm3-p.1